T0284120

Southwest Train Robberies

Hijacking the Tracks along the Southern Corridor

Doug Hocking

TWODOT®

ESSEX, CONNECTICUT
HELENA, MONTANA

TWODOT®

GUILFORD CONNECTICUT
HELENA, MONTANA

An imprint of Globe Pequot, the trade division of
The Rowman & Littlefield Publishing Group, Inc.
4501 Forbes Blvd., Ste. 200
Lanham, MD 20706
www.rowman.com

Distributed by NATIONAL BOOK NETWORK

Copyright © 2023 by Doug Hocking

All rights reserved. No part of this book may be reproduced in any form or by any electronic or mechanical means, including information storage and retrieval systems, without written permission from the publisher, except by a reviewer who may quote passages in a review.

British Library Cataloguing in Publication Information available

Library of Congress Cataloging-in-Publication Data Available
ISBN 978-1-4930-7110-4 (pbk. : alk. paper)
ISBN 978-1-4930-7111-1 (electronic)

♾️™ The paper used in this publication meets the minimum requirements of American National Standard for Information Sciences—Permanence of Paper for Printed Library Materials, ANSI/NISO Z39.48-1992.

To my wife, Debbie, who puts up with it and who reads my daily output to discover if it's intelligible. And to my friend Dennis "Nevada" Smith, because he helped, too, and it will make him happy. And to Gene, Rosanna, and Ilona, the ever helpful.

CONTENTS

Acknowledgments

Kathy Klump of the Sulphur Springs Valley Historical Society and Chiricahua Mountains Museum in Willcox helped a great deal with her archive of materials no one else has saved and with hints about other stories. The Klumps and Kathy's family have been in Cochise County about as long as there has been a Cochise County, and they are related to most of the cattlemen and outlaws. Chuck and Jean Smith helped with a bit of history along the Gila River, where they live and their families have lived since the nineteenth century. Chuck came up with the story of the 1916 train robbery at Apache and with connections to folks who have collected information about the Fulchers. Chuck put me in contact with Troy Thygerson, who has been studying the Fulchers and collecting information on their once friendly relationship with the Bradberrys. Nobody in Cochise County had heard of this one, and it proved an interesting tale. Alan Day, little brother of Justice Sandra Day O'Connor, is old enough to remember the Fulchers and tell me they were tough guys, and the word was not to mess with them. Lynn Wiese Sneyd makes sure that Alan gets about where I can enjoy both their company. The Cochise County Corral, Silver City Corral, the Prescott Corral, and the Apache Junction Public Library and the Empire Ranch have all been kind enough to have me speak about the train robberies, which has helped immensely with finding ways to tell the story. Stuart Rosebrook at *True West* is a true friend who has always been helpful. Bob Nilson at the Benson Visitor Center provided hints toward many stories, especially those involving Benson. Sorry, Bob, a case of Spam still doesn't count as a train robbery. The trains still roll through Benson, interrupting conversation approximately every ten minutes. A few years ago, Chris Enss introduced me to a publisher, and I can never thank her enough for that introduction. I need to thank Gerald Ahnert, who knows more than anyone about the Overland Mail and thus has unsurpassed deep knowledge of the southern overland trail. Gerry sent along a book of train robberies on the Southern Pacific Railroad. As always, I need to thank Debra Chatham at the Sierra Vista Public Library, who finds material I can't find and bends the rules a bit to get me more than the library generally allows. Bunker de France, Harry Alexander, Russell True, and again Alan Day, who do the *Cowboy Up* and *Voices of the West* podcasts from Russell's White Stallion Ranch—these hombres are always fun to talk with, and any excuse to visit White Stallion Ranch is worthwhile. I especially want to thank the folks at the Southern Arizona Transportation Museum at 414 N. Toole in Tucson. Kenneth V. Karrels is their director, and Steve Anderson and Randy Hill were exceptionally helpful. I urge you to visit their museum, where you can board a locomotive and see the statues of Doc Holliday and Wyatt Earp. A word might also be said for the Amigos and Ladies of the West, who gather in one booth at the Tucson Festival of Books each year and generally have a good time: Rod Timanus, Chris Enns, Melody Groves, Gil Storms, Bill Markley, Manuela Schneider, and Lowell Volk, as well as our official balladeer, Carol Markstrom, and the fellow who does our stunts, Bunker de France.

There are some great folks and points of interest along the way that you might want to visit. The Southern Arizona Transportation Museum has some of the friendliest folks you'll meet anywhere. Located near the Tucson railway station, they have the famous statue of Wyatt Earp and Doc Holliday and a steam engine where you can climb into the cab, and they'll show you how the controls work. Colossal Cave is open, and you can tour. At the Visitor Center in Benson, they have railroad artifacts in a replica of the station, and Bob Nilson has a miniature train set connected to a real railroad control panel. If you're nice, he'll let you drive his train. In Willcox, the Chiricahua Regional Museum is located on Maley Street just off Railroad Ave. across from Big Tex, where barbeque is served in a railroad dining car. Steins is still there and may be open as a tourist attraction/museum. It is worth the side trip to visit the Silver City Museum, and back on the main line the Deming Museum is a must-see.

INTRODUCTION

IN THE LATE SUMMER, I STOOD BETWEEN THE CARS ON THE CUMBRES and Toltec Railway blinking sparks and soot out of my eyes. It was already fall in the high country between New Mexico and Colorado, and autumn colors had appeared after an early frost the night before. The train crawled slowly up a 4 percent grade behind Engine 487, a K class 2-8-2, one of the last operational coal-burning locomotives built in the 1920s. I blinked a hot cinder out of my eye and looked back on a utility vehicle following a half mile behind to put out fires the sparks might ignite. Fires had been a very real hazard in the days of steam, especially in the arid Southwest. Looking down on trout streams and deep gorges, rocking from side to side on rails scarcely thirty-six inches apart, the narrow-gauge train crawled through autumn splendor as it inched around tight curves. The narrow gauge handled the mountain curves more easily than a wider gauge might have.

This was my first trip on the Cumbres and Toltec Railroad, but I knew her. I had seen her in my youth when she still ran from Alamosa to Silverton passing through my hometown, Dulce, New Mexico, as she headed for Chama, New Mexico, or Arboles, Colorado. She was known then as the Denver & Rio Grande Western. We were told that this railroad was the last commercially operating narrow-gauge railway in the country. We were also told that at ten thousand feet in the Cumbres Pass, this is the highest elevation achieved by any railroad in the United States. Track was laid in 1880 and extended all the way to Silverton by 1882. Until 1951, the *San Juan Express*, a daily passenger service, ran on these tracks. She was a luxury train with dining service and parlor car, making the trip from Durango to Alamosa in nine hours. The *San Juan Express* was the pride of all narrow-gauge passenger trains. In the 1960s, she was only run a few times hauling tourists. At other times the train chugged and puffed up Amargo Canyon under a huge cloud of steam hauling a few ancient box cars.[1]

The US Army has secrets no one knows and mysterious ways of learning about one's past. Perhaps knowing that I'd grown up along the tracks of the last commercially operating steam railroad in the country, they assigned me to the 714th TBROS&DE (Transportation Battalion, Railway Operating, Steam and Diesel Electric). The men of the battalion were mostly recently drafted railroad workers. By then, America's railroads were diesel electric, and no one knew what to do with a steam locomotive. The acting sergeant (paid as a private) in charge of repairing them was a knowledgeable amateur enthusiast who couldn't have been happier. The Vietnam War was raging, and he got to repair steam locomotives instead of visiting Southeast Asia. Having laid track to Alaska during World War II and kept the trains running on time in Korea, the battalion had a proud history and received a number of unit citations. Apparently, laying track through swamp and permafrost isn't much fun, nor is riding a train when enemy aircraft are overhead.

All of the railroad robberies along the Southern Corridor between Yuma, Arizona, and El Paso, Texas, took place in the age of steam. Riding the Cumbres and Toltec was a homecoming of sorts, but it also provided afresh that special feel of steam, the clacking, chugging, and swaying side to side along with the cloud of smoke and sparks. Gilbert Lathrop recalled the *Rio Grande Glory Days* at the end of the nineteenth century on the same road, saying, "The mellow sound of a steam locomotive whistle. [The engine] chuckling deep in her diamond stack, with whisps of black smoke kissing the cab roof and wafting its delightful aroma inside. I have always loved the bouquet of smoke, valve oil, and steam as they came from the stack of a working locomotive."[2]

Of course, the folks who ran the railroad put the passenger cars as far back as possible to avoid this same bouquet that I rubbed from tender eyes. They led the passenger cars with the smoking car. However, having the baggage cars and express car up front was convenient for outlaws.

There is something special about the southeast corner of Arizona and the "bootheel" of New Mexico. In the days of steam, the Southern Pacific

Railroad, without providing any numbers, claimed that train robbery was so profitable that both territories needed to make it a hanging offense. Despite newspaper claims at the time, the evidence is to the contrary. The outlaws didn't get much, but they did do thousands of dollars' worth of damage to railway equipment and Wells, Fargo and Company safes.

In 1846, the United States fought a war with Mexico and sent General Stephen Watts Kearny and the Army of the West to secure the Southern Corridor along the 32nd parallel as a transcontinental route for trains, wagons, and the US mail. In 1854, Lieutenant John Parke of the Corps of Topographical Engineers surveyed a route for the railroad. Many years would pass before the road that blood and money had acquired was built. Although the Southern Pacific Railroad extended to the Colorado River at Yuma on April 29, 1877, it wasn't until September 1880 that the first track was laid across the Arizona–New Mexico line. Construction continued until January 12, 1883, before the Southern Pacific tracks from Los Angeles officially met the Galveston, Harrisburg, and San Antonio Railway and completed the transcontinental run. That it took until January 1883 to complete the railroad probably explains why there wasn't a train robbery in the Southern Corridor between Yuma and El Paso until November 24 of that year. The date of the "last" train robbery is much less certain.

The only certainty is that, if I declare a last train robbery, then someone will come up with another one just to prove me wrong, and I worry that in desperation they might hold up a train themselves. Since commencing study and composing this account, I have already been advised of two new entrants for the last. But breaking into a boxcar parked on a siding to steal a case of Spam doesn't really count (I'm sorry, Benson, it really doesn't), and the other turned out to have occurred on May 12, 1922, three days prior to my last on May 15, although, inexplicably, the May 12 outlaws weren't tried in court until 1926.

In the process of gathering "lasts," Benson, not willing to be left out, came up with an almost robbery—in fact, two of them. In September 1899, the outlaws changed their minds and robbed the train at Cochise instead. At 11:30 p.m., August 14, 1889, outlaws succeeded in wrecking the No. 20 passenger train on the grade west of Benson, Arizona. They broke into a railroad equipment storage shed and took some tools to remove a fish plate and seven spikes. When the train came along, the tracks spread and the locomotive rolled down the embankment, twisting the express car sideways to the track in the process. Fortunately, no one was hurt. This incident does, however, point to two of the reasons train wrecking is not the best way to rob a train. Someone might be killed, and the valuable express car might be wrecked, not to mention wrecking takes more work than most outlaws are willing to expend. The outlaws were not seen, but their tracks were clear at a nearby telegraph pole where their horses had been tied and where they left behind a recent newspaper.[3] The whole debacle led the *Arizona Weekly Journal-Miner* to speculate on why the outlaws didn't stick around to rob the train. This incident will be addressed later.

Despite its failure to make the grade as scene of a train robbery, Benson, in Cochise County, Arizona, is at the heart of train robbing country in the Southwest. Almost all of the robberies, successful and otherwise, involve Cochise County one way or another, whether it occurs there, the outlaws flee to it, or lawmen pursue them through it or, alternately, are themselves the robbers.

Black Jack, actually Tom Ketchum, the only man ever hanged in New Mexico or Arizona for train robbery, was accused of robbing a train in Cochise County. Black Jack Christian and his High Five Gang were Cochise County cowboys, which is to say outlaws. Tom Ketchum, a bit out of his head, proclaimed himself "the one and only original Black Jack" and, in that capacity, to his regret, was hanged. The High Fives never did rob a train in Cochise County. However, they did twice rob an entire railroad town. Their haul included $2.50, five pounds of flour, two pounds of sugar, five pounds of beans, and some tobacco. Jesse "Three-Finger Jack" Dunlap, before he took to train robbery, was the last surviving member of the High Five Gang, perhaps expelled because he was digitally challenged.

Butch Cassidy and the Sundance Kid found inspiration in Cochise County. In 1895, Cochise County cowboys blew up the express car near Willcox, Arizona. It is unlikely to be mere coincidence that four years later, in 1899, Butch chose Wilcox, Wyoming, as the place to blow up an express car. In 1888, Cochise County cowboys charged, guns blazing, from a burning house into the fire of a company of Mexican *rurales*. Legend has it that Butch and Sundance, his friend, died charging from cover, their guns blazing, into the fire of a company of South American soldiers.

There is something special about this southeast corner of Arizona that attracts and inspires badmen. The Southern Corridor, the route along which Interstate 10 runs today, was recognized as necessary for an intercontinental railway as early as 1846, when General Stephen Kearny passed through with the Army of the West and Lieutenant William Emory as his Topographical Engineer (until the Civil War, the Topographical Engineers was an Army corps like infantry and artillery). The land south of the Gila River from the Colorado at Yuma to El Paso on the Rio Grande is what Gadsden purchased, but the focus of criminal activity against the railroad was Cochise County.

The United States stole New Mexico and Arizona from Mexico and then paid the Mexicans $17 million. The Mexicans then stole what would become the Gadsden Purchase from the United States through trickery and sleight of hand. The United States then paid an additional $10 million for the Gadsden Purchase, but months before the agreement was concluded, the surveyor, Lieutenant Parke, trespassed into Mexico and surveyed the right-of-way. In 1856, everything was ready for the United States to start laying track, but sectional rivalry led to a delay of twenty-seven years.

The 1850s were years of sectional squabbling during which Congress accomplished little. In the 1860s, war squandered money and men, thereby diverting attention from developing a transcontinental country. Thereafter, a triumphant Union was unwilling to benefit the defeated Confederacy with a southern railway connecting east and west coasts. Completion was further delayed by bankruptcy and the need for bridges. An ancestor of the Southern Pacific, the Galveston and Red River Railway, was chartered in 1848, but work on it languished. On April 29, 1877, the Southern Pacific coming east from Los Angeles arrived at the Colorado River across from Yuma, but it was Sunday, September 30, before the first locomotive to cross over the river blew its whistle on the Arizona side. More delays followed, and the tracks finally reached Tucson on March 17, 1880, perhaps due to prior planning on the part of Irish gandy dancers, section hands hired to build the railroad who were too drunk to lay track on Saint Paddy's Day. On September 22, 1880, the track crossed the Arizona border in Cochise County into New Mexico. On May 19, 1881, the tracks left New Mexico to arrive in El Paso. Finally, on January 12, 1883, the Southern Pacific was joined to the Galveston, Harrisburg, and San Antonio Railway by two sterling silver spikes at a location three miles west of the Pecos River near Langtry, in that vast wasteland the locals insisted on calling Texas. Langtry was home to Judge Roy Bean, known in Arizona and New Mexico as an outlaw, who in 1860 operated a store in Pinos Altos near what became Silver City.

The Santa Fe system wasn't one railroad but rather the joining of many short roads and thus referred to as the Short Line, as you may recall from playing Monopoly, a game inspired by the railroads. Unable to secure a port in California, the Santa Fe steered for Guaymas in Mexico. It entered the Gadsden Purchase near Hatch, New Mexico, and connected with the Southern Pacific at Deming, leaving again at Benson, Arizona, to head by way of Fairbank to Nogales, where the tracks entered Mexico.

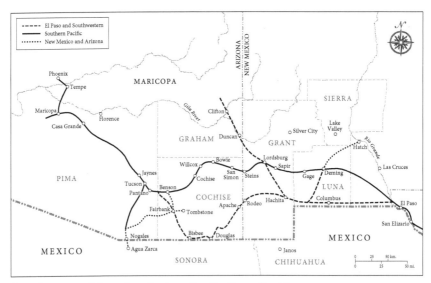

Overview map of the railroads along the Southern Corridor.

6

In 1892, there was a great drought in southern Arizona and New Mexico, and grass didn't come up. Ranchers attempted to sell their cattle and ship them to market and to other ranges, in order not to overgraze the land. Despite what the government today and legend would have you think, ranchers were by and large pretty good stewards of the land and understood what needed to be done to keep the range healthy. In the midst of this tribulation, the Southern Pacific raised shipping rates by 25 percent. Increased shipping rates made the SP quite unpopular with ranchers and with mine owners as well. The El Paso and Southwestern, part of which is the Arizona and Southeastern Railroad, built tracks from near Benson through Fairbank to Bisbee and El Paso with a line running northwest from Hachita, New Mexico, to Clifton, Arizona. This line was owned by the Phelps Dodge Mining Company as a way of telling the Southern Pacific to take its monopoly and shove it. Southern Pacific's rate manipulation was enough to make a cowboy think of taking up train robbing in revenge or of driving cattle to California. In 1892, the Vails, owners of the Empire Ranch, did just that, driving one thousand head to the Warner Ranch and Temecula in California, beating the SP and forcing them to reduce rates. Dislike for the railroad company lingered.

The railroads with the money to purchase legislators pushed through laws making train robbery a capital offense. Ranchers couldn't see the logic behind hanging a man who hadn't killed anyone. The law was very unpopular. In Arizona, only one train robber was ever sentenced to hang, and the governor, under popular pressure, commuted his sentence. In New Mexico, Tom Ketchum was sentenced to be hanged for train robbery, but Governor Miguel Antonio Otero seemed loath to go through with the execution, and there was even talk of an appeal to the Supreme Court. Tom Ketchum, who confessed to being the one and only, original Black Jack, was seriously in need of hanging. If he hadn't been hanged for train robbery, Arizona wanted to invite him to a necktie party over a murder in Camp Verde. His trail was twisted enough to raise doubts about being the one and only.

A pioneer could come to the Gadsden Purchase and lay claim to a homestead of 160 acres. That may sound like a lot of land to someone raised in a city high-rise, but it's barely enough to support one cow let alone her calf and a horse. If a man worked and improved the land for five years, he could file to get a patent, that is to say a deed. Some of the first ranchers to come into the area ran their cattle on "open range." No one owned it; they just used it. They might help some of their ranch hands to file homestead claims, especially around water sources, so that they could buy the land when the patent was filed. Henry Hooker of the Sierra Bonita Ranch started out this way, but it was a slow process. And it was a violent one. Running cattle on open range, one had to use a pistol to stave off others who wanted to use the land.

As part of their incentive to build, the railroads were given huge tracts of land by the government. If a rancher had the money, large tracts could be purchased from the railways. Much of the land acquired this way went to eastern investors, who often managed their ranches from a distance. The Erie Cattle Company in Cochise County was one such outfit, and George Hearst, father of newspaper magnate William Randolph Hearst, owned huge swaths of land along the San Pedro River, including the Boquillas Land Grant. For smaller ranches, owing mortgage payments to the railroad did nothing to increase the railroads' popularity with the debtors. We all love someone to whom we owe money . . . not!

In the 1860s and 1870s, before ranching got well started in the area, large cattle drives came up from Texas to feed the army posts, Indian reservations, and later the mining towns. Rough men hired on as drovers. Many were wanted in Texas, or to look at it another way, they were unwanted. They had to protect the herd from Indians and rustlers. When they arrived in southern Arizona and New Mexico, the drive ended, and they were paid off. They spent their money on wine, loose women, song, and gambling and wasted the rest until they had nothing left and no way to get back to Texas even if the Texas Rangers weren't looking for them. There were no jobs; therefore, they robbed stagecoaches and, when they became available, trains. They also rustled cattle and sold the beef cheap in the mining towns. Some, with a bit more ambition, rustled cattle from the big ranches to start their own spreads in and around the big out-fits like Henry Hooker's Sierra Bonita and Texas John Slaughter's San Bernardino. Given their common origin, this population of small ranchers was often sympathetic to their brothers from Texas and the South. The population, as Virgil Earp noted, was friendly to rustlers and hostile to railroads.

In 1882, Virgil Earp also suggested there was something special about the population. He talked to the *San Francisco Examiner*:

> *The Cowboys at one time numbered about 200, but during the last two years about fifty of them have been killed. The most of them are what we call "saddlers," living almost wholly in the saddle, and largely engaged in raiding into Sonora and adjacent country and stealing cattle, which they sell in Tombstone. . . . The cowboys are collected from all parts of the Western country, from which they have been crowded by advancing civilization, and they know that Arizona is about the only place left for them to operate in as an organization. With a complete breaking up of their company threatened in event of losing their hold where they are now, they resist official interference with the greatest desperation.[4]*

"Cowboys," often rendered "Cow Boys" in the nineteenth century, referred to outlaws. Decent fellows were drovers, stockmen, and cattlemen. Cowboys and saddlers, however, were outlaws. In Texas, where many drovers and drives originated, the Hoodoo Wars had left many with an urgent need to leave. Some would argue that an isolated rancher confronted with an outlaw or outlaw gang would have no choice except to provide hospitality or face evil consequences. Nonetheless, after the outlaws had gone, Cochise County ranchers showed themselves remarkably reluctant to provide information to officers of the law. In fact, on occasion, it appears the owlhoots were welcomed as heroes striking back at Northerners, Republicans, and the evil railroads.

The Gadsden Purchase was known for its sky islands—cool, wooded mountain ranges separated by a sea of grassy, desert plains. The mountains were a welcoming home and hideout for outlaws. The other "four corners" where New Mexico and Arizona come together with Sonora and Chihuahua, Mexico, made it easy to hop from one jurisdiction to another. Another factor of welcome was not so obvious. This area was a major population center where valuables were moving on the railroad. Silver City, New Mexico, and Tombstone and Bisbee in Arizona were some of the largest and richest towns between St. Louis and San Francisco. Mining brought population and sent gold, silver, and payrolls moving down the tracks. Payrolls were especially important.

One could carry on horse or burro back enough gold or silver to make oneself rich for life. Copper was more problematic, as it was valued by the ton rather than the ounce. Imagine taking away enough pennies on horseback to make oneself rich. Copper waited for the railroad and traveled in ton lots. To thwart thieves, mining companies poured molten gold and silver into ingots and bars weighing 50 pounds or more, making it inconvenient to carry away in saddlebags. The payroll, in coin or paper, was the thing to steal. Outlaws held up the stagecoaches on their way into town, not out.

Train robbing wasn't much of a crime. It wasn't like stealing a horse or killing someone. The governor commuted sentences and juries turned criminals loose rather than see them hang. Folks greeted Grant Wheeler, ranch hand and rodeo cowboy, as a hero after he robbed a train. He eluded five posses for a month while he toured the ranches of Cochise County. Around the campfire, he told his friends that if he ever got tired to cowboying and rodeoing, he'd turn to train robbery, for he was pretty sure he knew how to do it well.

Robbing a train was an art, and one that Hollywood never mastered. You wouldn't want to chase after a train on horseback and try to catch up. As they say in the navy, a stern chase is a long chase. Besides, your horse would likely be unwilling to run along the ties or get close enough to the train for you to latch on to it. If the horse cooperated, you'd likely fall to your death, and if you didn't, you would end up in the caboose confronted by an angry and armed train crew. Escaping these folks, you could make your way over the top of the cars, leaping between them, until you came to the engine and could order the engineer to stop the train. Alternately, you could jump onto the train at a cut or from a bridge. In the unlikely event that you survived, you could again run along the top of the train jumping from car to car until you fell beneath the wheels. Both approaches make excellent cinema, but this writer has never found a case where either method was ever successful or even attempted, but someone, somewhere is bound to have tried it sometime and probably died in the process. I watched Audie Murphy use both methods in an old movie.

However, there is an exception. Sheriff C. S. Fly, the famous photographer, tried to catch a train by running after it on foot.

Hollywood often portrays the passengers as the object of robbery. Certainly, in a time before credit cards and travelers' checks, the passengers carried great amounts of cash and jewelry. But they were also difficult to control and might be armed, and would-be robbers never knew who might be on the train. Only two cases where passengers were robbed have been found. In one, a curious passenger made his way to the express car to see what was going on. The other did not occur until 1910 when the Beardless Boy Bandits broke with tradition by robbing travelers and in other ways that led to the discovery that they were beardless. Lucky for them they did not try to rob a train in California in 2022, or they'd have been hanged for not wearing masks. This did not prevent passengers from panicking when the train was stopped unexpectedly, as the *Arizona Range News*[5] reported in Willcox in 1897:

> *Tucson parties state that A.E. Stoeger, of St. Louis, who has been posing as a hero and claiming credit for having prevented a collision between the Limited and Train 20 at Steins Pass on the night of the hold up, exhibited the reverse of bravery on that occasion. He ran back and forth through the car imploring the ladies to lie down on the floor to escape being killed and made himself generally ridiculous.*[6]

Despite train robbery conventions that led outlaws to ignore them, passengers did not want to believe they weren't the target of robbery, as the *Arizona Weekly Citizen* noted in 1888:

> *SCENES ON THE TRAIN.*
>
> *The train was an unusually large one, three Pullman sleepers filled with wealthy eastern people in addition to the regular train. As soon as the shots were fired and the passengers realized that the train was being taken in, every woman in the three sleepers fainted, and the cars were soon redolent with the odors of a dozen different kinds of restoratives. Men were pale and excited, and were deftly stowing away their valuables in out of the way places. If the robbers had ever*

entered those cars they would have had a picnic. It is very singular, but it happened that there was not a single firearm among any of the passengers. This would probably not happen again in years.[7]

Outlaws in the know went after the express car, which was also usually the mail car. Inside was a lone express messenger and, although armed, he was unlikely to resist, especially if the badmen threatened to shoot the engineer or fireman. If the express messenger did resist, or if the bandits had misplaced the crew, the wise outlaw brought along giant powder (dynamite) to blow the door off the car. The express messenger was in charge of valuables and of the Wells, Fargo and Company strongbox. In the movies and in novels, they call him the "shotgun guard." Sometimes the express messenger was a tough lawman or ex-lawman, but often he was an elderly man in glasses with a long history of being honest and trusted.

In those days of yore, registered mail often contained money and valuables. If the outlaw was lucky, he might score a payroll in a Wells, Fargo and Company strongbox bound for some intermediate station, though shipping times for payrolls were deliberately varied and difficult to predict. There might be a safe or strongbox to which the messenger had access, but the biggest rewards were protected by the "through safe," the keys to which were kept at the ends of the line. The express messenger could not be forced to open the through safe, for he had no key. It had to be blown. The knowledgeable outlaw, though, wanted the through safe. It held the big money, and its keys were kept in El Paso and Los Angeles.

Blowing the safe was no easy chore. Most outlaws didn't have the equipment or the time to drill into the locking mechanism and place a liquid charge, usually difficult-to-handle nitroglycerine. The alternative was to tamp the explosion, that is, to control its direction by placing sticks of giant powder on top of the safe and then placing something heavy on top of the sticks. The result was spectacular, literally cracking the safe and usually blowing the remnants of the express car all over the place.

Train organization was convenient. At the front was the locomotive, followed by its tender full of wood or coal for fuel and water. Behind the tender came the baggage car, and just behind it was the express car.

Farther back were the passenger cars. Perhaps this organization was to minimize the effects of sparks and smoke on the passengers, but outlaws found it opportune. If they could succeed in getting the locomotive to stop, they could have the brakeman disconnect the passenger cars, which could then be left behind so the express car could be taken farther down the tracks to be robbed in peace and privacy without the interference of pesky passengers.

Outlaws might board the locomotive when it stopped in some town or whistle-stop, a small community where the engine took on wood and water. Pulling a pistol on the engineer, the owlhoot would instruct him to start the train moving. Out beyond town, the train might be stopped so they could dispose of the passenger cars. Unfortunately, the entire town was apt to know that the train had been taken, and law enforcement might be notified. The key was to find a town with no law enforcement. Steins, pronounced *steens*,[8] on the New Mexico border next to Cochise County, Arizona, was just the ticket and the frequent scene of robbery. Willcox, Arizona, was another favored spot, for the population, mostly men from small ranches, was unlikely to inform law enforcement, and if they did, the local constable was apt to be one of the conspirators.

If the outlaws were familiar with railroad operations, as many were, having previously worked on trains, they might put out three torpedoes, small explosive charges. Like firecrackers, these exploded as the train rolled over them. *Bang-bang* meant slow down, danger ahead, and *bang-bang-bang* meant stop. If no torpedo was available, a bullet placed on the track would do nicely. The noise would be accompanied by waving a red lantern, which notified the engineer either of extreme danger or of a brothel ahead. In either case, the engineer was apt to bring the train to a halt. Sources on the Internet (so they must be true) claim that early railroad workers took red lanterns with them when they visited brothels and hung them outside so their crew could find them in the event of an emergency—thus, the origin of the term "red light district." The technique of waving a red lantern was so frequently employed that there must be something to the legend.

Bold outlaws might ride the "blind baggage," the end of the baggage car with no door, as "dead heads," emerging once the train was underway to climb over the tender to the locomotive. There was a danger of being detected as they climbed aboard, but they were most likely to be taken for hobos rather than robbers. The move from blind baggage over the tender was not nearly so dangerous, nor so lengthy, as attempting to climb over cars from farther back in the train.

Digging up the track or placing an obstruction over it was another technique train robbers used. It took more effort than most outlaws, being inherently lazy, were willing to expend. Why, they would ask themselves, expend so much effort in robbing a train when the whole point was to avoid labor. Nonetheless, this technique was occasionally used, but it, too, had its dangers. The engineer might spot the obstruction too early and bring the train to a halt short of where the outlaws were waiting. The train crew would then be on guard and difficult to handle. If the locomotive did hit the obstruction, the engine might tip over and kill the engineer and fireman, or it might explode. The express car might be wrecked, making its contents difficult to acquire. Even so, as we'll see, it was a popular technique.

DRAMATIS PERSONAE

Perhaps a word or two should be said about the people who operated trains in the late nineteenth century.

The Train Crew

The Conductor was the man in charge of passengers and freight. He ran the train, and, on freight trains, the caboose was his office. He kept track of cargo and collected fare or tickets from the passengers while keeping the train running on time. He was an interesting target for outlaws, who often stole his watch.

The Engineer, of course, operated the train and was tasked with making repairs in remote areas and with keeping the engine lubricated—with oil, not alcohol. In the days before sealed bearings, lubricating the moving parts was a big job, and moving parts required constant attention.

The Fireman was not tasked with putting out fires. He kept the fire in the firebox going. He loaded wood and later loaded coal, keeping everything in order so that he could feed forty to two hundred pounds of fuel to the engine every mile. Another job of the fireman was to keep the cylinders on the drive wheels oiled while the train was underway by climbing out on the running boards and creeping forward alongside the hot boiler to pour tallow on the valves.

The Brakemen were charged with coupling and uncoupling the cars. Prior to 1872, when George Westinghouse patented the fail-safe brake system, they ran along the top of the cars and leaped from car to car to set the brake wheel manually when the train needed to slow down. Otherwise, the engine applied the brakes while the cars kept going, causing a horrible mess.

The Expressman or Express Messenger was in charge of the Wells, Fargo and Company safe and the mail. We often see him in the movies as the shotgun guard, which was part of his job, too. He kept track of mail and money.

Although not part of the crew that rode the train, both Wells, Fargo and Company and the Southern Pacific Railroad employed detectives. Some, such as Bob Paul, Billy Breakenridge, and John Thacker, were famous and had been successful sheriffs and deputy sheriffs. Both Wells, Fargo and Company and the railroads as well as the US Post Office offered rewards for the arrest and conviction of train robbers. The offer was made for arrest and conviction, not for a body, dead or alive. The reward went to railroad detectives, to city constables, and to county sheriffs, who divided it with the members of their posses and with any snitches. While substantial for the times, the rewards were never as big as the movies would have it, and they—the rewards, not the movies— had to be divided. It's hard to imagine anyone making money collecting bounties for a living although many lawmen found rewards an important supplement to pay.

While we're at it, we should consider the other important figures that enter into the tale. Of course, the railroads, Wells, Fargo and Company, and the Post Office all had detectives or inspectors. Towns had constables or marshals. The latter create some confusion because the federal government in the territories, which New Mexico and Arizona remained until January 6 and February 14, 1912, respectively, appointed marshals who hired deputy marshals. We never knew if Matt Dillon was a federal or a town marshal, although he often acted like he was sheriff. Towns didn't have sheriffs, which was a county position. The sheriff's principal duty was collection of property tax, but he was also a law enforcement officer. Later in our story, we will encounter two Marshal Dillons working the same case. Fortunately, neither was named Matt. The term "constable" has been subject to many definitions. Today the constable is often a mere process server. In the nineteenth and early twentieth centuries in New Mexico and Arizona, the constable was a city policeman.

The Arizona Rangers formed in 1902 and were disbanded in 1909 by the legislature, which felt they were striking too close to home. The Rangers (the name had been used before and has been used after) were the famed "26 Men." Their jurisdiction was the entire Territory of Arizona. Most, more than twenty of them, were assigned to Cochise County.

In law enforcement, jurisdiction was important. A city marshal's jurisdiction ended at the edge of town, while the sheriff's ended at the edge of his county. The sheriff resided and had his office in the county seat. In Cochise County, that was Tombstone; in Santa Cruz County, it was Nogales; and in Pima County, it was Tucson. The Grant County seat was Silver City. Prior to the Civil War, New Mexico south of Socorro was all Doña Ana County, and the county seat was at Mesilla on the Rio Grande. During the Civil War, Arizona Territory was split off from New Mexico along an east–west line, and Doña Ana County became Confederate Arizona. Not to be outdone, President Abe Lincoln split Arizona from New Mexico along a north–south line along the 109th meridian of longitude, and that portion of Doña Ana County west of the line became Pima County in 1864.

As population increased, new counties were created. In 1875, the northern part of Pima County became Pinal County, with the county seat at Florence. Maricopa and Maricopa Wells became part of Pinal County, while Maricopa County was north of the Gila River with its seat at Phoenix. In 1881, the southeast corner of Pima County became Cochise County with its seat at Tombstone, while up along the Gila River the land became Graham County. In 1899, the southern part of Pima County became Santa Cruz County with its seat at Nogales. Finally, in 1909, the legislature created Greenlee County with its seat at

Clifton, virtually the only populated place in the county. Why is county organization important? When a train was robbed near Nogales in 1888, the sheriff had to come from Tucson, but after 1899, the sheriff would have had his office in Nogales. When outlaws took over the train at Maricopa in Pinal County, they rode it north across the Gila, and the Maricopa County sheriff pursued from Phoenix.

Similarly, New Mexico divided up Doña Ana County. In 1868, the western half became Grant County with its seat at Silver City. In 1884, Sierra County got a bit of northeast Grant County. In 1901, Luna County with its seat at Deming was created out of the southeastern part of Grant County and the western part of Doña Ana. Finally, in 1920, the southwest corner of Grant County became Hidalgo County with its seat at Lordsburg. If somewhere along the line, you feel the urge to correct me as to which county some event occurred in, check back here first. Remember the immortal words of Emperor Nero: "You gotta have a program. You can't tell the Christians from the lions without a program."

METHOD

I need to say a word or two about method. In this book, I relied heavily on newspaper articles. I recognize that many people claim the newspapers always get it wrong, and that's certainly true when it comes to spelling the names of people and places. However, I've found the old newspapers remarkable in their accuracy. They often printed verbatim letters from actual participants in events. They interviewed people shortly after the events they were writing about, and although they occasionally misunderstood what was being said, more often than not, they reported things with as much accuracy as many participants and bystanders would have.

Bias in a newspaper is always an issue, and sometimes it's obvious. When criminals were on trial, the Phoenix newspaper *Arizona Republican* was apt to cry, "Hang 'em high!" But the Tucson *Citizen* was more likely to say, "Have pity; he's a poor boy." However, when not editorializing, both were likely to report with all the accuracy we would expect from eyewitnesses, and they often reported in detail on testimony given in court. Certainly, different people tend to see different things as important, sometimes blinding themselves to matters that are obvious to others.

Old newspapers—that is, anything published before we all connected to the Internet—are horrible when they recite history rather than current events. The story of the 1916 train robbery at Apache, included herein, was originally seen in a contemporaneous news story that recited a brief history of earlier train robberies in the area, which unfortunately appears to have been the source used by local historians, for they included all the same errors in relation to the 1899 robbery at Cochise, which was conflated with the 1895 robbery at Willcox. In the end, they had the wrong man shot and the wrong man executed. Newspapermen often aren't especially good researchers. It may be that they're pressed for deadlines. Before the Internet, they had to rely on the newspaper morgue if the paper had one. Often, they relied on memory, their own and that of "old-timers." Not being constantly immersed in different historical periods, they were and are subject to anachronistic thinking and anachronisms in general.

One of the ways we can spot errors is by looking for anachronisms, the chronological misplacing of persons, events, objects, or customs in regard to each other. We should consider the wider world around the account we are reading and see if the account is in tune with that world. We test what we think we know by looking for things that might disprove it.

Deeds, court filings, official documents, and military reports were all written with the intent that they be accepted as true and correct. Where they are available, they are invaluable. Memoirs are primary resources, that is, the accounts of participants in events. There are two kinds of memoir. One is a private record that reflects what the writer believed to be true, and these are excellent sources. The other is the memoir that was written for publication with the hope of selling lots of copies and making money. By 1880, the publishing industry had been cursed with the "Ned Buntline effect." Ned wrote dime novels, the nineteenth-century equivalent of comic books. The public came to expect the Wild West and the kind of action Ned had written into his stories. Successful memoirs gave the public this sort of action. One such is the memoir of Billy Breakenridge.

Billy Breakenridge was a peace officer in various capacities. In the 1920s, he produced *Helldorado, Bringing Law to the Mesquite*, which will be quoted sparingly and with trepidation herein. Anything Billy had to say has to be checked against other sources. The title should have warned us. Billy is his own hero. He is also relying on memories forty years old. He tells a story of getting Curly Bill Brocious to help him collect taxes from cattle rustlers in their hidden camps. Unfortunately, the taxes being collected were real estate taxes, and if you didn't own any land, you didn't pay tax on it. If you did own land, its location was registered. Rustlers didn't pay taxes even if Curly Bill showed you where they're hiding. Does this mean that we should reject everything that Billy says? Of course not. He's still a primary source, but like everything else, what he says needs to be checked against other sources. The more general point is that memoirs can be trusted about as far as the newspaper can be. To reject everything Billy Breakenridge said because of one or two misstatements would constitute an ad hominem, an argument against the man rather than against what he has written.

CHAPTER ONE

Kit Carson Is the First to Rob a Train

Gage, New Mexico, 1883

IN AUGUST 1861, LIEUTENANT COLONEL JOHN BAYLOR, COMMANDING a battalion of the Second Texas Cavalry Regiment of the Confederate States Army, announced the formation of the Confederate State of Arizona with himself as governor. He was a bit premature, for the Confederate States did not follow his lead until January 18, 1862. The state stretched from Mesilla on the Rio Grande to Yuma on the Colorado River and included everything south of Socorro, New Mexico. Confederate Arizona included most of the Gadsden Purchase and thus future Grant, Pima, Cochise, and Pinal Counties, known as the Southern Corridor. Even Confederate acknowledgment of the new state was a bit premature, for all soon-to-be-relieved Colonel Baylor controlled was the Mesilla Valley. Nonetheless, it was a start, and it recognized a geographical reality. These southern realms, including the towns of Mesilla, Pinos Altos, Tucson, and Tubac, had more in common with each other than with points farther north. When mining towns, such as Tombstone, Bisbee, Galeyville, Santa Rita, and Silver City, began to blossom and were joined by other railroad towns, such as Deming, Lordsburg, Steins, Willcox, and Benson, they too became part of this southern realm. Cochise and Grant, the two counties along the border between territories, had much in common.

For instance, both claimed the Continental Divide. Grant County placed it along a line from Silver City to Gage. You'll pass over it if you drive on I-10 between Lordsburg and Deming. However, if you ride

Highway 80 between Tombstone and Bisbee, and as you pass through the Mule Pass Tunnel (locals call it the Time Tunnel), you will see above you on Old Divide Road a monument claiming to mark the true location of the Continental Divide. Bisbee's claim at the top of Mule Pass would seem to be superior since Grant County places it in the flat prairie between Separ and Gage. The Bisbee divide is not connected to the one in New Mexico, but Arizona State Governor Hunt put up the marker, using prison labor apparently under his direct supervision, so it must be correct.

The Apache problem, still an issue in the early years of this account, was shared between the two counties. In the spring of 1882, Colonel Sandy Forsyth with a regiment of cavalry chased War Leader Loco's Apaches from Separ (near Gage) to Steins Pass in New Mexico and then across Cochise County's San Simon Valley to Fort Bowie. The newspapers claimed that the entire town of Galeyville had been wiped out. Meanwhile, Cochise County Sheriff Johnny Behan with a Cow Boy posse was chasing the Earp federal posse from Tombstone toward the San Simon[1] Valley. Meanwhile, in Washington, President Chester A. Arthur and his cabinet argued about what should be done to get those wicked Cochise County Cow Boys under control. In the meantime, the Earps and Doc Holliday escaped across Grant County to Colorado.

The sky-island terrain, flat playas, dry lakes, and tall mountains are found in both, as are the mines of gold, silver, and copper, Chiricahua Apaches, and cattle ranches. In the 1880s, the range was still open. Some ranches controlled water sources and had a few acres, mostly of hay to feed their horses, under cultivation. Ownership of cattle was determined by brand. The cattlemen watched to see the brand on the cow a calf suckled, and the calf would receive the same brand. As the song says: "We rope 'em and brand 'em and cut off their . . ." Well, not tails, but if you've ever dined on mountain oysters, you now know how they were collected.

Roundup required a good deal of cooperation between cattlemen. The drovers knew each other. In a land without fences, they ranged far and wide rounding up strays and driving them into the roundup to be separated. Roundup was a time of long days, hard work, and relaxing around the campfire. The hands were likely to know each other across a very wide area. Lots of hands were needed at roundup, but not as many at other

GAGE, NEW MEXICO, NEAR THE SITE OF THE 1883 ROBBERY. JUST ONE OR TWO BUILDINGS AND A
CORRAL.. CREDIT: PHOTO COURTESY OF THE SOUTHERN ARIZONA TRANSPORTATION MUSEUM

times, so ranch hands tended to drift from ranch to ranch and to get into
trouble when not employed. There was also a need for weapons to defend
the cattle from predators, both animal and human. Cattlemen had to
command respect, often with arms, to defend their tenuous claims to water
and grass they did not own. Violence was inherent on the open range.

During the morning of Saturday, November 24, 1883, two men
dressed as cowboys rode up to Eaton's hay camp near Gage, a dusty whistle-stop thirty miles or so west of Deming. The younger of the two, riding
a horse, leaned over in the saddle to greet Albert Eaton and another man,
who were bent over repairing the Gage corral and wondering why they
bothered. The young man had two broken front teeth. His blond partner,
a few years older, rode a mule and had a facial quirk. In conversation, his
large mouth was wreathed in smiles when he spoke. The younger man
wanted to know when the trains ran east and west. The men at the hay
camp told them that the eastbound passenger train should pass through
after 4 p.m. The questions weren't unusual. Gage had a tiny train station,
cattle pens and loading ramp, a water tower, and telegraph key. It was flat,
dusty, and windswept with vistas that stretched away to craggy brown
hills in the distance. The riders thanked him and rode away to the east.

Gage was located on the continental divide, the Big Divide, between Separ, a place few people had ever heard of, and Deming, where the Atchison, Topeka, and Santa Fe (ATSF) Railroad joined the Southern Pacific. Separ does have some minor notoriety. During the Apache wars, a colonel loaded his cavalry regiment on the train at Separ to move them to Cochise, Arizona. This was the first time a train had been used to tactically move cavalry to thwart the Apaches. Later, the High Five Gang twice robbed the entire town. From Gage, the Santa Fe shared tracks with the Southern Pacific as far as Benson. Gage was there because the old wood-burning locomotives needed water just about every fifteen miles. Then someone thought: "The train has to stop anyway. I'll bet if I put a corral here and a loading ramp . . ." That was pretty much as far as the thought got. Before the days of powerful electric generating stations, the telegraph, which frequently tagged along with the railroad, used bell-jar batteries. These weren't very powerful, so the message had to be resent about every fifteen miles.

Six miles east of Gage, the two riders from Gage, Kit Carson Joy and Frank Taggert, met two compadres, Texan Mitch Lee and George Washington Cleveland. It was early days for train robbers as well as for the express service. Both train robbers and the express companies would learn from this first encounter. Having only the most basic tools, the boys dug under the crossties and separated a rail from the bed. It was a lot of work. Future outlaws usually disdained the labor or used tools to pulls spikes and unbolt fishplates, thereby leaving the rail loose but in place and less visible to approaching trains. A few minutes after 4 p.m., they cut the telegraph wire. "At first, only the whistle of the approaching train could be heard, but soon came the sound of exhausts, growing ever louder, until abruptly the locomotive snout rounded the last curve" and hove into sight.[2]

The train came on "chuckling deep in her diamond stack, with whisps of black smoke kissing the cab roof and wafting its delightful aroma inside . . . [while Engineer Webster's] expert hand was on the straight air valve, his practiced touch on the water brake, and his keen eyes focused on the track ahead."[3] At 4:20, as the train approached from the west six miles east of Gage, Fireman W. Thomas North noticed the missing rail and cried out, "My God there's a hole in the track!"[4]

Engineer Theophelus C. Webster hastened to reverse the engine and apply the air brakes. Giant steel wheels stopped and then began to turn in reverse, skidding over the rails as sparks flew and metal screamed. Too late! The locomotive slid off the last rail and bumped over the unprotected ties as the engine began to topple to one side. Webster and North jumped through their windows on opposite sides of the cab. As he jumped, Webster saw two riders approaching. It was the last thing he would ever see. One raised a pistol and aimed at the engineer. The other knocked the weapon aside with a large black

Silver City Courthouse, where Kit Carson Joy was tried and where the gang was held.
COURTESY OF THE SILVER CITY HISTORICAL SOCIETY

hand. Mitch Lee aimed his pistol again and shot Webster through the heart.[5]

On the opposite side of the tracks, someone fired two shots at North, who, unaware of Webster's fate, hid himself in a ditch. Brakeman Thomas Scott ran for Gage, only a few miles behind, where the telegrapher could send word of the incident over the wires. Kit Joy and his friends had cut the wire between Gage and Deming. The message would go west to Lordsburg instead of east to Deming. From there it might have had to go still farther west before it could be sent north, east, and south to Silver City, where the sheriff was located, and Deming. Delayed, the message arrived in Deming after 7 p.m.[6]

The outlaws rode to the express car and opened fire. Four shots rang out as bullets pierced the wooden door. Inside the car, wood splinters

showered Postal Agent W. O. Swan and Express Messenger George Hodgkins[7] as they listened to the whine of bullets passing close by. Swan gaped down in surprise as a hole appeared in the sleeve of his coat. Eyes wide as Swan displayed his ruined sleeve, Express messenger George C. Hodgkins cried out for the badmen to cease fire. Then he opened the door.

The leader, Kit Joy, sometimes known as Kid Joy, climbed into the car. As he did so, the mask slid from his face. Undaunted, he made no move to replace it. Instead, he grinned and displayed his chipped front

Kit Carson Joy.
COURTESY OF THE SILVER CITY HISTORICAL SOCIETY

teeth. Opening a drawer, he discovered some walnuts, sat down, and drew his new Bowie knife. Pleased with himself, he sat cracking and eating walnuts for several minutes. One of his allies demanded the keys to the safe and express box. Hodgkins surrendered them immediately, and the outlaw opened the safe. It was early days for the railroad and Wells, Fargo, and Company, for they were not yet using a through safe. The gang got eight hundred dollars. It doesn't sound like much today, but then a top hand was making thirty dollars a month, so this amount was two years' pay. Joy's companion rifled the mail. Postal clerk Swan described the boys as amateurs, saying:

> *They were novices concerning Uncle Sam's valuable mail matter. The registered mail pouch was lying near the mailing table, but was not noticed by them. The leader of the gang opened a drawer where there were some nuts and taking them out he cracked them and picked out the meats with his bowie knife while the others were searching the car for valuables. As far as the mail agent knows there was nothing removed from his car. The passenger coaches were unmolested.*[8]

On the ground outside, Conductor Zack Vail approached from the passenger cars joined by curious passenger Charles Gaskill of the US Publishing House out of Chicago. As the pair confronted the banditos, the outlaws demanded that they throw up their hands. The gang relieved Vail of two hundred dollars, mostly passenger fares, and the gold watch he used to keep the train running on time, while Gaskill surrendered $155. They took Gaskill's silver watch as well, but he pleaded for its return, saying that it was a gift. The outlaws returned the watch.[9]

With shots fired, the train stopped in the middle of nowhere, and the conductor absent, pandemonium reigned in the passenger cars. The *Black Range* wrote:

> *The alacrity exhibited by some of the passengers in secreting their valuables is said to be wonderful. One gentleman from New York secreted over $1,000 in his shoe. Watches, rings and other valuables were dropped in the water coolers, in the coal-boxes, behind the hot water pipes, in pillow boxes and in fact in every conceivable place in*

the coaches and sleeping car. One man even attempted to secrete himself in the linen in the sleeper.[10]

Before the cowboys rode away into the gathering dusk, the train crew had observed enough to assist posses in hunting them. The leader had chipped teeth and a new, identifiable Bowie knife. Another was a blond with a "large mouth, which, while in conversation was always wreathed in smiles." Still another spoke with a Texas accent. The last was a "large, ugly looking negro, about six-feet in height, as black as Erebus." As few have ever seen the deity who stands at the gates of Hades and returned to tell of it, one has to wonder just how useful this description was. Ugly may also have been added for alliteration. In time it would be found that folks remembered this group being in Silver City on November 19. From there they went to Mr. Whitehill's ranch, and Sheriff Howard H. Whitehill knew them. Onward they went to Ferguson's ranch and then to Eaton's hay camp. They were remembered, and their trail led to the Southern Pacific tracks at Gage. Both horse and mule tracks were found at the scene of the robbery. Later in Silver City, Albert Eaton would recognize a familiar mule as one belonging to these four.[11]

Relief, although close at hand in Deming, was slow in coming as word did not arrive until 7 p.m. that late fall evening. The line to Deming had been cut, and the message had to travel a circuitous route, resent every fifteen or twenty miles. "There was no electricity . . . in those days except that generated by blue vitriol and zinc in glass jars in the telegraph office."[12] The message went from station to station before finally arriving at Deming. As a result, relief would not reach the scene until hours later:

About seven o'clock a telegram came from Gage, stating that the train had been wrecked by train robbers and that the engineer and express messenger had been killed. A special train consisting of one flat car and two emigrant sleeper[s] was made up as soon as possible, and started for the scene of the robbery with about fifty well-armed men and Doctors Keefe and McChesney to render medical or surgical aid if necessary. After a cautious run of a little over half an hour, during which time a sharp lookout was kept for obstructions on the track and torn up rails.[13]

Wells, Fargo and Company was quick to pledge one thousand dollars per head for "arrest and conviction" of the train robbers. The Southern Pacific quickly followed suit with a similar pledge of one thousand dollars per head. The railroad was undoubtedly upset by the damage to their tracks and locomotive. The US Post Office, somewhat more parsimonious, limited itself to an offer of two hundred dollars per head. Thus, the combined agencies offered $8,800 for the quartet. This was enough to set a man up for life if only he could bring all four to justice by himself. It amounts to $232,680.71 in today's money.[14]

With eight hundred dollars in their pockets and having in their ignorance left a great deal more behind, the cowboys rode away to the west, away from Deming and toward Cochise County, Arizona. There they were perhaps glimpsed by the people of San Simon, already alerted to the possibility that the perpetrators of the Bisbee Massacre, bloody of fang and claw, might be headed their way. Indeed, some of that latter crew did pass by on their way north to Safford, Morenci, and capture. Eventually, one of the Gage outlaws, Frank Taggert, the fellow who couldn't stop smiling, headed north to a Mormon town on Arizona's Colorado Plateau while the rest of the bandits passed through Lake Valley on their way to Socorro.

The morning after the robbery, the posse came from Deming and found a cold trail. Hoofprints were lost in the many prints to be found on the Deming and Silver City roads. The ex-sheriff, Howard H. Whitehill, then serving as constable of Silver City, would have to use detective work to apprehend the boys. Suspicious characters were rounded up. Pete Spence, one of those involved in the 1882 murder of Wyatt Earp's brother Morgan Earp in Tombstone, was arrested in Lake Valley.[15] In June 1883, while serving as a deputy sheriff (or constable) in Georgetown, New Mexico, northwest of Silver City, Pete pistol-whipped a man to death. One of his misdeeds landed him in Arizona's Yuma Territorial Prison. There is some confusion in the record as Spence was already serving time in Yuma. Also, why would he be sent to an Arizona prison for a crime done in New Mexico? There could have been two different men with the same name.

A bloody picture appears on the canvas comprising Grant and Cochise Counties. In March 1883, only a handful of miles from Gage,

Chato's Apache raiders slew Judge Hamilton McComas and his wife on the road between Silver City and Lordsburg. Six-year-old son Charlie was never seen again. Geronimo was on the loose, and only a year prior to the train robbery, he had fought five hundred cavalrymen under Colonel Sandy Forsythe a few miles north of the railway. At the same time, Wyatt Earp was leading his Vendetta Posse across Cochise County. It should come as no surprise that in November 1883, when the railroad became available for robbery, the murdering robbers from the Bisbee Massacre fled toward Grant County, while the Grant County outlaws, having robbed a train, fled toward Cochise County and the two gangs might perhaps have crossed paths and been mistaken for each other. Looking at affairs in isolation, one fails to appreciate just how wild the Wild West could be and how closely the Southern Corridor was tied together.

In the fall of 1883, while enjoying the hospitality of a miner's cabin near Rucker Canyon, John Heath proposed a plan to his cohort. Big Dan Dowd, Billy Delaney, Tex Howard, Red Sample, and Yorkie Kelly intended to steal the Copper Queen Mine payroll as it arrived in Bisbee. The payroll would be housed overnight in the safe, the only one in town, at the Casteñda and Goldwater[16] Store. Heath would head into Bisbee weeks before to learn when the payroll would arrive and to open a dance hall at the head of the Gulch, a few doors down from the store. The grand opening would coincide with the arrival of the payroll and draw folks away from the store.

On December 8, 1883, everything was going along swimmingly until the stagecoach carrying the payroll lost a wheel, making it hours late in arriving in Bisbee. The boys grew impatient and rode into town looking for signs that the payroll had arrived. They rode up and down the street, and folks wondered about them. Finally, able to contain themselves no longer, they barged into the store with their pistols drawn. Two waited outside while the others plundered the folks inside and ordered the safe opened. They got a few hundred dollars and a watch that was later identified.

Meanwhile outside, the boys on guard were growing anxious. Seeing a drunk walking down the street, they ordered staggering Tex Nolley to get back inside the saloon. He responded that he'd be damned if he would. And so they obliged him with a bullet through the heart. Whether he was damned or entered the Pearly Gates is open to debate. John Tappeiner, a mining engineer, was shot next, and then pregnant Annie Roberts, sitting just inside her café. Deputy Sheriff Tom Smith attempted to end the episode and got a bullet for his trouble. The boys now rode out of town at high speed, leaving the dead of the Bisbee Massacre behind.

A posse soon formed, and John Heath volunteered. The rest of the posse became suspicious, for he seemed to be trying to mislead them. John eventually headed toward Tombstone, while the rest of the posse found their way to the miner's cabin near Rucker Canyon, where the miner informed them that Heath was the leader of the gang and the principal planner.

Soon afterward, a party of tough-looking men rode through San Simon. The locals figured they were badmen come from the Bisbee Massacre. No, the strangers replied, they hadn't come from Bisbee, and if they ran into them Bisbee varmints, they'd kill 'em. They looked mean enough to do it. There was speculation that perhaps they'd ridden in from Gage, where the Southern Pacific Train had been robbed and the engineer wantonly murdered. The confusion was understandable. Yorkie Kelly (York Kelley) was pursued into Grant County, New Mexico, and captured at Silver City.[17]

The Bisbee outlaws were soon rounded up and jailed at the new courthouse in Tombstone. On February 19, 1884, they were sentenced to hang. Entrepreneurs erected bleachers and sold tickets to what promised to be exciting family entertainment. Hangings were rare enough, and five at one time was unheard of. As the bleachers went up, Nelly Cashman, the Angel of the Camp, erected a wall between the bleachers and the scaffold. On March 28, the five left this world in dignity and without spectacle.

Meanwhile, John Heath, who planned the operation, was convicted of second-degree murder and sentenced to time in Yuma Territorial Prison. The Bisbee mob thought his sentence didn't sound fair since he was the leader and planner. On February 22, the mob "borrowed" Heath from the jail and suspended him from a telegraph pole while famed photographer C. S. Fly took pictures to sell as souvenirs. The city fathers, concerned that a town that had a lynching might not prosper, consulted with Doctor George Goodfellow. He had a solution. The death certificate read: "Died of emphysema, a constriction of the lungs at high altitude."[18] The Rough Bunch that had been mistaken for the Bisbee Gang at San Simon were probably glad to get back to Grant County.

If the four bandits had stayed together as far as Cochise County, they soon parted ways. Kit Joy, George Cleveland, and Mitch Lee headed back across Grant County toward Socorro, while Taggert went north toward St. Johns, Arizona.

George Washington Cleveland, later described as "a fine specimen of the mulatto, six feet two inches in height," from Llano County, Texas, took up gambling in Silver City and then headed northeast to Lake Valley, Kingston, Geronimo Springs, and Socorro. He had money, and people noticed it. Word got around. Perhaps lured by the huge reward, ex-sheriff Constable Howard Whitehill all but abandoned his duties in Silver City to hunt bandits. While he was away on the owlhoot trail, the city council voted to fire him. He had the scent, and enlisting the aid of Sheriff Pete A. Simpson in Socorro, he went after Cleveland and found him at the Sturgis House.[19]

Despite what Hollywood portrays in the movies, a large black man with money to burn found himself welcomed in New Mexico's gambling hells. He then left a trail as he headed northeast through Lake Valley and on to Kingston and Geronimo Springs. As long as he had money, he was welcome. He was also noticed for having an awful lot of money for a simple cowhand. Cleveland was apparently a country boy lacking

The Sturgis House,

SOCORRO, N. M.
A FIRST-CLASS HOTEL.
Headquarters for Mining Men. Recently Re-opened by
R. C. Dougherty, Proprietor.

AD FOR THE STURGIS HOUSE, A FIRST-CLASS HOTEL IN SOCORRO, WHERE GEORGE WASHINGTON CLEVELAND WAS ARRESTED. THE HOTEL WELCOMED BLACK COWBOYS LOOKING TO GAMBLE, BUT NOT IF THEY USED STOLEN MONEY. PUBLIC DOMAIN in street smarts. Whitehill told him that his buddies had ratted him out, naming him as the murderer of Engineer Webster and telling Cleveland that he surely would hang for killing him.

Whitehill told Cleveland, "Your buddies have confessed and say you shot Engineer Webster. You planned the whole robbery."

To which George replied, "No, no sir, it wasn't me. Kit Joy planned the whole thing, and it was Mitch Lee done shot the Engine Man, him an' Frank Taggert."[20]

Cleveland immediately claimed that he'd tried to save the engineer. It was Mitch Lee who shot him. He gave the two lawmen everything he knew about his friends, their names and descriptions. Sheriff Whitehill knew them. Mitch Lee was described as a "mere boy, but a perfect type of the Billy the Kid stamp of desperados" whose father was a wealthy cattleman at Uvalde, Texas. Kit Joy, with the chipped front teeth, was the son of David Joy of Cerrillos in Santa Fe County, while Frank Taggert came from Illinois to reside in Apache County, Arizona.[21]

George Cleveland's arrival in Silver City was news:

> *A little excitement was created on Saturday when the train from Deming arrived and Sheriff P.A. Simpson, of Socorro, and H.H. Whitehill stepped out of the cars on the platform with George Cleveland, one of the reputed train wreckers and murderers of the engineer, T.C. Webster, on the 24th of November, about four miles east of Gage station on the Southern Pacific railroad, in Grant county. George Cleveland is a colored man, 24 years of age, born in Lano [Llano] county, Texas, which he left four years ago, and three years since came to New Mexico. Your scribe being on the train with the colored man obtained a full confession in writing as dictated by him. Owing to the fact that three others of the gang whose names are given by him as connected with the robbery, and one of which is the real murderer, are at large with officers in pursuit, they are omitted from this letter.[22]*

Grant County from Mesilla to Steins on the Arizona border, between Deming in the south and Silver City in the north, is a broad, flat plain punctuated by the occasional hill. To the north, the land rises into the high mountains and the headwaters of the Gila River, while in the south, green hills and valleys stretch away like spread fingers to Mexico. Much of the land today won't support more than "four units" (four cows and their calves) per section, 640 acres. The grazing may have been better in the nineteenth century, which was cooler and wetter and before the government introduced erosion control grasses that aren't nutritious to cattle. Grazing was better in the higher country and in the valleys with running water. A man could homestead a quarter section, 160 acres, and if he worked it and made improvements, in five years he could get a government patent, a deed. Men claimed land along rivers and streams where they could keep their horses close and grow some hay and vegetables. On this particularly rich and rare land, a man might raise a few head of cattle, three or four, which were hardly enough to live on. He needed open range.

There, on land that didn't belong to anyone except the government and perhaps the Apache, a man could run cattle on thousands of acres. He could control as much land as he pleased until he started crowding his neighbors. Then he needed tough ranch hands to back his claim. These were men armed to protect the cattle against predators, including Indians, sodbusters, and other ranchers. Ranchers found that cooperation was more productive than open hostility, and they soon came to understandings as to which part of the open range belonged to whom. Cooperation was backed by superior firepower.

But cattle roamed, and the cattlemen had to chase after them. The *corriente* cattle that the Spanish introduced into the Southwest were pretty good at looking after themselves. In fact, they were fearsome beasts that didn't take kindly to coddling, milking, or predators. They were allowed to roam and didn't require close looking after like other European breeds. This free roaming meant that in spring and fall they had to be rounded up, and it was understood that the calf would get the same brand as its mother. Cowboys from all the ranches gathered for the roundup and the branding. They ate around the chuckwagon at night and dawn. A few were appointed referees to make sure the branding was done fairly.

"We'd take them off their mothers and wean 'em, rope 'em and brand 'em and turn 'em out in the pasture. Then, when they was two-year-olds, we'd forefoot 'em and cut the studs and turn 'em out in that 120-section pasture."[23]

They cut the studs to turn them into steers so they'd grow big and fat and not too vicious. The cows were kept to make more calves and grow the herd, while sometime in their second year the steers would be sold for meat and hide. Gathering at roundups meant that the ranch hands from a wide area got to know and recognize each other, each other's saddles, bowie knives, horses, and chipped teeth. A man might think twice about turning an armed comrade over to the law unless there was a really big reward.

The newspapers gave two vague accounts of the capture of Mitch Lee and Kit Joy. One story said that Sheriff Pete Simpson captured them near Lake Valley between Rincon and Nutt. The other reported that four cowboys, among them A. J. Best and Charles C. Perry, captured the outlaws near Horse Springs, 120 miles west of Socorro.[24] Neither Christopher Carson Joy, aka Kit Joy, nor Mitch Lee was regarded as particularly dangerous or as a murderer. "Among the 'Gila men'[,] that Kit Joy was not regarded as a murderer or train robber, but as a bold courageous fellow, never seeking a difficulty, but making friends where he went."[25] They rejected the despicable accusation against the two ranch hands Joy and Lee, saying, "We have known both of the boys long and well, that they have always borne the best of characters, and we do not hesitate to express our utter disbelief of their guilt or complicity in any manner whatever, in the alleged crime."[26] Nonetheless, the newspapers tended to bill the outlaws as the reincarnation of Billy the Kid and the Regulators.

The Las Vegas, New Mexico, papers thought that the liberal reward of $2,500 per head might have been a motivating factor when former friendly acquaintances turned them in. H. H. Whitehill, who was the former sheriff of Grant County, was then working as a Silver City constable and as a bounty hunter hot on Cleveland's trail. The real bounty hunters of the Old West were usually lawmen and railroad or express company detectives. They went after bounties to supplement their pay. Possemen got a share distributed by the leading lawman. Those providing evidence also got a share.

Sheriff/Constable Whitehill, who lost his job while on the trail of the outlaws.
COURTESY OF THE SILVER CITY HISTORICAL SOCIETY

Taggert was another matter.

"Taggart is the type of regulation cowboy. He could not be anything else, except possibly a robber and murderer, which he is. He is about twenty-two years of age, five feet eight and one-half inches high, weight 150 pounds; has light hair and mustache, blue eyes, and a large mouth, which, while in conversation is always wreathed in smiles."[27]

Whitehill talked of the capture of Taggert: "After I had captured Cleveland and wrung from him that confession I laid all the testimony against Taggert before Judge Bristol and he informed me that the circumstantial evidence was strong enough to convict the whole party. I then determined to hunt up this man. I had heard that he was loafing about Holbrook and St. Johns and so of course decided on visiting those towns."[28]

Armed with a writ, Whitehill, along with his seventeen-year-old son and Deputy Sheriff Gilmore, headed to Holbrook, Arizona, a Mormon town. Mormons were suspicious of outsiders and protective of their own. Their mythology had them wrongly chased from Ohio to Missouri to Illinois and then to Utah, where finally, beyond the mountains and beyond the reach of government and civilization, they set up a theo-democracy. The church owned everything, and the people got to vote to elect the one candidate the church presented.

In Holbrook, Whitehill learned that folks thought the outlaw had gone to the neighboring American Valley in New Mexico. Whitehill found Taggert, capturing him at Fort Agua del Frio. Whitehill took his captive back to St. Johns to make the formal arrest. He and his son were promptly arrested for kidnapping Taggert, and Taggert was released. After several days of presenting writs and notifying other authorities, they were eventually released, but the authorities still refused to give them Taggert. The writ of habeas corpus was refused. He was able to capture Taggert again but then faced townspeople who didn't want the outlaw arrested. "Whitehill hired a wagon and then by using a good deal of force succeeded in getting Taggart into the conveyance. . . . The drive to Holbrook was a long and tiresome one, but they at last reached that station and took the Atlantic & Pacific for this city [Albuquerque]."[29]

Kit Joy was so popular with the local ranchers that the former sheriff thought he might never catch him. After his harrowing escape from Mormon jail, former sheriff and constable Whitehill reflected on the popularity of the outlaws, little realizing that Lee and Joy were already behind bars in Silver City. "Just before the train started for Deming Sheriff Whitehill stated that another one of the robbers known as the 'Kid,' was well known to him. That the 'Kid' had once worked for him but that he despaired of ever capturing him, as he was confident that he had escaped into old Mexico."[30]

By March 10, 1884, the four cowboys had grown tired of the Silver City jail and perhaps a bit nervous, for the town's populace was in a hanging mood. They had new companions incarcerated with them. Carlos Chavez had already been sentenced to be hanged for the murder of Yum Kee. Another prisoner, name unknown, was charged with murder

Kit Carson Joy and his gang broke out of the jail in Silver City.
COURTESY OF THE SILVER CITY HISTORICAL SOCIETY

and even worse, horse stealing. About ten o'clock in the morning, two guards took the six manacled men into the yard for exercise.

The six had planned their escape. The shackled prisoners rushed the pair of armed warders, overpowering the jailers and wresting their weapons from them. The outlaws bound the guards hand and foot and, securing the keys, unlocked their manacles. Searching the jail, the former prisoners soon secured three shotguns, plus a Winchester rifle and pistol for each. Heavily armed, they made their way to the Elephant Corral, which kept horses, not mastodons. There they were about to discover one of the lessons of nineteenth-century city life.

In town, no one kept horses. There just wasn't room on a town lot for them, and it was expensive to feed and maintain an animal that one rarely used. People lived near their work. There were stores every few blocks so that one could stock up on fresh food daily. There was no refrigeration. Butchers went to the edge of town, where at an abattoir animals were slaughtered daily and divided among the shopkeepers so that townspeople could purchase fresh meat for that day's table. The horses that were available were kept at livery stables like the Elephant. In October 1881, fifty men volunteered for the Tombstone Militia to go and fight Geronimo, then nearby. They could only come up with twenty-five horses, and some of those would have been more useful to the knacker than in combat.

At the Elephant Corral, the fearsomely outfitted escapees ordered the livery attendants to saddle up six good ponies. Spotting an old friend, Mitch Lee was overcome with joy. "Here's my old pony! I know I can trust him. Saddle him up."[31] Alas, despite Lee's good fortune, only five good horses were secured. Noble George Cleveland, willing to risk the noose to save his friends, volunteered to stay behind.

"I don't really want to go," he said.

Kit Joy replied for the group. "Oh, yes, you will. We are going to kill you anyhow, but don't care to do it right here." Gesturing with a shotgun, Kit continued, "Get on behind Taggart!" Cleveland did as he was told.[32]

The six hombres charged through the streets of Silver City, firing wildly at all who poked their heads out. In moments, the town was on full alert. Shots were fired after the fleeing band. Horses were gathered from other stables. Frank Jackson had a horse to hand, and mounting became one of the first in pursuit. Keeping the outlaws in sight, he fired with little hope of hitting any of them, but with the intent to alert others following to the direction taken. Joseph N. Laffer, a widower raising six children on his own, soon joined the chase, and when he got too close, Kit Joy blasted him from the saddle.[33]

Five miles from town, the gathering posse found the body of George Cleveland; a shotgun blast had relieved him of his head. Some concluded that Kit Joy, unforgiving of Cleveland's faux pas in ratting out the gang, had kept his promise, although, with the posse gaining on them, Taggart may have wanted to lighten the load on his horse.

With their horses tiring, Mitch Lee and Frank Taggart along with Carlos Chavez went to ground firing at the posse, while Kit Joy and the nameless horse thief made good their escape, at least temporarily. A gun battle ensued during which Mitch was shot through the hips and Chavez was slain.[34] Deputy Charles Cantley took the two train wreckers into custody while the sheriff continued the pursuit of Kit Joy, soon losing him in the high country northeast of Silver City. The horse thief, whose name was discovered to be Charles Spencer, soon joined the deputy's party.

When the sheriff returned, he discovered that Mitch and Frank had met with an accident involving a length of rope and an oak tree. Spencer survived a split decision by the posse-turned-lynch-mob, which had relieved Cantley of his prisoners over the deputy's objections. Even though Charles Spencer was a horse thief, pending a regular trial, they let him live.

In the meantime, Kit Joy roamed free in the high country that he loved, but he needed food.

The outlaw began "borrowing" food from the ranch of Erichus "Rackety" Smith on the Gila River thirty miles northwest of Silver City. Rackety, enticed by the rewards being offered, informed friends that Kit was nearby. These included Sam Houston, a nephew of the Texas governor, Mike Maguire, and Sterling Ashby. Sam Houston approached Kit Carson Joy to lure him to Rackety's cabin. Ten days after the jailbreak, on Thursday, March 20, Joy was supposed to arrive to receive succor, but he didn't show up. The next morning at about eleven o'clock, the folks at Rackety's cabin saw Kit Joy crossing open ground three hundred yards from the cabin. A shot rang out and struck Kit above the knee, shattering the bone. Two days later, the four took Joy to Silver City, where his leg was removed.[35]

On November 15, 1884, Kit was taken from the Lake Valley jail, which had recently acquired three fine iron cages guaranteed to ensure that prisoners stuck around for the trial. Although on crutches and missing his left leg, Kit was taken under heavy guard for fear that he might attempt another daring escape.[36]

On November 20, 1884, Kit Joy, went to trial at Hillsboro in Sierra County. Why he was tried in Sierra County on a Grant County case is not entirely clear, but connections both friendly and otherwise in Grant County may have made a change of venue advisable. The case began with arguments that Kit was only guilty, if the facts were proved, of second-degree murder, not first degree as the indictment charged. With this technicality cleared up, the government presented its evidence for second-degree murder.

THE TESTIMONY on the part of the State showed that Kit Joy, Mitch Lee, Frank Taggart and George Cleveland (colored) were together at Silver City on the 19th of November; thence they went to Mr. Whitehill's ranch on the 21st; thence to Ferguson's ranch, in the direction of Gage station. According to the testimony of Harris, two of the band, Kit Joy and Mitch Lee went to Eaton's hay camp, still nearer the railroad, and opposite the point where the train was attacked. At the hay camp these two men enquired as to how the trains ran east and west, and the exact time the passenger express would pass. They learned that it did not stop at the switch after passing Gage either east or west; they also learned that the train afterwards attacked passed the switch about 5 p.m. San Francisco time, which would make it about dusk. Harris also testified that Mitch Lee rode a mule and Kit Joy a horse; that he examined the ground on either side of the track where the robbery took place and found horse and mule tracks. On the morning of the 24th, Kit Joy and Lee were at Eaton's hay camp, at which time they made the enquiries about the times the trains passed the switch. On the evening of November 24th, about dusk, the east-bound passenger passed Gage, and on reaching the switch about four miles east, the conductor saw that something was wrong, and then discovered that a portion of the train had been thrown from the track.[37]

Kit Joy attempted to call Pete Spence, then said to be operating a dance hall at Lake Valley, as a character witness. Given that Pete, as a deputy in Cochise County, had pistol-whipped a man to death and was then serving time in Yuma Penitentiary, this valuable testimony to Kit's character was denied him.[46] On November 29, the jury returned its verdict:

At the Hillsboro court, the jury in the Kit Joy case returned a verdict of murder in the second degree. This was owing to the Judge's charge, in which he said that the finding was all the evidence warranted. In spite of this charge, however, five of the jurors voted for the death penalty on the first ballot. Joy's sentence is imprisonment for life in the penitentiary, and meets with generally approval from all quarters.[38]

Kit continued to protest his innocence:

Kit Joy, the Gage train-robber, was sentenced to imprisonment for life. He claims to be innocent, and after his sentence had been pronounced, he said: "I am not guilty. The evidence against me was false and manufactured by railroad officials, but I believe the jury acted honestly. I will go to the penitentiary and try to perform whatever duty may be assigned me, and I hope by an honorable course to regain my liberty through the pardon of the governor.[39]

It seemed obvious to Kit Carson Joy that he'd been railroaded. In the spring of 1896, Governor Thornton of New Mexico Territory commuted Kit's sentence to time served, and on April 3, Joy was released from prison.[37] He ended up at Fort Huachuca in Cochise County working as the post tailor, a trade he had acquired in prison.[40] All of these stories seem to come back to Cochise County, Arizona, one way or another. In

1926, for six months, he became a guest of the county after entering a guilty plea for violation of the national prohibition act.[41] On April 14, 1936, Kit Joy passed away at age seventy-six and was interred in Bisbee's Evergreen Cemetery.[42]

With Kit Joy safely locked away in the new iron cells in Lake Valley, posse members gathered to collect the large reward. When the going gets tough, the tough get going, and so did the US Post Office. Realizing that there were multiple claimants to the reward—the men who identified the boys at Gage, Whitehill and company who'd made a number of arrests, those who made the arrests at Horse Springs, Sheriff Pete Simpson, various witnesses, those involved in rounding up the escaped prisoners after the jailbreak, and "Rackety" Smith—the Post Office got going and fled threatened lawsuits, withdrawing its offer of reward. After all, the Post Office officials reasoned, the outlaws hadn't really molested the mails all that much.

Still, the vultures gathered seeking reward:

C.C. Perry, of Socorro county, one of the captors of Mitch Lee and Kit Joy, now resides about three miles east of this city. It will be remembered that the original captors of the train robbers received only two-thirds of the reward, and they have now decided to sue the county or the sheriff of the county for the balance of the reward which amounts to about $1,600. H.H. Whitehill, John Gilmore, C.C. Perry and Jack Best are the original [c]aptors. Elliot, Pickett & Elliott, have been employed to bring the suit. All of the reward money, except for the capture of Kit Joy, has been paid. The Gila people, who re-captured Kit Joy, have entered suit for one-third of the reward which they will be allowed, unless Judge Wilson decides the case differently than his predecessor.–S.C. Enterprise." [43]

We are left to imagine that the final disposition of this case might have ended in a conversation between Rackety Smith and his lawyer.

Attorney: Mr. Smith, after final adjudication your share comes to fifty dollars.

Rackety: Fifty dollars! 'Twern't hardly worth my time and risk!

Attorney: No, no, Mr. Smith. Fifty dollars is what you still owe me.

CHAPTER TWO

The New Mexico and Arizona Railroad

FAIRBANK, ARIZONA, IN COCHISE COUNTY, WOULD HAVE TO WAIT UNTIL 1900 for its hour in the sun, but prior to that it contributed mightily to many confusions. We might start with its name, Fairbank, and be assured that Fairbanks (with an -s) is in Alaska. The town in Arizona was built at the point where Walnut Gulch, descending from Tombstone, meets the Babocomari River at its mouth on the San Pedro. There was once a dam on the San Pedro and a lake there where people from Tombstone went to enjoy a row and a picnic in the shadow of mighty cottonwood trees. The Mormon Battalion passed this way in 1846 and saw the dam and lake. They fished for eighteen-inch "salmon trout," probably Gila chub or cutthroat trout, which had pink flesh like salmon. It is here also that the famed original First Battle of Bull Run was fought. Colonel Cooke named the Babocomari River "Bull Run" in the account of his battalion's exploits. They passed through lands that had been Mexican land grants. The Apache drove out the Mexican rancheros and they left behind their corriente cattle, a relative of the longhorn. The Mormons of the battalion, although admonished not to by Colonel Cooke, tried to hunt the cattle. The Apache had killed and eaten the cows, leaving behind sexually frustrated bulls. The Mormons shot and wounded a bull, and in retaliation the bulls attacked. The Mormons suffered numerous casualties before retreating, their blood on the ground and their wagons overturned. The herd, bereft of cows, soon died out. The Mormons, with a plethora of females, did not. After 1861, the battle was renamed the Battle of the Bulls. It's unclear who won, but today there are plenty of Mormons and no wild bulls in the area.

Fairbank was a town built for spite and primed with confusion. In 1880, the Arizona and Mexico Railroad was incorporated, with Colonel Henry Hooker at its head and local Cochise County businessmen backing its construction.[1] Its plans were spectacular if undecided. The railroad might run from Benson to Fairbank and then down the west bank to the San Pedro River to Mexico, or it might run down the San Pedro to Fairbank and then up Walnut Gulch to Tombstone and on to New Mexico. To say the railroad was never built would not be correct. It was started. The company constructed key cuts and fills, before undercapitalization grabbed it by the cojones. The questionable ownership of the developed cuts and fills delayed the building of a railroad to Tombstone until the early twentieth century.

Meanwhile, the New Mexico and Arizona Railroad was built in 1881 and 1882 from Benson, to Fairbank, to Crittendon, to Nogales, and on, under a Mexican name and incorporation, to Guaymas. The Atchison, Topeka, and Santa Fe (ATSF), known in the game of Monopoly as the Short Line or just as the Santa Fe, carved its way to Deming, shared tracks with the Southern Pacific, and then, unable to get port privileges in California, headed south at Benson to Guaymas, Mexico, on the Gulf of California or Sea of Cortez. The Santa Fe is the Short Line because it doesn't have just one line from coast to coast. It is an agglomeration of numerous short lines into one system. Crittenden is eight miles south of Camp Crittenden (1868–1873), abandoned long before the railroad was built. Patagonia, three miles south of Crittenden, was soon found to be more convenient to the mines.[2] The Santa Fe in building this railroad was spiting the Southern Pacific, much in the manner of Davy Crockett, who, losing an election, told the voters, "You go to Hell. I'll go to Texas." So the Southern Pacific won California, and the Santa Fe, implying that the SP could go to Hades, went to Mexico.

Later, when the Southern Pacific raised its rates, the Phelps-Dodge Corporation with its main stake at Bisbee in the then Copper Queen Mine, decided that the Southern Pacific could go to Hell and Phelps-Dodge would go to Bisbee, though which is worse is yet to be determined. The corporation built a railroad from Mescal on the Southern Pacific track, west of Benson, to Bisbee and finally, following the border, on to El Paso, christening it the El Paso and Southwestern, or maybe the El Paso and Southeastern, perhaps depending on where you were standing at the time.[3] The Southeastern was the southwestern branch built in the 1890s, and the Southwestern was the southeastern branch built after 1900.

All of four railroads came together at Fairbank, which, as if its name weren't confusing enough, also had a spur line out to a nearby stamp mill and two railroad stations, one on Main Street and one nearer to the San Pedro River.

The New Mexico and Arizona Railroad, which went to Mexico, but not to New Mexico, was built largely with Chinese labor known as "gandy dancers." This makes the following piece, which ran on May 17, 1882, in the *Arizona Daily Star*, extremely odd:

> *New York, May 16.—A special from Laredo, Texas, says: Information has been received that a railroad mob has taken forcible possession of the railroad at Crittenden, New Mexico, the cause of the riot being the presence of Chinese laborers. They drove the Chinamen from the camp and then seizing Scott, the superintendent of construction, they hanged him to a telegraph pole until he promised to hire no more Chinamen.[4]*

The New York papers claimed they got the story from a Texas newspaper, which said the event occurred in New Mexico although Crittenden was in Arizona. The railroad was under construction at that time at Crittenden, but the crew was all Chinese. Strangely, no local account of the riot at Crittenden, apart from the repetition of the New York City story, can be found. It doesn't appear in the Tombstone, Bisbee, Tucson, or Nogales newspapers. Since chasing away the Chinese workmen would have resulted in the railroad never being built, it is highly unlikely ever to have occurred. More likely, this story is an early example of the eastern papers claiming that folks in the West were extremely wild and hated Mexicans, blacks, Indians, and Chinese. In the early days, they needed each other, tolerated each other, and even the peaceful Indians got along with the rest. In truth, the murder rate in Tombstone was lower than that in New York City, and the gunfight on Fremont Street near the O.K. Corral shocked the citizens of Tombstone.

In 1860, an educated man and mining engineer, Raphael Pumpelly, arrived in Arizona by stagecoach. He would later write about his experiences. Upon arrival in Tucson, after sleepless weeks on the stage, he collapsed on the floor of a saloon, where he slept for the next day and a half. He experienced numerous harrowing adventures watching friends and acquaintances being slain by Apaches. In company with Charles Poston, he escaped over the aptly named *Camino del Diablo*, the Devil's Highway. As a result, he suffered for the rest of his life what today we would call PTSD.[5] In 1884, he had occasion to return to Arizona and ride on the newly built New Mexico and Arizona Railroad:

> *In the night between Benson and Magdalena, we were sitting together in the center of the car. When the conductor called out "Crittenden" I turned to my companion, saying: "Gooch, we're only twenty miles from my old stamping ground. I never thought to come so near and get away again." In the same instant there rang out the sound of a rifle, and the ball, entering the window just ahead on the other side of the car, passed in front of Gooch's nose and just back of my head, scattering glass on us on its way. The only other passengers were some officers and their wives at the end of the car. One of the ladies, by the light of the flash, saw a man fire the shot.[6]*

We don't know who fired the shot or why, although Pumpelly seemed to think it was deliberately aimed at him. It might have been a railroad worker still upset at being underbid by the Chinese, a drunken cowboy, an Apache out for some fun, or an assassin who had waited patiently for over twenty years for Raphael to return to his old haunts.

There was one occasion when the rowdy behavior of workers and others on the New Mexico and Arizona line accidentally chased away willing workers. Calabasas was located where Sonoita Creek joins the Santa Cruz River north of Nogales. A Prescott newspaper, the *Arizona Weekly Miner*, reported the event:

> *Calabasas, the proposed junction of the Arizona and New Mexico railroad and the Sonora railroad is, from all accounts, a pretty*

*lively town, and the jolly railroaders, when their day's work is done,
are inclined to become merry. A few evenings since a few specimen
members of the genuine Arizona miner visited the town, and the
natives waxed merry in their honor. The best whisky the town affords
was consumed without regard to price or quantity; and various were
the feats of horsemanship performed and devilish tricks perpetrated.
The day previous to the visit of the miners some of the young ladies of
miscellaneous affinities that are known to abound in Tucson removed
to Calabasas on a business trip. The evening after the arrival of the
ladies (?) and the same evening on which the miners and railroaders
were holding forth four Chinamen arrived. This was genuine game for
the rather unscrupulous combination. The Chinamen were instantly
seized upon, stripped naked and ordered to perform a dance on the
green lawn fronting the big hotel. At that identical moment the
soiled fair ones from Tucson were making an informal inspection of
the partially completed caravansary. They appeared at the window
and a glance taught them not as much through the force of knowledge as the intuition of genius, that a genuine frontier "circus" was
in progress beneath them. They smiled approval, and with many
nods, winks and other peculiarities calculated to establish feminine
pleasantry, gave the weight of their influence to the performance. One
of the crowd suggested that the celestials ought to have partners; that
a stage dance never was and never could be an agreeable entertainment, and wound up by saying that in his humble opinion the ladies
ought to be invited down to take part. This speech was received with
cheers, and on motion of a miner, seconded by a railroader, a committee was appointed to enter the hotel and bring the females down.
The committee performed their duty without any unnecessary loss of
time, and the ladies appeared on the lawns, beauteous with paint,
and sparkling with jewelry. A motion was made by a railroader,
and seconded by a miner, that the ladies be ordered to disrobe. This was
carried unanimously, and a committee was appointed by the drunk-
est man in the crowd to aid the ladies to divest themselves of their
garments. It was done, and in the midst of the cracking of whips and
shooting of pistols the dance was again renewed. Three Chinamen and*

four girls took part in the dance, all arrayed in Eden habiliments. For an hour the dance continued, to the intense delight of the assembled crowd, when on motion the festivities adjourned, and the dancers were ordered to dress. This being done, it was moved by a miner, and seconded by a railroader, that a collection be taken up and the dancers rewarded. One hundred and thirteen dollars was collected, of which $25 was given to the Chinamen and the rest given to the girls. It was previously understood that the girls had come to stay, but to the consternation and disappointment of all the unmarried men in the vicinity they quietly left for Tucson in the ordinary farm wagon, not having the courage or patience to wait for the stage that was expected on the following morning.[7]

In these early days of Arizona railroading, the outlaws had not yet figured out that there were many less labor-intensive ways to rob the train than pulling spikes and wrecking the engine. As time went on, they would learn.

In August 1885, a rancher who lived near Huachuca Siding, later known as Camp Stone and Huachuca City, heard strange noises and went out to investigate. The siding was famous for the amenities provided to soldiers from nearby Fort Huachuca, among them a fine hog ranch and other dens of iniquity. Stepping from his house about three miles east of the siding, the rancher watched three men hastily ride away. Suspicions aroused, he headed toward the siding, where the message was telegraphed to trainmen in Fairbank and Nogales.

The next day, not far from the rancher's house, an alert engineer on the northbound train saw three mounted men. He quickly applied the brakes and reversed the throttle, backing the train to Huachuca Siding. The conductor was sent to walk ahead of the train as it again set out for Fairbank, though moving very slowly. He found the spot where the spikes had been pulled up. Pulling spikes and loosening rails would have wrecked the train had the crew not been warned and alert. The tracks were quickly repaired, and the train went on its way.

Huachuca Siding near Fort Huachuca, Arizona, on the NMAZ.
COURTESY OF THE SOUTHERN ARIZONA TRANSPORTATION MUSEUM

In a passenger car onboard, three sporting men departing a successful run at Nogales feared they might be the target of the attack. Hastily, they hid seven thousand dollars in coin, the proceeds of their winning streak, in the stove.

It would be years before the New Mexico and Arizona Railroad was again a target. By then, the outlaws had developed better robbery skills.

Chapter Three

Supernatural Heists

Pantano, located on the brink of Cienega Creek at the base of the western approach to the pass between the Rincon and Whetstone Mountains, was a whistle-stop, a place for trains to take on fuel and water. The two passes that follow—up to Mescal, down to Benson, then up to Dragoon Summit, and down to Willcox—are the steepest grades on the Southern Pacific Railroad. If you are driving west today from Benson to Tucson, as you cross the bridge at the low point over Cienega Creek, look north. If you're lucky, you'll catch a glimpse of the rusting water tower at Pantano two miles to the north.

Cienega Creek is joined by Davidson Canyon to form Pantano Wash, eight miles west of Pantano, and this stream in turn is joined many miles away by Tanque Verde Wash to form the Rillito, which flows north around Tucson, where it joins the Santa Cruz River. These intermittent streams reveal themselves on the surface accidentally, unless it's raining. None of this information would be important except that the general flow of the streams is north and west, and Tucson is south of the Rillito and west of Pantano Wash. The Southern Pacific entered Cienega Creek west of Pantano and climbed out again on a rickety trestle in Pantano Wash. The slow-moving train, on a dangerous trestle, and near a town too small to have a constable, was an open invitation to train robbers.

I first read about the Pantano robbery, or Colossal Cave Treasure, in the early 1960s, and I still have the book, *Lost Treasure Trails*, that

THE GRADE AT PANTANO.
COURTESY OF THE SOUTHERN ARIZONA TRANSPORTATION MUSEUM

tells the exciting story of Sheriff Bob Leatherwood, his posse, and four outlaws. The badmen boarded the train at Pantano and made off with a railroad payroll of sixty-two thousand dollars in gold. They rode north into the Rincon Mountains to an "unimpressive-looking hole which appeared to be the entrance to a small cave."[1] The sheriff and posse picked up the trail and soon discovered the outlaws' horses nearby.

The braver (or less sane) members of the posse ventured into the cave only to be met with a volley of gunfire. Electric flashlights and miners' carbide lanterns had not yet been invented, so they ventured in by candlelight, which did more to illuminate the holder as a target than to allow him to pick out targets at any distance. Bullets ricocheting from stalactite to stalagmite, men wading through bat guano and hiding in rimstone dams, leaping bottomless pits, sliding over flowstone, the fight continued, all of it illumed by candle and the flash of gunfire. Finally, Sheriff Leatherwood sounded the recall and brought the posse back out of the cave, reasoning that the badmen would have to emerge sooner or later for food and water. For two weeks, the bored posse camped outside the cave, playing poker because no one had brought a setup for the then popular game faro.

Then one day, word came for the Pima County sheriff, Leatherwood, from Willcox in Cochise County that the outlaws were enjoying themselves and spending money. Mounting up his posse, unconcerned with jurisdictional limitations, Leatherwood headed for Willcox, where at the corner of Maley and Railroad (Rex Allen Drive had not yet been designated), a gun battle ensued. Soon three bandits lay dead, and the fourth lay wounded. The wounded man revealed what Leatherwood had begun to suspect. The cave had a second entrance by which the gang escaped while the posse waited patiently out front. Avowing only that the gang had buried the loot in Colossal Cave and refusing to divulge the location, the outlaw was packed off to Yuma Territorial Prison.

Folks searched the cave for the buried loot to no avail.

Years later, time served, the outlaw was released though carefully watched by Wells, Fargo and Company detectives. One day, he slipped away, but the detectives soon picked up his trail near the cave. This time they guarded both entrances, but he never emerged. The sixty-two thousand dollars was never found, and the bandit was never seen again. The detectives reasoned that he must have fallen into a bottomless pit.[2]

In 1988, I visited Colossal Cave for the first time and was shown the empty money sacks where the gang had divided and buried the loot and the bottomless pit where the last man had fallen. In 2021, the money sacks are no longer available at the cave, perhaps given to some museum for preservation. The treasure has never been found, probably because it was never there. The outlaws did disappear near Colossal Cave, not once, but twice, but probably never entered the cavern.

On April 27, 1887, the westbound Southern Pacific passenger train due into Tucson at 10:45 p.m. had left Pantano Station on time. Although light on a dark night can be seen for miles across the desert, after midnight, the headlight on the train was still not in sight. Railroad officials naturally concluded that something serious had occurred. Then word came from Pantano. The train had been attacked!

An hour earlier, Engineer William Harper on the westbound Southern Pacific had been startled by three successive small explosions under the wheels of his locomotive. Torpedoes! Ahead, in the gloom, a man frantically waved a red lantern, signaling danger.[3] The engineer slammed on the brakes and reversed the throttle. Behind him cars jammed into each other, and sleeping passengers were thrown from seats. Two men with drawn pistols approached the cab.

Colonel Harper, as the engineer was known, recalled:

The man on the left side said "G—d d—n you, get down." I did so and he put a giant cartridge in my right hand and the red lantern in my left, and said, "Take that and light it and put it in the express car." He marched me to the car with his revolvers in hand, while the other covered the fireman. I told him it was no use to do this as I could get the men out of the cars without hurting any one. I got the mail agent to come out by telling him what was up. I was then taken to the express car and told, "Now d—n you, get that man out of that car, or I'll kill you." I told the express messenger to open his doors, and get out, as I had a giant cartridge in my hand and was covered with revolvers; if he did not open the car he would be blown up and both of us killed; that they were putting a dynamite cartridge on the platform.[4]

Inside the express car, Messenger Charles F. Smith hastily hid five thousand dollars in an unlit stove before opening the door. The bandits got three thousand dollars and $1,500 in Mexican silver. Two packages of railroad money were also taken and an unknowable amount, but probably a great deal of money, taken from registered mail.

Two of the outlaws now took Harper back to the engine:

They then marched me to the engine, to see about the water in the engine, for I told them it needed it. When we got there he said there was enough there as he looked at the gauge, showing that he had been on an engine before. He said, "I suppose you recognize us fellows." I said "no; I don't recognize anybody; I am doing what I am told to do."

One man then took the fireman back to cut the train between the express car and the sleeper, leaving the engine mail and express cars.[5]

Harper tried to give misleading instructions as he pulled ahead three car-lengths, but it became clear to him that these men knew more about the train than they were letting on.[6] Disconnecting the express car from the locomotive, the outlaws mounted the cab and piloted the engine westward toward Tucson only a few miles distant. Harper's account continues: "I was then made to show them how to work the levers and then was told to start it easy and after it was going to jump off, which I did. As the express car passed me, one of the robbers standing on the rear platform bade me a pleasant 'good night.'"[7]

In Tucson, there was concern for an overdue train. Undersheriff Charles A. Shibell was alerted and formed a posse that included Dr. John Handy. Mounting a special train, they rode eastward. Six miles west of the scene of the robbery, near Papago Station, the posse encountered an abandoned locomotive, its boiler now cool, its engine lever now reversed, making it unserviceable. Papago Indian[8] trackers, the best to be had, were called out and searched the ground around the engine for over a mile, but no tracks were found. The outlaws had vanished without leaving trace or trail.

The Southern Pacific offered one thousand dollars for arrest and conviction of each of the four men responsible, while Wells, Fargo and Company put up the same and the US Post Office offered two hundred dollars.[9] In an early example of the use of New Math, the *Arizona Weekly Journal-Min*er trumpeted: "The rewards offered for the arrest and conviction of the Pantano stage robbers in this territory amounts to $2,300 each, or a total reward of $11,500."[10]

These were the days when lawmen were still qualified to collect bounties. Deputy Sheriff Matthew Shaw and Undersheriff Charlie Shibell were on the case with Papago trackers and a troop of cavalry and were joined by company detectives Jim Hume and John Thacker.[11] The huge reward soon got the desired attention as the usual suspects were rounded up.

The Four Train Robbers Captured at Bowie by Marshal Meade
United States Marshal Meade passed Benson Monday evening having in his custody three of the men who robbed the train near Pantano. Mr. Meade also told a prominent railroad official that he had the

other one located, and could place his hands on him at any time. The
three men were captured at Bowie Station, and proved to be three
well known railroad men, and the fourth is also said to be a former
employe [sic] of the Southern Pacific.[12]

Unfortunately for US Marshal for Arizona William K. Meade, as it
turned out, these weren't the right men. It seemed clear, even this early
on, that railroad men must have been involved. They knew how to signal
a train to stop and knew how to disconnect the cars and had a pretty clear
idea of how to operate the engine. For now, the gang had mysteriously
disappeared.

Arizona State Historian Marshall Trimble wrote, "A search train
was sent from Tucson to find the late train. They found the engine and
Express car in the desert a few miles from town. But there was no sign of
the train robbers. Further down the tracks they found crew and passengers. They brought in Tohono O'odham Indian trackers who tried to cut
a trail. Several posses scoured the country but *the bandits seemed to have
vanished into thin air.*"[13]

No one had any idea who the outlaws were at this point, including
Marshal Meade, who had the wrong men in custody. They were will-o-
the-wisps who could vanish into the night. Later it would be learned
that a gang had formed around notorious "Cowboy Bob" Rennick.
Among its members were Jack "Kid" Smith and John "Dick" Maier,
a pair of hardcase former railroad brakemen who had met in El Paso,
Texas. On January 4, 1886, Smith and Rennick robbed and murdered
a merchant, Jules Boisselier. On July 9, they held up El Paso's Gem
Saloon,[14] and on March 15, 1887, Kid Smith shot an El Paso police
officer. Smith and Maier were joined by J. M. "Doc" Smart and George
Green in fleeing to Arizona. Two railroad friends, brakeman William
Skidmore and freight conductor Alfred Syndor, would join them.[15]

In August, the Silver City newspaper, *Southwest Sentinel*, noted the
activities of the gang, who also seemed to have been active in Texas.

There has been more train robbing in the southwest this year than
has ever been [before now] in the same length of time, and the
robbers have been more successful than is usual in such cases in

evading the officers. On April 27, the west bound Southern Pacific train was robbed near Pantano station, about 20 miles east of Tucson, and three robberies followed in quick succession in Texas. Last Wednesday night the Southern Pacific train going west, was stopped and robbed near the place where the robbery was committed last April.[16]

On August 10, 1887, the telegraph buzzed that the westbound Southern Pacific express had passed Pantano Station on time and in good shape. As midnight approached in Tucson, it was clear that the train was hours overdue. The company sent out a reserve locomotive to see what misfortune had befallen. As the engine neared Papago Station, the man at the controls was startled by the rapid firing of a revolver in the night. He immediately reversed his controls and started backing toward Tucson. Out of the night, rapidly gaining on him, came a speeding handcar manned

Pantano Station was the scene of more than one robbery.
COURTESY OF THE SOUTHERN ARIZONA TRANSPORTATION MUSEUM

by Conductor Gillespie and W. G. Whorf. They brought news of a fresh holdup "near the same spot." In Tucson, Deputy US Marshal Underwood and Deputy Sheriff Shibell assembled a posse.

Hours before, as Engineer James Guthrie and Fireman R. T. Bradford piloted the train up the grade from Cienega Creek, they passed the spindly trestle and then watched looming canyon walls on their left and on the right the steep drop to the creek far below. It was then that the gloom was split by the explosion of three torpedoes and a red light flashing ahead. Guthrie, knowing the danger, "endeavored to stop, by throwing the full force of the air brake against the wheels."[17] Sparks flew as steel wheels screamed and slid over steel rails. But too late! A gravel switch had been thrown, and momentum carried the locomotive forward unto an unfinished siding where it bumped over ties without rails and then began to roll over down the cliffside. Guthrie sprang out and landed in the arms of a thorny mesquite tree fifty feet below. The fireman tried to follow, "but before Bradford could follow the engine and tender had so closed as to bar exit in that direction. He then jumped through the cab window but kept his hold till his feet touched the ground, when he let go and rolled down to the bottom of the embankment."[18] Breaking free of the "briar patch," the pair scrambled away as the engine crushed the mesquite.

From the dark, a voice called out Conductor Gillespie's name. He had boasted that no robber would ever dare hold up his train. Circumstances were proving him wrong. Above the train, outlaws fired a number of shots into the express car and sleeper.[19] As two robbers approached the express car, they demanded that those inside open the door. Courageous Express Messenger Charles F. Smith and Route Agent A. M. Gault of the Wells, Fargo and Company refused them entry. Not having a handy engineer to threaten, the outlaws hung a stick of giant powder[20] against the door and blew it open. Recognizing Smith, an outlaw jocosely said, "Smithy, that stove racket don't go this time." He then demanded that Smith open the safe. The express agent refused and for his trouble got rapped a number of times on the head with a pistol until he chose to comply. The badmen cleaned out the American money and Mexican coin before departing into the night.

Deputy Sheriff Shibell, arriving in the morning, got the first of several surprises. The outlaws providing covering fire from above had left their dusters behind. It was then concluded that, in fact, they had never been there at all. In the dark night, the shots that pierced the cars had come from somewhere else. There had been only two robbers, not four. The newspapers loved it. From a place of concealment, Guthrie and Bradford had heard the departing robbers say, "Our meeting place is further up." The trail was followed "further up" and across the canyon bottom to a knoll where horses had been tied, and the Pima County sheriff discovered his second surprise: one thousand dollars in Mexican pesos were found abandoned. "Two linen dusters, one American $20 gold piece, one silver dollar and one half dollar American money were also found."[21] A clear trail led into the Rincon Mountains to the north. Two and half miles farther on, a great many money express packages had been opened, the paper and sacks having been left on the ground. The outlaws were thought to have got away with twenty to thirty thousand dollars. The trail was followed to a small cave, a few hundred yards from Colossal Cave, twelve miles from the point of the robbery. There someone had been living for a time and apparently observing the movement of the trains below. The posse found cooking utensils and provisions.[22] Thus, a legend was born and grew over the next century. The *Arizona Weekly Citizen* wrote: "The large cave found in the Rincons by the posse hunting for the train robbers on Wednesday last in the Rincon mountains, has long been known to several of the residents of this city. They report it large and spacious with well-formed chambers at different intervals, but on the whole it most resembles a great fisure [*sic*] in the mountain. Although penetrated for a long distance the end has never been reached."[23]

The trail continued at a point where the canyon runs toward the San Pedro River, where the bandit party divided, two going one way and two the other into Cochise County.[24] The posse continued to follow the trail, but in Cochise County, even the weather does not cooperate. Heavy August monsoon thunderstorms soon obliterated the trail. The four outlaws got away scot-free. The newspapers tried to understand the seemingly supernatural disappearing outlaws.

"At first it was five robbers who took in the railroad train near Pantano; later on there were two men and two dusters; now there are only the two dusters and by next week they too will have dusted. The 'dust' they raised has probably been safely consigned to the dust, until such time as they can in safety to dust return."[25]

Major Noyes sent fifteen US cavalrymen to join the pursuit while the railway and express companies each offered two thousand dollars' reward per man. The railway and express companies, as usual, were tight-lipped about their losses, claiming far less than the newspapers speculated. "It is not known how much money was stolen, Wells, Fargo & Co. admit $3000—but as the robbers got the entire contents of safe, the general belief is that it was much more."[26]

Fred Dodge, friend of Wyatt Earp, who claimed to have been "undercover for Wells Fargo" in Tombstone, joined the chase as a Wells Fargo detective. With him was Virgil Earp, sans elbow joint, the bone having been "misplaced" during an 1882 operation to save his arm, his forearm flopping merrily about as they galloped along. They followed a trail that, like the outlaws, disappeared. Fred recovered a biscuit in a rock shelter near Colossal Cave where the outlaws had camped. He was able to identify the baker of the biscuit and thus the outlaw who had purchased it.[27]

The powers of the outlaws to multiply their numbers, to disappear without a trace, to hide in caves, and to erase their trails seemed to make them almost supernatural. A good story grew in the retelling. Suspicion turned toward El Paso outlaws as the culprits. The *St. Johns Herald* reported:

> The El Paso Inter-Republica *says the railroad detectives have dis-covered clues that lead them to believe that "Tex." Harris and one Donapin, two hard characters of Arizona, have been engaged in the recent train robberies. Donapin formerly flourished about El Paso, and is a gambling-house tough. A few days before the robbery he went into Tucson and bought a can of ham of a peculiar brand—little sold. A can of similar sort was found lying in the cave where the robbers had rested. In addition to this he has been extremely flush of*

late, and a $20 bill with stitch holes through the end such as express companies use to secure their packages, has been traced to him. The recent rains have obliterated the trail and it is supposed that the robbers are camped in the Rincon mountains.[28]

In September, there may have been another attempt to rob the train at the old Cienega cut. A repair crew sent to fix a washout caused by monsoon rains, passing the spot where the robberies had taken place between Pantano and Papago Station, found the switch lock broken and a number of spikes removed from the track.[29]

You may have realized by now that the same gang was responsible for these robberies and that they understood railroad operations. They were apprehended on their third attempt. How ironic it would have been that the express agent who brought them to justice would have been their implacable enemy, the clever Smith who hid money in the stove, who with the third robbery had just had enough, if not too much. Alas, it was not to be. The third express car contained a Smith, Messenger J. Earnest Smith, not the one and only original Messenger Charles F. Smith. Nonetheless, J. Earnest was not a man to be trifled with.

In the evening of October 14, 1887, two men crouched unseen in the blind baggage as Engineer John Lohner took the eastbound out of El Paso toward the Southern Pacific's junction with the Texas Pacific Railroad at Sierra Blanca. When the train had gone about a mile, the two donned cloth masks and climbing the tender stood with a revolver in each hand ordering the engineer to the stop the train at the next curve.

Imagine the dramatic scene, if you will. Here are two gunmen, probably dressed in cowboy clothing topped with black Stetsons, standing high atop the swaying tender, using a pistol in each hand for balance with thick black smoke from the locomotive blowing directly into their faces, the whole scene illuminated by the flickering red glow from the firebox. The outlaws ordered the train brought to a halt before momentum on the curve could pitch them overboard. Standing fast as statutes, the sudden braking and jerking of the train did not dislodge the wraiths. The engineer and fireman must have thought they were gazing into a scene straight from hell. Descending into the cab, the pistoleros escorted Lohner and his fireman back to the express car.[30]

Nearing the express car, the badmen fired their weapons in the air. The sound alerted the express agent, J. Earnest Smith, that something was up. Closing the car door, he placed his pistol out of sight behind it. He and J. R. Beardsley, clerk of the Wells, Fargo and Company office in Fort Worth, put out the lights and took cover in the rear of the car, for the outlaws threatened to blow the door open. This they did with sticks of giant powder, the resultant explosion blowing a hole in the door, breaking glass, and tossing the two occupants about. The robbers ordered Smith and Beardsley to put up their hands and come out. The outlaws searched the men and then ordered Smith back into the car to light a lantern. Smitty had enough. Climbing back in, he seized his pistol, put it to an outlaw's breast, and fired a bullet through the man's heart. As he fell, probably already dead, the robber fired twice, ineffectually.

Messenger Smith and the dead man's partner exchanged a few polite rounds as the robber tried to drag his dead comrade up into the cab of the locomotive. Apparently, he intended to uncouple the cars and make his escape into darkest West Texas. Smith retrieved his double-barreled messenger shotgun and leaning from the damaged car fired into the night. The outlaw fell and then sprang up and ran off into the gloom, content to make his escape on foot.

The engineer backed the train to El Paso, where Deputy US Marshals Van Ripper and Ross took the trail of the missing badman. Securing the best and most experienced Mexican trackers, they headed to the scene of the attempted robbery. Their skill on display, they had soon followed the trail fifty yards to the dead body of the second robber. Inspection showed that only one buckshot had struck him, but entering at the shoulder it had traversed his body and severed his aorta.[31]

Are Charles F. Smith and J. Earnest Smith the same man, merely misidentified by the newspapers, as was all too common? It would be fitting. J. Earnest was greeted with a hero's welcome in El Paso. The paper noted that he was thirty-four years old, from St. Louis, and was then living in San Antonio. He had been in the employ of Wells, Fargo and Company for four years and then was assigned the run between

San Antonio and El Paso. This latter datum probably rules out his being assigned to the Tucson run. The citizens of El Paso presented him with a suit of clothes and raised over one hundred dollars for a medal.

J. W. Nicholls, superintendent of Wells, Fargo and Company for Texas and Louisiana, telegraphed Smith to congratulate him on his victory, saying that if his example were followed train robbery would soon be a thing of the past. Alas, the robbers were just getting started and perfecting their technique. The gang that had robbed the two Smiths was, however, done.

The bodies of the two men, both about twenty-five years of age, were taken to El Paso for identification. One carried an express receipt for J. W. Emerson, and the other was missing the third finger on his right hand. Time was running out for the gang. The El Paso authorities made tentative identification of the bodies and began looking into the activities of their associates. The officers learned that a group of men had been meeting in Caboose 44, which was controlled by freight conductor A. W. Syndor.

In November, Joe Smith and George Green were apprehended in Gainesville and taken to Tucson on a charge of train robbing in Arizona. It was reported that Green had confessed; however, when he was interviewed at the jail, he said, "It is simply a false charge trumped up against me by some of my enemies, that is all." Meanwhile, back in El Paso, his mother, Mrs. Green, was reported as being frantic. She said that her son was a good boy until he got acquainted with the Smith-Meyer Gang and that perhaps they had led him astray.[32]

By December, the two dead men had been identified as Jake Smith and Maier[33] (Meyers, John Mayar). "Doc" Smart was soon arrested, demoralizing the gang. A Wm. Joseph Wright, a former railroad employee working as head brakeman under Conductor W. T. Skidmore, was also arrested although he was registered at the Vendome Hotel as W. J. Wilson.[34] Here we encounter for the first but not the last time Wells, Fargo and Company detective J. N. Thacker. Thacker interviewed Green's mother, who admitted her son was in Arizona at the time of the robberies, and she gave the names of all parties, identifying the two dead men and others associated with her son.[35] The gang's railroad connections also included a Conductor Syndor (A. W. Sydner, Snider), who ended up in court alongside W. T. Skidmore and Doc Smart. Syndor had been the conductor on Caboose 44, which apparently had become a home for some of the outlaws and a place of meeting. It seems Syndor had managed to have the railroad tow it between Tucson and El Paso as the gang conducted reconnaissance.[36] Among the witnesses against the trio were Mrs. Green and her son George, whose true name was George D. Wills. He was one of the confederates.

Most of Mr. Wills's testimony was reported in full in the *Arizona Weekly Star* of January 19, 1888:

> *Next night after the conversation Myers, Smith, Doc Smart and myself met near the Pierson hotel. Doc Smart proposed robbing the express office near the depot. I remarked: "That is foolishness to talk any such way." . . .*
>
> *Smart remarked: "Will you three boys go up to Arizona and stop a while and I will come as soon as I can without creating suspicion?" Smith and Myers remarked to me aside that we would go and leave the s-n of a b——h behind. We stopped two weeks in the mountains about five miles from town. We used to come to town every night. We sent Myers to town to see when Skid would be in. Myers returned and reported that Skid was in town on caboose No. 44. We then came to town that night, without seeing Smart. We all three of us went direct to caboose 44, and met Skid and Sidner."*

George Wills (Mrs. Green's favorite son) went into the planning for the first Pantano robbery. Finally, on April 17, 1887, he told the court, they went into action.

> *About noon we saw the bridge gang eating dinner on the bridge. After arranging the giant cartridges Smith came to me and said: "You and Dick Myers will put the ties on the track if I don't fire my pistol; if I should fire my pistol it would be a signal for a freight train." Smith walked down the track. We saw a train coming and hearing no pistol shot, placed the ties on the track together with the red lantern and*

then went up on the bank, one on each side of the track. The train came to a stop at the ties. Myers remarked: "Don't move, you s-n of a b-h, for the train is taken in." And then we all commenced firing and Smith remarked: "Get back you s—s of b———s, don't put your heads out." Smith and Myers came up to the engineer, Smith put his gun up and requested the engineer and fireman to get out, which they did. Smith remarked: "get you hands up and walk in front of me." They walked down to the mail car and requested them to open up, which they did. The mail clerk jumped out and said: "boys, we are rather light to-night." They then took all parties to tell the messenger to open up. The messenger remarked: "who are you?" The answer was: "I am Harper, the engineer and covered with arms." Smith told him to tell the messenger to open up or "we will blow the d——d door off or open." Smith then handed the engineer a giant cartridge and told him to touch it off and blow the s— of a b——— up. The door was then opened. . . .

Smith made the engineer show him how to work the engine and moved up a short distance. Smith told me to get on the back end, which I did. Myers and Smith carried these men back on the train, all but the engineer. We then pulled out leaving the engineer standing there. As we passed by the engineer he remarked: "good-by boys, hope you will have a good time." I answered "good night."

We took the train a short distance above there, about three miles. Smith requested me to go down the road towards the passenger [cars] to keep watch, while Smith and Myers went through the cars. About half an hour afterwards they called me up to the engine. We then all got into the engine and pulled out for Tucson. Smith put out the head-light about nine or ten miles from Tucson. We got off and Smith reversed the engine and sent it back. The engine started back alone. We heard it running back for about five minutes.[37]

The puzzle of the ghost train or disappearing robbers was solved. The outlaws had set the locomotive in motion with no one aboard. They had already debarked, and so their tracks were not found where the engine, running out of steam, came to rest. It was a fairly large gang and may

Sheriff John Slaughter of Cochise County, who chased train robbers and employed at least one as a deputy.

COURTESY OF SULPHUR SPRINGS VALLEY HISTORICAL SOCIETY

have included other members who dodged both conviction and death. Doc Smart and George Green were found guilty, and Syndor (Snyder) and Skidmore were acquitted.[38]

During the trial, Syndor had made Caboose 44 famous as a meeting place and mobile home for the gang, towed back and forth between El Paso and Tucson by the Southern Pacific. With the trial over, nine of the twelve jurors rode Caboose 44 eastward to homes in Cochise County.[39]

Elected in 1886, "Texas John" Slaughter, at age forty-five, was sheriff of Cochise County for four years. Legend has it that dissatisfied with the courts releasing the guilty, Slaughter devised a new method of ridding the county of outlaws. He would return from the hunt with the word that "they left the county." And the outlaws would never be seen again anywhere. According to the *Tombstone Prospector*, within three months of being elected he already had nineteen prisoners confined in the county jail and had plans to restrain thirty more horse and cattle thieves.[40] The courts may have found incarcerating so many ne'er-do-wells excessive, though this being Cochise County, it might have been impossible to find twelve men "good and true" to convict these men, there being an unwillingness to cast the first stone.

John Slaughter was a former Texas Ranger who had come to Arizona as a cattleman. He eventually acquired the San Bernardino Ranch in the southeast corner of the county and northeast corner of Sonora. He was frequently accused of illegally importing Mexican beef but explained that he was only moving the cattle from his south range, in Sonora, to the north range, in Arizona. Slaughter occasionally employed Tombstone thug and snitch Burt Alvord as a posseman since he was willing to shoot to kill. Some said he was a regular deputy. Slaughter denied it. Alvord would eventually accept employment as the constable in Willcox and would almost immediately kill a cowboy under suspicious circumstances.

Slaughter was neither the first nor the last to try to clean up Cochise County. Eventually, it would take twenty-six men, the Arizona Rangers, to complete the job so Arizona could become a state. In gratitude, and perhaps trepidation, the Democrat-dominated legislature disbanded the Rangers. In 1887, Texas John had suspicions. The gang conducting train robberies seemed to be passing through his county just a bit too often.

He thought they might be hiding up Willcox way. On August 27, 1887, he, Virgil Earp, and Constable Fred Dodge surprised a gang of five men at Steins Pass. Virgil is described as galloping after the badmen with his arm, missing a length of bone since an 1882 ambush in Tombstone, flapping at his side. It's unclear if they were in Cochise County or just over the border in New Mexico. It's doubtful that the sheriff with his broad sense of justice would have cared, but it might have mattered to the courts later. The gang had been hiding on Hughes's ranch, and Slaughter surprised them, making a quick, bloodless capture. Hughes escaped, while another outlaw rode hard clutching at liberty. Slaughter's cutting horse proved faster, and he overtook the runaway. The sheriff fired two shots and the man surrendered. The sheriff took J. T. Blunt, Thomas J. "Dick" Johnson, Joseph Brooks, and L. M. "Red Larry" Sheehan as unwilling guests.[41]

The bandits arrested have been described as being under the leadership of notorious Jimmy Hughes, sweetheart of the San Simon gang of John Kinney, New Mexico's "King of Rustlers." Thomas J. "Dick" Johnson was said variously to have ridden with Presley "Toppy" Johnson and to be his son. Toppy was known to "old-timers." In Arizona at the time, old-timers were folks who had been there before 1870. They were indeed a tough crew.[42]

The sheriff conducted Johnson, Joseph Brooks, and Red Larry Sheehan to Tucson. After a preliminary hearing, Sheehan was held, briefly as it turned out. The grand jury failed to find an indictment, and he was discharged.[43] Upon their release, Brooks and Johnson remarked to Pima County Sheriff Matthew Shaw, "We have never robbed any trains yet, but as long as we have been accused, we are going to get busy and rob one for luck."[44]

Chapter Four

Robbing a Train for Luck

Steins Pass, New Mexico, 1888

THE YEAR 1887 WAS A BANNER YEAR FOR TRAIN ROBBERY. THE SAME gang had robbed the trains three times, twice "mysteriously" disappearing. There would be more robberies in 1888. Between 1888 and 1894, train robbery in Arizona went into hiatus after the legislature passed the notoriously unpopular "hanging law" for train robbery.

In the nineteenth century, a man was known by his clothes and the way his muscles developed. Sailors had highly developed forearms, like Popeye, from pulling on ropes. Masons wore leather aprons to protect their clothes. "I see by your outfit that you are a cowboy" was no joke. High-heeled riding boots with spurs, chaps, a .44 Colt slung in a holster, a bandana to fight dust, and wide-brimmed sombrero to keep off the sun and rain would have been common among this class of men. The shirt and hat would have been stained with sweat and dust and the leather battered and scuffed. Easterners, knowing these men from the works of Ned Buntline, would have seen them as unsavory and dangerous.

In the fall of 1887, sometime after the third train robbery, two such men stood on the platform in the Tucson rail yard near the spot where Wyatt Earp and his Vendetta Posse had shot Frank Stilwell to "Swiss cheese" only a few years before. One of them, "Red Larry" Sheehan, about twenty-five years of age, was tall and rawboned with a face red as a beet and smothered in freckles. Winchester rifle in hand, he turned to his partner, a shorter man and thick set. Dick Hart was a regular rounder who gambled and drank and looked for easy money. Unlike his friend,

68

he was well educated and smart. The two laughed over some joke. As the pair stood by the depot, the westbound passenger train puffed and readied itself while passengers from the east, tourists, walked up and down taking in the sights, oohing and aahing over the spot where Stilwell fell. Larry hoisted his rifle to his shoulder and, pointing it down the platform at the crowd, called out: "Get on board, G—- d—— you— hurry up." Easterners rushed the boarding steps and knocked each other aside trying to board. Larry and his friend thought it a fine joke.[1]

Fooling around probably accounted for Larry's failure to appear at Steins Pass with his fellow outlaws. Wells, Fargo and Company detective Johnny Thacker spotted Sheehan in Chihuahua City, four hundred miles to the southwest of Steins Pass, buying horses and equipment. The detective said that Sheehan's red, freckled face was unmistakable. When Thacker heard about the train robbery shortly after, he was certain he knew who the culprits were. Through no fault of his own, Red Larry didn't make it to Steins. He shot himself in the kneecap doing something unwise with his weapon. Legend says he was practicing his quick draw, but this seems unlikely. Hollywood hadn't as yet invented the fast draw. Sheehan was left behind to recover at the Palotado Ranch (Pallotterro).[2]

Steins—a hotel, saloon, railroad platform, and an outhouse on the Arizona–New Mexico border.
PUBLIC DOMAIN

In 1895, the *Arizona Republican* carried the following disjointed account of the 1888 robbery: "TUCSON, Ariz., Feb. 26—The bandits who attempted to hold up the overland [express train] at Stein's Pass, N.M., last night have taken to the mountains and are still at large.

"In 1888 a train was held up at the same point by five men who got $40,000, but were followed into Mexico by a Posse and killed."[3]

I suppose we must forgive newspapermen of yore. Indications are that newspapers did not as yet maintain "morgues" of old newspapers. If they did, it must have taken quite an effort to dig through the pile, but at the time, newspaper writers were not known for their industry. They relied on what folks told them they remembered, which was almost always completely wrong. Not to be overly critical, newspapers often recorded current events correctly, with the exception of universally misspelling names. It is when they made forays into the past that confusion reigned.

Steins Pass, pronounced *steens*, was about to become a favored focal point for outlaw mayhem. It really should be Stein's or Steen's as it's named for Major Enoch Steen, who, as far as we know, never visited, passing, in 1856, through the Peloncillo Mountains at Doubtful Canyon nine miles farther north. Located in Grant County—this portion of Grant is now Hidalgo County—Steins was on the boundary between New Mexico and Cochise County, Arizona. When outlaws took over a train in Grant County and rode it into Cochise County to rob it, they confounded law enforcement over who had jurisdiction and who got first crack at the outlaws for bounties and in court. Conveniently located, Steins was about as far from the county seats, where the sheriffs were located, as one could get and had no law enforcement of its own. It was also close to both Chihuahua and Sonora in Mexico. It could not have been better situated for ambitious outlaws.

Steins Pass had started out as a quarry from whence came ballast for the railbeds. When the line was completed, the railroad realized that a water stop was needed at Steins. Unfortunately, the pass was dry, and water too deep for a well. The railroad was forced to bring in water in tanker cars. With water provided, the town blossomed and soon had a mercantile or general store, a hotel, a rail depot, a saloon, and an outhouse. It was without jail or constable. It was an urban paradise for outlaws.

We can't know, but it seems likely, that just weeks before he shot himself in the knee, Red Larry Sheehan had been sitting around a table playing cards with Jimmy Hughes, Dick Johnson, and Dick Hart in the Steins Pass saloon. Someone, possibly Hart, who was rated smarter than the rest and their leader, glanced around at the surrounding town and said something like, "Wouldn't this be a great place to steal a train? The nearest law is in Silver City."

Another responded, "Wouldn't that be something? And we could take the train over into Cochise County to rob it right in Slaughter's backyard. We'd sure show him."

"Heck, [actual words have been sanitized] that'd teach him a lesson and might even cost him the next election!"

They gathered equipment in Chihuahua City, far enough away so as not to arouse suspicion, and leaving Larry to convalesce at Palotado Ranch, they planned their escape route by scouting it from there to Steins Pass. They staked their horses a few miles from the pass out in Cochise County's San Simon Valley and walked into Steins for a few drinks and perhaps some dinner. At around 8 p.m. on February 22, 1888, the No. 20 westbound stopped to take on wood and water. It also received two unticketed passengers who ducked into the blind end of the mail car just behind the tender.

Head brakeman Jerry Cerrano saw the two "tramps" and ran forward as the train pulled out of the station. Coming alongside the unwanted passengers, he shouted for them to get off his train. He was greeted by two rifles and told to back off. Cerrano decided to stay in Steins Pass and await developments. The tramps, he said, were five feet eight inches and heavyset and five feet four inches and slender. These were not the only tramps riding that night.

As the train crossed the border into Arizona, two men carrying Winchesters climbed over the tender to the locomotive. Colonel William Harper, the engineer, had plenty of practice and experience in what came next. He'd been engineer on two of the trains robbed the year before, and third time is the charm, as they say. He cursed under his breath that fate had it in for him and then stopped the train to uncouple the passenger cars. Two tramps poked their heads out of hiding, and the bandits put them to work as well with the uncoupling.[4]

As they worked on the coupling, the conductor, McLellan, and some of the passengers came forward to see why the train had stopped. Brakeman C. A. Jackson, known as El Paso Jack, recalled that the outlaws fired three shots into the ground and told folks to get back in the cars. With the forward part of the train unhitched from the passenger cars, the badmen ordered the engineer to take them a few miles farther out. And so for the first, but far from the last time, the order was heard, "Take this train to Cochise County!"

Left behind were four Pullman sleepers full of passengers from the east. Red Larry would have enjoyed himself. L. Shapers, a picture man from Minneapolis, was scared so badly he later told a news reporter, "I faint twice at one times." Two New Mexico miners, William Dickson and R. Ross, on their way to Tombstone told the *Epitaph* that the trainmen were a disgrace. There were seven of them and only two robbers. They could have stood them off. The two would-be heroes and other passengers were armed and willing to join a fight against the two outlaws, who hadn't even bothered to wear masks. "Backbone seemed to be lacking."[5]

The bad hombres ordered the train stopped and rifled the express. Speculation had it that they got off with between one and fifty thousand dollars. The truth was probably closer to two thousand. The newspapers speculated that a closer estimate was impossible because people chronically undervalued their shipments to beat shipping costs. Neither Wells, Fargo and Company nor the Southern Pacific were ever forthcoming about their losses. Claiming a large value for their loss would have damaged trust and stock prices. The outlaws departed on foot with their newfound wealth. The trainmen believed the bandits were on foot. As it turned out, the spot where they robbed the train was near where they'd staked their horses.[6]

The locomotive backed toward Steins Pass to pick up its abandoned Pullman sleepers and to telegraph word of the robbery to Tucson and Silver City. In Tucson, US Marshal W. K. Meade and Sheriff William Shaw Sr. of Pima County mounted an expedition. The posse included Len Harris, the celebrated railroad detective W. G. Worf, and Deputy Marshal Will Smith. The posse took along engineer Harper, the two tramps who'd uncoupled the cars, and four Papago Indian trailers. A special train was put together, and the posse loaded its horses and headed for the scene. Unfortunately, thinking that this would be a short chase after men afoot, they failed to take food and water, coats, and proper warrants. The February weather was cold. Arriving in the dark, the posse waited for morning to pursue and were twelve hours behind the outlaws when they set out.[7]

These were the days when lawmen, not bounty hunters or even possemen, were the great collectors of bounties offered by Wells, Fargo and Company, the Southern Pacific Railroad, and the U.S. Post Office. Meade and Shaw undoubtedly saw the main chance to beat Sheriff John Slaughter to the scene where the outlaws were, so they'd been informed, on foot. They were sure to catch the badmen.

They trailed the bandits down the San Simon Valley and through the Peloncillo Mountains, probably by way of Skeleton Canyon, duplicating in reverse the route Geronimo had used on his surrender just two years before. Arriving cold and hungry at the border with Chihuahua, Mexico, Len Harris had had enough. He turned back to Tucson, where he learned that Johnny Thacker, Wells, Fargo and Company detective, had been in Chihuahua City, where he saw Red Larry buying horses. Returning to El Paso, Thacker learned about the robbery and headed into Mexico in pursuit.[8]

Why was Sheriff Shaw of Pima County operating so far outside his jurisdiction, first in Cochise County and then in New Mexico and Chihuahua, Mexico? In those days lawmen could still collect bounties in addition to their salary. Perhaps he saw the main chance. In Tucson, he was among the first to get word of the robbery, even before Sheriff Slaughter in Tombstone, and he had a railroad at his disposal while rail lines would not reach Tombstone for another fifteen years. A special train delivered Sheriff Shaw to San Simon, where he planned to arrive ahead of everyone, chasing outlaws who were presumed to be on foot.

Penetrating Chihuahua, Shaw and Meade finally concluded that they needed food and had probably better let the Mexican authorities know that they were visiting their fine country. They notified the Mexican authorities at Janos, Chihuahua. The Mexicans learned that the posse was without proper documentation of any kind. On March 10, 1888, the

Mexican authorities promptly arrested the posse for illegally importing horses and weapons into Mexico and threw the posse into a dungeon, or so the American newspapers described it.[9] Later accounts described them as under house arrest and allowed the freedom of the town. The *St. Johns Herald* wrote:

> *US Marshal Meade has made a full report to the Secretary of State, of his arrest and detention at Janos Chihuahua, while in pursuit of the Steins Pass train robbers, which is not complimentary to the Mexican officers who made the arrest, and subjected him and his party to unnecessary insults and indignities. His report has already become the subject of much criticism and controversy, some of which savors of extreme partisanship [sic]. It reads like a simple, unvarnished statement of facts, with no attempt at self-laudation or complaint of personal nature, and should merit due consideration.*[10]

Meanwhile, Hart and Johnson were leisurely making their way back to Palotado Ranch, 125 miles west of Chihuahua City, far to the south of Janos. They camped for four days at Piedras Verdras (*piedras verduras*, rocks green like vegetables), eighty miles south of Janos, resting themselves and their horses, unaware that in Janos the posse was in jail.[11] Bob Paul, Southern Pacific railroad detective, thought the posse lucky to be in the lockup, for if the outlaws had known that they were being followed, they'd certainly have lain in ambush in rough country perfectly suited to the enterprise. The *St. Johns Herald* carried the following:

> *Detective Paul, who led the posse which killed the Steins Peak train robbers, is of the opinion that Marshal Meade and his party would have been ambushed and killed, if they had not been detained at Janos, as the country through which they passed was rugged, and presented many advantageous points for ambush. Such may have been the case, but it does not mitigate the outrage of their incarceration by Mexicans.*[12]

Robert H. "Bob" Paul was a tall westerner raised in California. In 1880, he ran for sheriff of Pima County. Skullduggery on the part of Ike Clanton and Johnny Ringo at the San Simon polling place led to one hundred more votes than there were voters (104 votes in all) being turned in. All of the votes were for Sheriff Charlie Shibell. The election was eventually overturned and Bob Paul elected. In the interim, Paul worked as a shotgun guard on the stagecoach from Tombstone that was ambushed on March 15, 1881, and the driver slain. Paul famously told the outlaws, "I halt for no man," and drove on through a hail of lead. Wyatt Earp, his brothers, and Doc Holliday pursued the would-be assassins. Even though the court overturned the election, Charlie Shibell refused to vacate the sheriff's office. The *Epitaph* called Bob "gallant ex-sheriff Paul" and said that a more efficient officer never lived.[13]

On March 24, 1888, after securing the proper paperwork, railroad detective Paul went to El Paso, crossed into Chihuahua, and headed for Chihuahua City to talk to the governor. He hired, or was loaned, a Mexican orderly sergeant, a duty sergeant, and four privates. Together they headed for Palotado Ranch. There a local Mexican came to their assistance. While Paul and his men waited out of sight, the Mexican went in and scouted the rancho. He found the three robbers

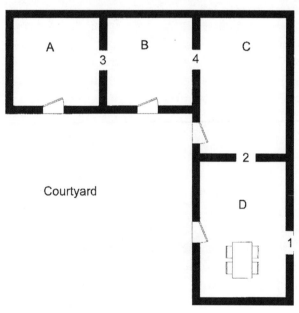

Diagram of multifamily house in Chihuahua, Mexico.
AUTHOR'S DIAGRAM

having dinner in the room marked D, while their rifles had been left in A. He rounded up two of the weapons and returned to Bob Paul with them, telling the officer what he'd learned. The four rooms of the adobe house all had their only doors opening into the interior courtyard. There were no exterior doors or windows, and no doors connected the four rooms internally. Rooms C and D were full of women and children, twenty-one of them in all.

The Mexican then volunteered to go back in and secure the third rifle that he'd been unable to locate on his previous visit. Searching Room A, he finally located the rifle on a shelf just as the outlaws returned and wanted to know what he was doing. Alarmed that his Mexican ally was long overdue and fearing for his safety, Bob Paul ordered his men forward and stationed them alongside the outer walls of A and D, where they could cover the courtyard with weapons fire and prevent the outlaws from moving between the rooms. His ally had been captured and taken as a hostage.

The duty sergeant saw the robbers ducking into Room A and rushed the door only to be shot through the heart for his trouble and courage. The outlaws dragged his body inside and barred the door. Paul was afraid to have his men fire. There were people inside, including his brave Mexican collaborator. The detective sent for the alcalde.

An alcalde was a Mexican official who combined the offices of mayor, sheriff, judge, and officer of the local militia, all in one person. Combining all of these functions in one officer might be seen as very efficient and certainly saved on salaries. Learning that a Mexican sergeant had been slain by the pistoleros, the alcalde was anxious to help and brought additional armed men.

Paul stationed his men around the building so there could be no escape, and through the night, he called to them frequently to ensure that they remained awake and alert. The outlaws had their brave Mexican prisoner start digging a hole into Room B at the spot marked 3 on the diagram to provide them with more options. They would then attempt to dig through at 4 into Room C, where most of the women and children were trapped, for the outlaws wouldn't let these noncombatants out across the courtyard. If the badmen could get to the women and children, they could use their new hostages as cover to escape.

The alcalde had his own idea. He had his men dig a hole through the adobe wall at 1 into Room D, and then he evacuated the people from that room and began digging at 2 into Room C. The bandits and the alcalde were both attempting to access Room C. The race was on, and the alcalde won by a nose. He evacuated the women and children. As the last woman was coming through 2, the outlaws broke through at 4 and fired on her, putting a hole through her dress. This act of deliberate savagery enraged the alcalde and the local men. The word went out that no quarter was to be given.

The alcalde now had his people scrape the adobe off the roof to reveal the bark shavings covering the *latillas* and *vigas* that made up the lower, wooden part of the roof and ceiling. He lit them on fire.

With the roof now in flames, Paul called on the outlaws to come forth. They answered in lead. Sheehan, hobbling on his wounded leg, tried to make a break and was shot dead by fire from a dozen rifles. With the women and children safe, Paul's men and the alcalde's men were now free to fire on the outlaws. Hart opened a door to fire back at the Mexicans outside and closed the door after each shot. He was shot through the door, lead mixing with splinters. The raging fire was too hot for Johnson, who rushed forth, his clothing smoking and his guns blazing. Return fire came from all sides. He went down hard and clawed his way up on his elbows, still firing until his two six-shooters had been emptied and his life spent, leaking blood into Mexican clay.

Bob Paul searched Johnson's body and found six hundred dollars and some jewelry. By the time he got to Hart, his Mexican soldiers had already beat him to the prize. He thought it best to let them have it as this was their reward and would encourage their cooperation in the future. No mention is made of Sheehan. Either he had no money, the Mexican soldiers got it, or he was too badly burned for Paul to recover anything.[14]

Detective Bob Paul sent the following message to Superintendent J. J. E. Lindberg of the El Paso division of the Southern Pacific:

Our posse found the Steins Pass robbers, Sheehan, Hart and Johnson, about one hundred and twenty miles west of Chihuahua, on the night of the 16th. We called on them to surrender and they took refuge in *an adobe house where they were attacked by us. They killed one man; burnt them our [sic] after 18 hours fight. All three men were killed fighting. The bodies were brought here and we recovered about $600 and jewelry. Can not say when I can leave here. The inquest will be held to-day. Will advise you later. R.H. Paul*[15]

Having been discovered by outlaws, there would be more robberies at Steins Pass. Sheehan and friends may have inspired other outlaws—picture Butch Cassidy and the Sundance Kid—to seek similar, dramatic ends to their lives. The year 1888 would host another bloody train robbery before the railroad and the legislature would act.

CHAPTER FIVE

Sheriff John Slaughter and the Massacre at Agua Zarca

TIES TO COCHISE COUNTY

Nogales, Arizona 1888

IN 1888, THE RAILROADS WERE PUSHING HARD THROUGH LEGISLATORS IN their debt to have something done about the train robberies. They arranged to have train robbery and train molesting made a capital offense in Arizona and New Mexico. At various times, the army had the authority to cross the Mexican border in hot pursuit of Apaches. Now the railroads wanted something similar. The *Tucson Citizen* wrote: "Wells, Fargo & Co, the Atchison, Topeka and Santa Fe and the Southern Pacific Company have petitioned Secretary Bayard to negotiate a treaty with Mexico which will allow the officers of either country to cross the border line in pursuit of criminals engaged in train robbery."[1]

Jean Tullier, alias J. J. "Jack" Taylor, was not a very nice person. We might forgive him the alias, often a sign of ill intent, since it appears to be the anglicization of his name. We might also forgive him for skipping Willcox owing money while taking along another man's wife. The wife didn't receive mention while he was in Nogales, so perhaps she'd already jumped ship on Jack. Her husband doesn't seem to have come looking for her, so perhaps he thought himself better off without her. Perhaps the aggrieved husband had been reading Rudyard Kipling, for the poet informs us: "Let 'im take 'er and keep 'er: that's Hell for them both."[2]

What we might not forgive is the company he kept both in Willcox and in Nogales.[3]

Tullier worked as a freighter on the Willcox to Globe Road and as a blacksmith. Both should have provided steady income, but he found it necessary to move from Silver City, New Mexico, to Willcox, Arizona, and then to Nogales.[4] The people he associated with were nothing to admire and may explain some of the difficulties he had in business. His employees in Nogales were nothing short of a murderous crew. He owed money to Conrad Rohling of Willcox, who would go on to do time in Yuma Territorial Prison and upon his release return to Willcox to collect on a minor debt, pick a fight, and wind up dead. Rohling was not someone to whom you wanted to owe money. Unlike modern loan sharks, rather than break your legs to force payment, he'd kill you and write the note off as a bad debt.

On May 11, 1888, Con Rohling went to Nogales to collect from Jack Taylor, but Taylor said, "I haven't got any money now, but I will let you have it in the morning." He left his residence at four o'clock in the afternoon and returned the following morning, paying Rohling off in Mexican silver dollars.[5] Considering subsequent developments, we must assume that the debt was quite small.

The Santa Fe Railroad, the Short Line, ran as the New Mexico and Arizona Railroad from Benson to Nogales, where it changed its name and continued to Guaymas, Sonora, as a Mexican road. It was rare for this line or its passengers to carry very much money, but the pay car had just arrived at Nogales and was supposed to be attached to the train as it headed south again. Unfortunately for Jack, it wasn't attached. In any event, the paymaster had paid the railroad's employees on the trip north to the border and had little left. The pay car was devoid of cash. The train departed with two passenger coaches, a baggage car, express and mail car, and five freight cars. About twelve miles to the south in Mexico, Jack Taylor and four of his dastardly employees waited in ambush at Agua Zarca siding, where the train would halt briefly.[6]

An outlaw leapt aboard the locomotive and ordered the engineer, James Gray, to throw up his hands. The engineer complied instantly. Seeing his distress, fireman Forbes jumped to his aid and received a shotgun blast for his effort.[7] He fell dead in the passage between engine and tender. Gray plunged out the window and hid under the train. Meanwhile, two other bandits headed for the express mail car, where a door had been left unlocked, perhaps because the car carried nothing of significance. Entering the car, one of the bandits shot messenger Ira Hay in the head. A second shot went through his body, passing through his kidneys. Hay fell to the floor and with very little effort feigned death. The robbers were frustrated in their attempt to open the safe. They found keys, but still unable to open the box, they took it with them.

Conductor Lewis Atkinson, in the baggage car, stepped out of the door to see what was afoot. He was shot for his effort and died on the return journey to Nogales. Passengers rushed forward to intervene but were blocked by two gunmen, who held the passengers at bay in the second-class passenger car, ordering them not to interfere. W. H. French, formerly a conductor on the Sonora Road and now working on the Mexican Central and riding as a passenger, was shot through the body. Among the passengers were two Mexican customs agents in uniform. Covered by outlaw guns, they kept quiet. Later, they would be arrested for complicity but were soon released.

Firing back at the train, the outlaws rode away into the Mexican night. As they went, Jack Taylor lost his hat. Stopping nearby, the banditos broke into the strongbox and extracted 130 Mexican dollars. Divided five ways, that was twenty-six dollars apiece. Jack can't have owed Con Rohling very much, though, for the next day Con, apparently satisfied with the payment, rode north for Tucson. It wasn't much of a haul considering that it left two men dead and two more not expected to live.[8] The *Arizona Silver Belt* thought the affair shameful.

Taylor, formerly a blacksmith in Wilcox and subsequently a freighter on the Wilcox and Globe road. Taylor, whose wicked life is drawing to a close, is, or soon will be, on his funeral march to a Sonora grave, where as is the custom, in the grey morning, a volley of Mexican lead will tap his life blood as an atonement for his participation in that sordid, cruel and defenseless deed. Taylor was not alone in this work of death.[9]

Ad for J. J. Taylor's shop in Nogales, Arizona.
COURTESY OF SULPHUR SPRINGS VALLEY HISTORICAL SOCIETY

As they left the now empty strongbox, Jack confessed to the others that he'd lost his hat. Nieves Miranda said, "You losing your hat will lead to your detection and arrest, and to save your neck you'll give the rest of us away, and the only way to save ourselves is to kill you." Taylor fell to his knees, begging and pleading for his life. The others convinced Nieves to grant mercy, but he had been correct. Taylor was soon captured. His hat was recognized as one he'd worn about the city of Nogales on May 11.[10]

Taylor was cornered like the rat he was and proceeded to do just as Miranda predicted. The law soon had a description of three Mexicans.

The *Arizona Silver Belt* wrote: "Three Mexicans suspected—Geronimo [Nieves] Miranda, 35 or 30, 5'4", 130 lbs. Native of Morvis Sonora. Frederico, 25, 5'7" 145 lbs very dark with features like an Indian. Well known in Willcox. Manuel Orozco Robles, 34, 5'6" 155 or 160 lbs. known in Contention. Reward $3,300 apiece."[11]

Other sources suggested that four Mexicans were involved. The papers do not agree as to whether or not Rohling was implicated by Taylor, but considering that he was handed over to the Mexican authorities, it seems likely that he was.[12] However, he was not convicted and returned to the United States only to be arrested on other unrelated charges.

At this point, two Cochise County luminaries, Sheriff John Slaughter and Deputy Burt Alvord, entered the story. Slaughter was featured by Walt Disney as Texas John Slaughter, and his theme song touted, "Texas John Slaughter made 'em do like the ought'r, 'cause if they didn't, they died." Disney also had five-foot-four Slaughter played by six-foot-five Tom Tryon. Slaughter took a 99-year lease on the San Bernardino Mexican Land Grant as his ranch. It lay on both sides of the border. The proximity to the border brought him into confrontation with Mexican outlaws and revolutionaries, including Pancho Villa, as well as Geronimo and plenty of American-made owlhoots. He had a Mormon cowhand with a house on either side of the border and a wife in each. John was tough and no one to mess with, and no one, except Disney, called him Texas John, but the record shows that he stuck close to the law as sheriff of Cochise County, not Tombstone, which was only the county seat.

Burt Alvord was another matter. He will reappear several times in our account on both sides of the law. Erwin, Slaughter's biographer, wrote, "Slaughter had hired Burt because he knew Burt was well informed on outlaw activities. And he knew that Alvord would sell his best friend down the line for a fee."[13] He was Slaughter's deputy sheriff. Exactly what that meant in the 1880s is difficult to say. County records seem to indicate that the sheriff was paid a substantial salary, but deputies were not on the county payroll, suggesting that the sheriff paid them and that thus they were used on again, off again as possemen. Such a setup allowed the sheriff plausible deniability, for Slaughter seems to have said later on that Alvord was never a "regular" deputy. Others suggest that Slaughter liked and trusted Burt.[14] Alvord truthfully seems to have been a thug who'd sell his best friend, but one who had a bit of pluck and courage in the face of outlaw gunfire and was useful on a posse.[15]

Sheriff Slaughter and Deputy Alvord pursued the Agua Zarca outlaws. The *Tucson Citizen* wrote that "our plucky sheriff was equal to the emergency, and on Wednesday night accompanied by his tried and trusty Deputy Burt Alvord," they shot it out with several of the badmen in French Joe Canyon in the Whetstone Mountains.[16]

"Sheriff Slaughter has been trying to capture the men who committed the deed, and at the same time endeavored to murder parties on the train. They were tracked from Fairbank to Wilcox [Willcox] and Clifton, and from there to this place, where they stopped overnight some ten days ago. From here they returned to Contention and thence into the Whetstone mountains."[17]

In company with their tracker, Susano Lucero, the sheriff and his trusty deputy proceeded up French Joe Canyon until they could see the outlaws' campfire. When within eighty yards of the campsite, they took off their boots and proceeded barefoot in order not to alert the men, who were sleeping wrapped in their blankets, to the posse's presence. Closing to within a few feet of the campfire, his deputy with .45 Colt in hand, and Sheriff Slaughter, holding a shotgun, cried out, "Throw up your hands and surrender!"

One of the bandits replied, "Yes, without arms." And then they fired on the posse.

Guadalupe Robles, a brother of the outlaw Manuel, was killed instantly, dying with a six-shooter in his hand. Nieves Miranda ran up the steep hillside, firing back at the lawmen as he went. He got about forty feet before the sheriff brought him down with a load of buckshot. The other man, Manuel Robles, ran down canyon, passing Alvord, who running after him barefoot put two rounds into him. Slaughter and his deputy pursued the wounded man for over two miles through rugged terrain by following the blood trail that he left. The two dead men and the wounded outlaw were taken to Contention City, and the justice of the peace called in to conduct a coroner's inquest.[18]

Manuel Robles was put on a special train and transported to Nogales to face charges. He died en route.[19] His death left only Frederico, whose last name, if he had one, was unknown, on the loose somewhere in Sonora. In May 1893, the *Tombstone Epitaph* recorded his fate. Frederico, still without a last name, was convicted and shot by a firing squad at Hermosillo, Sonora, Mexico, the last surviving Agua Zarca outlaw. The paper also reported that Geronimo, the outlaw, not the Apache, was still on the loose. But Geronimo was actually Geronimo Nieves Miranda, or Nieves Doran, who had been shot by John Slaughter in French Joe Canyon in 1888 and died on the train.[20] Maybe. The *Arizona Range News* reported: "Frederico was sentenced to death and will be shot at Hermosillo in a few days. Nieves Doran was shot by Sheriff Slaughter's posse (Burt Alvord) in the Whetstone Mts. and died on the train while being brought to Nogales. Taylor was shot at Guaymas. Rohling was in jail for two years. Robles is still in jail, and Geronimo is the only one that has not been captured."[21]

The only thing we can be sure of is that by May 1894, four of the five Mexican outlaws were dead along with some of their relatives. And one outlaw might still have been at large somewhere in Sonora.

Hoping to use Jack Taylor as state's evidence or to get him to provide more information than he already had, the Mexican authorities held on to him until 1890. It was a vain hope, for he had already given up everything he knew. He turned out to have more lives than a cat. On August 30, 1888, the *Arizona Weekly Star* reported that Jack had been executed. On May 17, 1889, the *Santa Fe New Mexican* proclaimed that J. J. Taylor was "Not Hung Yet!" On May 25, 1889, the *Arizona Silver Belt* wrote: "J.J. Taylor, formerly a blacksmith of Silver City, who was sentenced to be shot for robbing a train in Sonora, is still alive. He is being held as a witness against two others who were implicated. Taylor's partner, Rohling, has been sentenced to ten years in the salt mines."

On October 5, 1889, the *Arizona Weekly Citizen* reported that Tallier (Taylor, Tullier) had been shot. However, on October 12, 1889, the *Arizona Silver Belt* wrote that he had "As Many Lives as a Cat" and was still alive. On January 4, 1890, the *Arizona Weekly Citizen* informed its readers with finality that official State Department sources said that as of December 9, 1889, Jean Tallier had been definitively shot by firing squad and was officially dead.[22]

Conrad Rohling never made it to the salt mines. Upon his return to the United States, he got in trouble with the law and did time at Yuma Territorial Prison. Returning to Willcox, he attempted to collect a debt

J. J. Taylor or Tullier.
COURTESY OF SULPHUR SPRINGS VALLEY HISTORICAL SOCIETY

and got in a fight over a busted wagon hub with Braulio Elias. Big Con tried to force a fight, but Elias wasn't having any, so Con went and got two pistols, giving one to his opponent, who promptly dropped it onto the ground. Enraged, Big Con took aim at Elias, at which his enemy drew his own weapon and shot Rohling dead. This was ruled justifiable homicide.[23]

BENSON ALMOST HAS A TRAIN ROBBERY
Benson, Arizona, 1889
After numerous train robberies and attempted robberies, the railroad companies and Wells, Fargo and Company were concerned. Considering the dangers outlaws were posing, the companies may have had difficulty finding new engineers and express messengers. On the other hand, they may have been concerned over the expense of wrecked locomotives and express cars. With a great many legislators in their debt, they were in a position to do something about it. On March 4, 1889, Governor Zulick signed a new law into effect.

> *Mr. Lewis Martin's bill, making train robbery a capital crime in this Territory punishable with death, became a law yesterday by receiving the signature of Governor Zulick. The law is a good one along the frontier or for that matter any where [sic] else, and it is to be hoped will be adopted in Texas, New Mexico and California immediately and along the northern frontier, that a stop may be put to the devilish and murderous operations of desperate men who hesitate at no loss of innocent life to carry out their purpose of robbery.*[24]

Had not the governor signed this bill into law, no telling what mayhem might have occurred at Benson in August 1889.

The story of the Great Benson Train Robbery is mentioned here because, otherwise, it would rate only a footnote. In later years, two lawmen planned to rob a train at Benson but changed their minds and settled on Cochise instead. Benson is a town of many "almosts" where both sides of the tracks might equally be described as the wrong side. With four surface-level crossings, the trains roar through town, continuously sounding their horns while seldom stopping. Benson can claim, both east and west of town, the steepest grades on the entire Southern Pacific Line, which is to say, not very steep at all. The tracks drop down to the level of the San Pedro River, which, as if hiding in shame, usually flows underground at Benson, sinking at St. David and rising again at Tres Alamos. Trains pass by on this busiest of railroads every few minutes, making conversation difficult.

On August 14, 1889, three men attempted to hold up a train on the grade west of Benson. Having more energy than common sense, they decided to wreck the train. "Borrowing" tools from a nearby railroad shed, they removed four bolts from a fish plate, seven spikes from the rails, and two curve braces. At 11:30 p.m., when the No. 20 train arrived, chugging up the grade beside a twenty-foot embankment, the tracks spread beneath it, and the engine tumbled down the slope. Miraculously, the engineer and fireman escaped injury. The mail car jumped the tracks and spun ninety degrees to the rails. According to the *Epitaph*:

> *The tracks of the villains who did the dastardly work were plain to be seen, leading up and down the embankment to a telegraph pole, where had been tied one or more horses. Whoever it may have been, they had evidently planned the deed previous to undertaking the execution, as they had broken open the tool house at Benson and taken a claw bar, with which the spikes were pulled and which was left at the wreck and picked up by the train men at the bottom of the embankment.*[25]

A one-thousand-dollar reward was offered by the railroad, but no one was ever apprehended. Wrecking a train was a dangerous thing to do at this particular time. Apart from having picked a spot to await the arrival that was at the bottom of the embankment where the locomotive rolled, there was the issue of events taking place in the 15th Legislative Assembly. Not only did the legislature propose statehood for Arizona, if only they could suppress outlawry in Cochise County, but the solons had made it a hanging offense to wreck trains. In Prescott, pronounced *press-kit*, the *Journal-Miner* speculated on the robbers' motivation:

The only clue to the identity of the men is the finding of a copy of the laws passed by the 15th Legislative Assembly near the scene of the wreck. There is a difference of opinion regarding the cause of their failure to rob the train. One faction claims that they had possibly been sitting around the telegraph pole waiting for the train to come along, and that each of the three agreed to read a piece out of it to pass the time away. Number 1 read the bill where an alien is not allowed to enter the hospital in case he is hurt. He being Mexican, became frightened lest he should get hurt, and skipped out. Number 2 read the train wrecking act and followed number 1. While number 3 turned to the act providing for the calling of a constitutional convention, and after finishing it concluded that Arizona must have increased greatly in population since he visited her last year, and wisely concluded he would be caught in such a thickly populated country, and picked up his hat and sauntered down the road to Benson and signed a petition in favor of statehood.[26]

Between 1864 and 1867 and again between 1877 and 1889, Prescott was the territorial capital and had reason to defend the fine work of the legislature. Mr. Martin's bill seemed to have been working.

THE DEATH PENALTY
Maricopa, Arizona, 1894

Outside of Benson, which has always been a bit slow to catch on, there were no train robberies along the Southern Corridor for over five years. And then, three fellows made bold at Maricopa. The newspapers speculated that 1894 might have amounted to unusual times, thus sparking robberies that might not otherwise have occurred. "There is an ugly rumor to the effect that the hold up was done by some of the democratic candidates of Maricopa county in their efforts to raise campaign expenses."[27]

In the aftermath of the Maricopa train robbery, there was new resistance to the hanging law. It went to the Arizona Supreme Court and through various appeals. A timely hanging of the Maricopa culprits was greatly delayed. The county sheriff begged relief from the responsibility of constructing a scaffold, and ultimately, the governor commuted the sentence. The result was predictable and resulted in a brand-new spate of train robberies.

Shortly before midnight on September 30, 1894, at Maricopa station, three masked men huddled in the blind baggage of the No. 19 eastbound passenger train. Lou Holliday, assisted by fireman Jim Smythe, was the engineer at the controls of locomotive No. 1327.[28] In the dim light of the station, Conductor Martin signaled the engineer to get underway.

Brakeman Jerry Cerino went from car to car along the train checking between them to make sure connections were secure. A short distance from the station, he stumbled upon three masked men. At first, he thought them hobos and ordered them off the train. They jerked pistols from holsters and ordered Jerry's hands aloft. Jerry had experience being train robbed and complied quickly. In 1888, at Steins Pass, he had mistaken other outlaws for hobos. Hearing the ruckus over the noise of the train, Lou Holliday slowed the engine. A small, unmasked man crawled over the tender and stood looking down into the cab with a Winchester pointed at Lou.

Looking much bigger perched above, he ordered, "Keep her going!"

"How far?" the engineer asked.

"None of your **** business but keep her moving!"

A mile and half farther on, the outlaw ordered a stop where the gang had left their horses. Confusion reigns at times like these, and the crew thought that two more badmen had joined the party. Only three banditos were ever identified, so it seems unlikely that there were more. As one crewman recalled, "They seemed to be everywhere at once."

A few cars back, Conductor Martin alighted to ascertain the trouble that had caused the unscheduled stop. Two bullets whistled past his head, and a voice called out, "Get back on the train, you little ***** *****, or we'll fill you full of lead!" He hastened to comply.[29] He had a schedule to keep but rationalized he couldn't very well do it if he were dead.

Finding the door to the express car closed, an outlaw escorted fireman Jim Smythe to the locomotive to retrieve a coal pick with which to open it. Returning, it took only two knocks before the door opened from within. Express messenger George Mitchell later recalled, "Be Jasus I thought they were bums, so I stuck me head out and he says, 'up goes your hands' and I says 'up they go.'"

As an outlaw climbed into the car, Mitchell patiently explained that the big money was in the through safe, the combination of which he did not know. It was known only to authorities at terminal points such as San Francisco, Los Angeles, and El Paso. Only $165 could be found in other drawers and containers. As a consolation prize, the badman relieved Mitchell of his watch. Stepping down from the car, the outlaw snarled at the express agent: "'You —- of —— you will learn to vote the republican ticket next time,' as much as to say they would not have been in that kind of business but for the hard times entailed on the country by the democrats."[30]

The unscheduled stop and the gunshots frightened passengers further back in the train.

"A passenger by name of J.F. Rawlings, from Bloomfield, Iowa, was dosing in his seat at the time the train came to a stand still. He woke up by hearing a shot fired, and the car seemed to be empty, but on investigation he found most of the passengers under the seats and he lost no time in keeping them company, but fortunately they were worse scared than hurt, as the road agents did not molest them."[31]

We cannot attribute this behavior to Hollywood, because in 1894 theaters were not yet screening movies, and the silent film about a train robbery wouldn't come along for many years. We must lay this panicked behavior at the doorstep of the pernicious influence of Ned Buntline and his numerous dime novels. Train robbers did not molest the passengers except in fanciful stories. Somewhere in the back of the train, a young maiden, wishful to break free of the restraints imposed on the fairer sex by Victorian mores, whispered to herself, "I hear the outlaws always ravish the ladies." It was not to be. However, when the train arrived in Tucson, it was noted that a number of people had been scared so badly that "their complexion will not be natural in color for several days." Some must have been rosy cheeked while others were quite pale.

Sheriff Lemuel K. Drais of Pinal County, where Maricopa is located, recruited a posse. Billy Breakenridge, enforcement officer of the Southern Pacific Railroad, left Tucson with a special engine and a boxcar carrying his saddle horse. He wired Casa Grande for Billy Stiles and Felix Mayhew to round up saddlehorses and join him at Maricopa.[32] The posse followed the trail north across the Gila River and approached the Salt River where, seven miles from Phoenix, the posse was joined by Sheriff James Murphy of Maricopa County.

Some readers will recall Billy Breakenridge as a deputy sheriff under Sheriff Johnny Behan of Cochise County, the nemesis of Wyatt Earp. He provides many fanciful stories about his time in Cochise County. Billy Stiles went on to a long career in law enforcement, and we will encounter him again in another chapter. He became constable of Pearce in Cochise

Billy Breakenridge.
COURTESY OF SULPHUR SPRINGS VALLEY HISTORICAL SOCIETY

County and an Arizona Ranger and died in the line of duty serving a warrant as a deputy sheriff in Nevada.

The posse closed in on the camp of three men in thick mesquite. Securing the bandits' horses, the posse moved in on the badmen and told them to throw up their hands. A brief, though sharp, fight ensued. Two outlaws made good their escape, on foot, through thick brush. The third, Frank Armour (or Armer) fell with five bullet holes piercing his body. None were fatal, and though severely wounded, he survived to stand trial and face the threat of departing the earth by the "rope route."

In the outlaws' camp, Billy Breakenridge discovered a poll tax receipt belonging to Oscar Rogers, whose true name, the lawman wrote, was Oscar Touraine (Torraino). Back in Maricopa, Breakenridge learned that three men had been hanging around town together. They were Oscar Rogers, Frank Armour, and Ed Donovan. The chase was on. A description of the outlaws was available as a result of investigations at Maricopa, the railroad waystation. The *Arizona Daily Star* wrote: "Oscar Rodgers is a Swede about 26 years old, six feet two or three inches high, light sandy mustache, prominent front teeth, and talks peculiarly. Donavan is about 30 years old, five feet eight or nine inches high, weighs 155 pounds, has scars over his face and ears. Frank Armour is about 22 years old, height five feet six or seven inches, weight about 145, freckled face, light complexion."[33]

A short time thereafter, Rogers walked into the station at Sentinel, Arizona. Sentinel was in the western desert of Arizona, many miles from where he was last seen on foot near Phoenix. It would have been a long, hungry, thirsty walk, so it seems likely that he was assisted along the way. Much of the way, he would have been close to the Salt and Gila Rivers, both of which were dry for long distances while elsewhere providing water for irrigation. At the station, he was told that he was one of three men wanted in connection with the Maricopa holdup. The newspaper was read to him, and he admitted that he was the Rogers referred to but denied having anything to do with the robbery. He soon disappeared again on foot into the desert pursued by local farmers. On Sunday morning after a twelve-mile chase, they caught him at Adonde, about twenty miles east of Yuma. He was shipped to Florence, county seat of Pinal.[34]

Donovan was still on the loose, pursued up near Tuba City north of the Little Colorado River by Sheriff Donahue of Coconino County and his deputies, Jonston and Matt Blakely.[35] On a trip up to Durango, Colorado, Billy Breakenridge learned that a man resembling Donovan was working over near Pagosa Springs, Colorado. Billy learned that the man was not Donovan but rather Ben Mitchel, who was wanted in Brown County, Texas. Billy arrested him and wired the sheriff, who sent for him at once. Donovan, on the other hand, was never found. In the days before fingerprints and ID cards, changing your identity was rather easy.[36]

Rogers and Armer went to trial. Armer pled guilty and was sentenced to thirty years in the penitentiary, his guilty plea allowing him to escape the noose. Rogers, who continued to insist on his innocence, could not convince a jury of the same. On Monday, December 10, the jury found him guilty. On Tuesday, December 11, at 8 p.m., Judge Rouse sentenced Rogers to hang on the eighth day of February, 1895.[37]

On February 9, 1895, the headline in the *Arizona Republic* screamed "He Still Lives." Although the eighth was meant to be his big day, a last-minute reprieve was granted and the execution delayed by appeals. The case would go to the Arizona Supreme Court to determine if hanging a man for train robbery was constitutional. Interestingly, although it seems somehow unfair, Judge Rouse also served on the Supreme Court, but fortunately would not be available to rule on this particular case.[38] Apparently, tired of the delay, Rogers, with the assistance of Kid Thompson, tried to break jail, but Sheriff Truman knew of the plot, and it was foiled.[39] On June 15, despite Rogers's best efforts, he was still in jail.[40] A few days later, the Arizona Supreme Court affirmed the sentence and a new date for the hanging was set.[41]

However, the tide of public opinion had turned. The hanging law for train robbery, although highly effective for five years, was no longer popular. In the early 1890s, Arizona suffered a severe drought. Ranchers attempted to ship their cattle to market and to other ranges. The Southern Pacific Railroad helped out by increasing shipping rates by 25 percent and thus became very unpopular. Imagine shipping cattle to market, paying the Southern Pacific, and then receiving less at market than the cost of shipping. A rancher can't stay in business for long doing this sort of business. Thousands of cattle died on the range in southeast Arizona. On August 19, 1896, the *Arizona Republic* noted that the Prescott-based *Journal-Miner* was the only paper in the territory that still desired Rogers's hanging. The *Republic* wrote: "The fact is before us in all its magnitude that Rogers shed no blood, deprived no fellow being of life, caused no bodily injury to a human being while he was pursuing an act in contravention of the laws of the land, and neither was there brought out in his trial any evidence showing such intent."[42]

Shooting at Conductor Mitchell didn't count. He was an employee of the Southern Pacific and, therefore, no longer to be considered a human being. Or perhaps the *Republic* editor thought Frank Armour had done all the shooting.

On September 5, 1896, in another last-minute reprieve, Governor Franklin commuted the sentence to thirty years.[43] The *Republic* reprinted an article from the *Silver Belt*:

> *Silver Belt: His excellency, Governor Franklin, in the plentitude of his power and profound consideration for the sensitive feelings of the sheriff of Pinal county, relieved him from the unpleasant duty of severing the earthly tie that gives Oscar Rogers a hold upon life. He has commuted the sentence imposed by Judge Rouse, for train robbery, that Rogers hang by the neck until dead, on the 11th inst. to a forty year imprisonment in the territorial bastile. At the termination of his incarceration, should the thread of life be still intact and the hand of executive clemency withheld, his limbs will be stiffened by age and his occupation as a pianist will have fled with the ebb of time.*[44]

Later on, Rogers's sentence was reduced to ten years, which he served. Armour also had his sentence reduced but was released due to ill-health.[45]

CHAPTER SIX

Billy Breakenridge Pursues Grant Wheeler

RODEO COWBOY

Willcox, Arizona, 1895

PRESCOTT, ARIZONA, CLAIMS TO HOLD THE WORLD'S OLDEST RODEO, with competition beginning on July 4, 1888. But even the folks at Prescott admit that "the act of rodeo is as old as cattle raising itself," thereby admitting that theirs isn't the oldest rodeo. What they're saying, in other words, is, "We were the first to fornicate, but the sex act has been around as long as there have been women." The author hopes this clears up for the reader the true origin of rodeo, though he's not certain that the above comparison is apt. Rodeo is certainly a lot of fun, as is fornication, but barring the objections of certain city folk, it is doubtful that rodeo is sinful.

We know the true origins of rodeo. At some point Mexican vaqueros, Texas drovers, or Arizona cowboys sitting around a campfire had a bit too much to drink. One of them said, "I'm the greatest rider here!"

To which another replied, "Oh yeah. I'll bet you can't ride that bull!"

And the rodeo was on.

I attended a Ranch Rodeo in Willcox. It was great fun and great people. The events were "unsanctioned," the way rodeo started out, and were said to reflect the real tasks that cowboys perform on the ranch. One event involved four men unscrambling tack, flagging down a horse, saddling up their ponies, and chasing down a range cow that was knocked on its side and milked. I'm sure that's how the day starts on most ranches as they head out to get milk for the breakfast table. If they chase the cow far enough, the butter comes prechurned.

Rodeo provides cowboys with wholesome heroes who love their country, mom, and apple pie and who go to church most Sundays, even when severely hungover. It always has. In 1895, one of those heroes was a cowboy named Grant Wheeler, who could rope, shoot, and ride and who had a unique retirement plan should he ever tire of rodeoing and cowboying.

Cochise County had a cowboy problem when "cowboy" meant outlaw, although even then there is evidence that they attended church and loved their country, mom, apple pie, and other folk's cattle. The Earps and their friends tried to clean up the county, but eventually the lawmen left the area pursued by the "law," with the problem only slightly ameliorated. "Texas John" Slaughter tried a few years later, but local juries were loath to convict. In 1894 and '95, even renowned photographer C. S. Fly took a turn as sheriff. You might remember him as the photographer who went along with General Crook and photographed Geronimo and his warriors.

In 1894, Grant Wheeler was already a Cochise County rodeo hero well liked by many cowhands and ranchers. He distributed signed photos of himself to pretty maidens, and these photos would be his undoing. According to folks in Willcox, "Grant Wheeler had been mentioned several times in the newspaper in the year before the robbery. He was known to his cowboy pals as a square, honest, well-meaning young fellow, and one of the best cowhands that ever roped a steer."[1] Grant is mentioned in an abortive horse race at Whitewater Ranch. The *Epitaph* reported:

> *James Bastian and John Woods had entered Sherman Clump's bay horse, Bunk, the winner of the quarter race at Bisbee on Christmas day last. Hugh MacDonald and Roy Sanderson entered J.H. Powers' two year old horse, Cricket. The purse was $140 and the distance 300 yards.*
>
> *Mr. MacDonald had made every arrangement to render the occasion a success and to have the best horse win. He had the track in perfect condition, the colt, Cricket, was in fine mettle and Mac was confident he would ride the winner.[2]*

We might conclude that Grant was there to ride Bunk, the fastest horse around, since he'd be noted as winning a race in August at Whitewater Ranch while mounted on the same animal. It was a 350-yard dash that paid off two hundred dollars against John Woods's bay mare, Maud. We might speculate on how Bunk got his name. In a rock-and-rye[3] fueled discussion, his owner said, "My horse is the fastest horse around!" To which a cowboy replied, "That's bunk!" Obviously, he was referring to a substance cowhands are loath to step in. However, the horse's owner responded, "Exactly! That's my horse Bunk!"

In February the *Tombstone Epitaph* reported: "Grant Wheeler the well known cow boy who won the steer tying contest at Bisbee, is at Mary Tack's suffering from a dislocated shoulder. He was making a quick turn and his animal fell, throwing him with great force to the ground."[4]

A cowboy with a hurt shoulder isn't often news. Visit a ranch on any given day, and you'll find that half the cowboys are suffering from injuries of one kind or another, including missing digits. A hurt shoulder doesn't mean much unless you're talking about a rodeo cowboy whose performance might be impaired and upon whose prowess one might place a bet.

In May 1894, Grant bought himself a new lariat, and thinking to try it out, he rode down Maley Street, swinging it overhead, when he espied a Chinese dishwasher named Lee who worked at the nearby Willcox Hotel. In a spirit of fun, Grant swung the rope as if to rope the Chinaman.[5] Lee ran into a restaurant and emerged on Haskell Avenue with Grant still in pursuit.

At this point, according to Grant, Lee displayed a gun, so the cowboy let fly and roped him in tight to a fence post as the Chinaman shouted, "Mucha bad cowboy!" Grant put spurs to his mount and galloped off, snapping his new lariat in two pieces. Lee grabbed one and headed for Judge Nichol's office to lodge a complaint against the bad cowboy. Meanwhile, Grant headed out to his camp outside of town to pick up his revolver. He then headed back to town to find Lee. Constable Howarth was on Grant's trail on a charge of abusing a Chinaman and caught up with his quarry at the corner of Maley and Haskell. Taking Grant by surprise, Howarth made the arrest and hauled Grant off to court, where he was fined thirty dollars for assault and battery and fifty dollars more for carrying deadly weapons in town.[6]

In 1894, Grant Wheeler and sometime deputy sheriff and Willcox constable Burt Alvord worked for rancher L. J. Overlock. In 1902, Overlock recalled, "Alvord was in my employ in 1895 [actually 1894] at the time Grant Wheeler worked for me. Wheeler afterward held up the train at Willcox. These two noted characters were not friendly when they worked for me, and Alvord, as a deputy sheriff, tried to capture Wheeler after he had held up the train."[7]

On October 5, 1894, the eastbound No. 19 passenger train with Lou Holliday at the throttle roared out of the yard at Maricopa only to be robbed shortly afterward by two armed men who had hidden in the blind baggage and climbed over the tender to take control of the locomotive.[8] This bold train robbery would have been the number one topic of conversation around the campfire at roundup.

"Grant Wheeler has been heard to often say that there was no use in living such a d——d life, that he would hold up a train and get something or they would get him. He also told on numerous occasions of how easy it could be done. 'I am not fool enough' said he 'to go to Mexico where I would get caught, the mountains are good enough for me.'"[9]

Arizona was still mostly open range. The unfenced land was still the possession of the government, although ranchers usually acknowledged each other's "rights and priorities," and most ranches included homestead claims of 160 acres on which the rancher's house, barn, and farm buildings and a water source were located. Some ranchers had begun acquiring other homesteads as well as larger holdings available from the government and railroads. Cattle mingled on the range, and at roundup they had to be sorted out and branded, dehorned, made into steers, and selected for sale. It was a cooperative effort, with cowboys from different outfits worked assigned sections to gather everyone's cattle. A calf received the same brand as the brand on the cow it was suckling. The bosses needed to be present to make sure they got a fair deal and to give the orders. They selected men they could trust as umpires and referees. Roundup was hard work.

In the evening, they gathered around the chuckwagon for their meals. Afterward, the cowhands settled down to brag, lie, and tell tall tales. It was at these gatherings that Grant bragged about retiring from cowboying on the Southern Pacific's dime. The SP wasn't popular with ranchers and cowhands in 1895 after SP's 25 percent rate hike during the terrible, cattle-killing drought. The ranchers struggled to move cattle to other ranges and to sell them off lest they overgraze and die. Everyone would have recalled the Maricopa train robbery, and most would have been sympathetic to Grant's scheme.

Wise cattlemen prohibited gambling and liquor at roundup. Both led to fights and gunplay. They needed men who were fresh and not hungover in the morning. Nonetheless, the *St. Johns Herald* reported,

> *On Saturday night at Si Baryant's [sic] ranch in the Swisshelm mountains the Whitewater round-up camped for the night. After a long, hard rids [sic] during the day, some of the boys accepted the invitation of one of the neighboring ranches to stop and take a drink.*
>
> *One drink followed another untill [sic] they were pretty full, and reached camp, in intoxicated condition. Ben Whiston, who was cooking at a camp fire, was the mark for one of the boys, Grant Wheeler, who became so noisy and dangerous that Si Bryant, who was in the house with ten or fifteen cowmen, thought best to go out and stop it.*[10]

Si learned the hard way that separating drunken, arguing cowhands is dangerous. Grant shot him in the belly with his "Colt's .45 caliber pistol." Thinking the boss dead, Grant jumped on behind a companion who was on horseback and the pair fled.

The ball entered Si to the right of his navel and skidded around under the flesh atop his stomach muscles and exited on the left side about six inches from where it had entered. Ranchers were made of stern stuff in those days. "I am shot through the body," said Bryant as he calmly walked into the ranch house. "The wounded man came at once to Tombstone, where his wound which proved to be only a flesh one, was dressed."[11] It was only a flesh wound? I thought Hollywood had come up with that.

Learning that Si had only a flesh wound, Grant Wheeler turned himself in and was placed under a five-hundred-dollar bond awaiting the action of the grand jury.[12] It may be sheer speculation, but he may have been more concerned with what Si Bryant might do in retribution than he was with the outcome of the grand jury. In any event, he decided that it was time to put his retirement plan into effect.

PURSUIT

Steins, 1895

In January 1895, Grant Wheeler with friend Joe George appeared in Willcox, many miles from Tombstone and from Whitewater Ranch, making purchases to enhance his retirement. On January 29, 1895, in "Willcox they purchased, among other things, large quantities of cartridges and sixteen pounds of giant powder."[13]

The man at the store on Railroad Avenue asked, "Why do you need all that giant powder?"

Joe George replied, "We're gonna blow some stumps."

In the evening dusk of January 30, 1895, Grant Wheeler and Joe George climbed aboard the blind baggage of westbound Southern Pacific passenger train No. 20 at the station in Willcox. They huddled close in the cold night air, hoping the darkness would conceal them. The train was arranged so that the engine was followed by the tender full of coal and water. Behind them came the baggage car, whose doorless forward end, known as the blind baggage, was a place of concealment for hobos and other nonpaying riders. The US Mail express car was located ahead of the passenger cars just beyond the baggage car. Perhaps the arrangement

Railroad Avenue, Willcox, Arizona in 1880.
COURTESY OF SULPHUR SPRINGS VALLEY HISTORICAL SOCIETY

distanced passengers from the smoke and sparks of the engine. Those with an eye to a stickup found this organization quite convenient.

Willcox was a cattle-shipping railhead in the Sulphur Springs Valley, midway between Benson and Steins, New Mexico, on the territorial border. It was a cowboy town with close ties to the ranches and vaquero traditions. In 1895, the town ran for three blocks along the rails and about four blocks north and south. When the train came through, the whole town was aware of it. It was also at the northern edge of what had been, until 1876, Cochise's Chiricahua Reservation.

Brakeman W. J. Young, passing down the line, detected noise and movement in the blind baggage. He stepped up to investigate and found two cowboys crouching there. Sheepishly, they offered to pay a dollar for passage as far as Dragoon Summit, but the brakeman, an honest man, declined. Two drawn and cocked six-shooters instantly confronted him.

The depot at Dragoon, Arizona.
COURTESY OF THE SOUTHERN ARIZONA TRANSPORTATION MUSEUM

Fireman O. J. Johnson soon joined them and likewise was taken captive by the two hobos and escorted to the engine, where engineer Zeigler was ordered to put the train in motion. In the crowded station, the armed men and early departure drew the attention of the whole town.[14]

Everyone knew, according to the *Morning Call* of San Francisco[15]—everyone except Sheriff C. S. Fly, the famed photographer turned lawman in Willcox from Tombstone, the county seat, on business. The Tucson papers said that he did nothing until the next morning.

> *If the reports concerning Sheriff Fly, of Cochise county are true he ought to be indicted and fired from office. If they are not true then a gross wrong is being done the man. He was, it is said, in Willcox at the time of the late railroad robbery, and although it was well known in that town, and to Fly among others, that a robbery was in progress, he made no attempt to go to the rescue of the train notwithstanding the hold up was within hearing and was a whole hour and a half in [consummation].[16]*

Perhaps Fly's response was casual, but subsequent accounts show him highly active in pursuit, although he did not have much luck. He may have been the only person in Willcox who was unaware of the robbery. The locals may have considered it unsportsmanlike to tell him. Learning of the robbery as the train began to pull away from the station, Sheriff Fly went looking for a horse. Unlike in the Western movies, there just weren't saddled horses standing around everywhere waiting for someone in need to ride away. Few townsmen owned horses. Owning one was expensive, and horses took up space that wasn't readily available. Folks didn't need them either. They lived within walking distance of their work. Visit an old town, and you'll find that every three or four blocks there's another mom-and-pop grocery, a baker, and even a saloon, or as the Brits say, "one's local." Even the livery stable wouldn't have had horses saddled and ready. Sheriff Camilus Fly could not find a saddled horse.

Local oral history, that is to say legend, says that Fly and his deputy flew into immediate action, pursuing the captive train for a about a mile on foot until it outran them or they ran out of steam.[17]

In any event, the train, Grant Wheeler and Joe George aboard, got away, only to halt about two miles out of town on the Willcox Playa,[18] where the cowboys ordered the passenger cars disconnected and left behind so as not to further discommode the paying customers. Meanwhile, aboard the express car, Wells, Fargo and Company messenger George Mitchell[19] was contemplating his ill luck as it had only been three months since he was held up near Maricopa. As the passenger cars were unhitched, he jumped off, taking the "local money" with him, and ran back toward Willcox, perhaps hoping to meet Sheriff Fly along the way. The train proceeded farther into the playa and stopped again. The brakeman was sent back along the track "to the train two miles away with the reassuring intelligence that the passengers and conductor need not feel apprehensive of bodily harm if they did not interfere with the proceedings in front."[20]

The train is said to have stopped by a small campfire where additional men, well known to those who had boarded the train, were in waiting. Initial stories gave the names and descriptions of five men. Wells, Fargo and Company offered three hundred dollars for the arrest and conviction of each, and the Southern Pacific Railroad put up two hundred dollars per head:

Joe George—about five feet eight or nine inches high, very slim, very dark and swarthy complexion, forefinger off right hand, 30 to 35 years old, weight 140 pounds.

Jim Yates—slim, dark complexion, about five feet nine inches high, 28 or 30 years of age, has very small sandy mustache, weight 145 to 150 pounds.

Grant Wheeler—about five feet seven inches high, dark complexion, dark eyes, weight 145 pounds, 30 or 35 years of age.

Mart Taylor—small man with lame leg.

John Woods—a tall man, light complexion, about six feet, weight about 180 pounds.[21]

In subsequent accounts, all but the names of Joe George and Grant Wheeler disappeared.

Out on the playa, the two outlaws escorted engineer Zeigler to the express car and directed him to demand that the messenger open the door lest the railroad employee be executed on the spot. As the Wells, Fargo and Company employee had already departed, running back toward the sheriff, no answer came from within. Rather than slay the engineer, Grant and Joe decided to employ some of their giant powder, that is to say, dynamite, on the door and blew it open. They had purchased the giant powder the day prior in Willcox, and that purchase led to their almost immediate identification. On opening the car, they were surprised to find it vacant. Undaunted, the cowboys proceeded to crack the through safe, to which the messenger would not have had access in any event and which contained the greatest prize in ill-gotten wealth, about forty thousand dollars, or so the newspapers wrote. In truth, the outlaws may have emptied the safe of as much as three or four hundred dollars, but the press never missed an opportunity to tell a good tale. In the car, they found twenty sacks of Mexican money, "dobie" dollars, then valued by the ton, although having a face value of twenty thousand dollars.[22] These were used as tamping to blow the safe, their heavy weight directing the explosion of the dynamite down toward the safe. As the *San Francisco Call* noted, "Among the coin was 18,000 'dobie' dollars. As Mexican money has little value in less than ton lots, and as the robbers had no drays with them they had no use for the stuff and so they made a heap of it, put a stick of dynamite under it and touched it off. Only 700 of the 18,000 dollars have been found. They went through telegraph poles, cars and, in fact, flew everywhere."[23]

What was left of the express car gave the appearance that it had been the target of a giant shotgun. The Mexican inhabitants of Willcox came out the next morning to gather their sudden bounty and collected thousands of pesos scattered about and stuck in telegraph poles and in fragments of the car. Despite their best efforts, pesos were still being found on the site in the 1960s.

As posses pursued, the two outlaws received aid and food at isolated ranches where perhaps the stockmen and their families feared retribution if they failed to assist. That's all well and good, but once the outlaws had left, they should have been safe enough to inform the posse by telling which way they'd gone. No one pointed in the right direction. No one had any love for the Southern Pacific, and Grant was a rodeo hero. The boys were welcomed and wined and dined in style. The five posses in the field couldn't find them, and the boys were rumored to have left the county if not the country. They rode a great circle around Cochise County, visiting friends while remaining invisible to the law. In an early account, before it was realized that only Joe and Grant were involved, the *Tombstone Epitaph* proclaimed, "The latest news received at the sheriff's office says that there were four men in the train robbery, and they are still together. There [*sic*] are given as Joe Scott [actually Joe George], Jim Yates, Grant Wheeler, and John Woods."

"Deputy Sheriff Graham left this morning with a posse to try and head off the train robbers, who held up the west bound train near Willcox last evening. They started south in the Sulphur Spring valley."[24]

Southern Pacific railroad detective William "Billy" Breakenridge joined the search. Some may recall him as Johnny Behan's wimpy deputy in the movie *Tombstone*. In reality, he was a tough and long-serving lawman. He knew the geography of the county well. The *Epitaph* reported,

> *There is absolutely nothing new from the pursuit of the train robbers. None of the pursuers have returned and no one has shown up who has seen any of them. A telegram from Breakenridge this morning from Willcox indicates that he has not been out with the posse which left there the day after the robbery.*
>
> *Several others are now believed to be implicated in the robbery. It is suspected that the outlaws went to Mulberry, just over the mountain, where they procured a fresh relay of horses in waiting for them, and kept on into Mexico.*
>
> *Others who know Wheeler well say he would not go to Mexico under any circumstances.*[25]

And so, two extraordinary cowboys disappeared into the dusty playa and mountains of Cochise County, passing up the opportunity to escape into Mexico and history for having conducted an apparently successful train robbery. How much they made off with remained a mystery. Wells, Fargo and Company and the Southern Pacific Railroad remained mute, though it was reliably whispered by some that "after using six sticks of dynamite the safe was finally blown open, the robbers securing about $2000."[26] On February 26, 1895, about a month after destroying an express car, Grant Wheeler and Joe George chose instead to seek even more glory at Steins Pass.

By 1895, the correct spelling of Major Enoch Steen's name forgotten, the Southern Pacific Railroad established first a quarry and then a whistle-stop providing wood and water and servicing a few local mines. Steins Pass, where I-10 runs today, although easy of passage, was not much used by wagon trains, for it was dry. The railroad had to bring in tanker cars of water to serve the tiny town. It was also too small a town to have its own officer of the law. Tombstone, county seat for Cochise, was one hundred miles to the southwest, and Silver City, where the Grant County sheriff was located, was almost as far to the northeast.

On Monday evening, February 25, 1895, Grant Wheeler and Joe George, guns drawn, mounted the locomotive of the westbound Southern Pacific Express No. 20. They directed engineer Jacky Burke (or Bruce)[27] to cut loose the cars. All was done with "alacrity and strictly according to instructions."[28] Proceeding westward from Steins, New Mexico, several miles into Arizona, the cowboys again issued orders, this time for the train to halt. Engineer Burke was handed a gunnysack and told to start filling it with stones and gravel. Supposing he "had fallen in with a band of escaped lunatics instead of train robbers," Burke followed orders. Curious, he asked, "What's that for?" The robber explained that the gravel was to be placed on top of the safe to offer greater resistance to the dynamite, tamping the ensuing explosion as effectively as in the express car on the Willcox Playa, cracking the safe like a walnut to expose the riches inside. To this Burke replied, "But we don't carry a safe in the cab." Only then did the bandit realize that the express car had been left behind, per his own orders, at Steins.[29]

At least one newspaper, the *Arizona Silver Belt* of Globe, thought there was more to it, running a story labeled "Heroic Brakeman": "The intentions of the robbers to rob the express was frustrated by the brakeman who purposely uncoupled the mail car and engine, leaving the express car behind at the station. When the engine and mail car had been run about three miles up the track, the 'mistake' was discovered, and the robbers foiled, lit out, intent only upon escape."[30]

What followed was wondrous and terrible to behold. It involved terms neither gynecological nor scatological, adhering entirely to the biblical and theological. Engineer Burke recalled that the leader of the gang indulged in the worst profanity that had been reported between ancient and modern times. Jacky considered himself an expert on profanity as an engineer of the Southern Pacific who had witnessed Captain Tevis losing at cards on a fine hand, been present when Barnes and Dunbar were sentenced to hang, and having served a term in the Arizona legislature. "Profanity on those occasions would pass for religious worship" by comparison.[31] The outlaw damned the Southern Pacific, starting with the president and chairman of the board and working his way down through the conductors, engineers, and fireman to the lowliest brakeman and Pullman porter. He then commenced on the track and crossties, working his way across the mainline and out onto the spurs and sidings. Even the rolling stock was not overlooked. He cursed the section hands, the bridges, and every foot of track from San Francisco to New Orleans. "The longer he swore the more eloquent and blasphemous he became."[32]

Even the Associated Press and the *Arizona Republican* were impressed: "The bandits indulged in considerable strong language and then mounting horses that were fastened to a tree near by they rode to the south. The engine and car returned to the rest of the train. The passengers as is always the case were scared nearly to death; many crawled under the seats and remained there till assured that the danger was over."[33]

It was now that the real problems began for Joe George and Grant Wheeler. Detective Billy Breakenridge was in pursuit, and he was persistent. Abandoning Wells, Fargo and Company detective John Thacker, Billy stayed on the trail.

I left him [Thacker] and returned to Tucson, where I had plenty to do. He stayed in the Tombstone vicinity for about a month and accomplished nothing, and then went back to San Francisco. One of his plans was to get one of the outlaw's friends to bring them a bottle of drugged whiskey, and, after they fell asleep, to hog-tie them and bring them to him in Tombstone. The friend told the bandits about it and they laughed about his trying to catch birds by putting salt on their tails.[34]

Grant Wheeler gave this photo to pretty girls, and Billy Breakenridge used it to track him down.

COURTESY OF SULPHUR SPRINGS VALLEY HISTORICAL SOCIETY

Breakenridge thought that many of the folks in Cochise County were in sympathy with the outlaws. Both Wells, Fargo and Company and the Southern Pacific were unpopular with the people, who thought their freight and express charges excessive. It's also probable that many had bought land from the railroad and were in debt to it. No one loves the leaseholder. Wheeler and George remained in hiding.

Billy Breakenridge needed a break and then heard a story about a photograph. "One of my cowboy friends told me that there was a young lady living in the Chiricahuas who had a photograph of Wheeler in her album, and I gave him $20 to get it for me. He brought it to me within a few days and I had a lot of copies of it made."[35]

From one of his sources, Billy heard a whisper that the boys had gone north to Durango, Colorado. He picked up the trail at Durango and followed it south to the vicinity of nearby Farmington, New Mexico, and the ranch of a man named Short. There Wheeler was identified from a photograph as "the man the children call the bad man." Pursuit continued to Shiprock and then on north to Cortez, Colorado, where, even after showing the photograph around, Billy lost all track of Grant. It was suggested that the outlaw may have headed for the Blue Mountains of Utah, where many men, such as the outlaw pair, were known to hide. Almost completing a circle route around Mesa Verde, Billy headed back to Durango to pick up his friend, the sheriff who knew those mountains. On the way, at Mancos, a farmer's wife recognized the man in the photo. Breakenridge planned to grab Grant Wheeler when he came to town to a saloon he was known to frequent. Billy wrote:

> *We saw him bring up his two horses, put a light pack on one and saddle the other. But instead of coming to town, he went into a gulch that ran down toward an irrigating ditch close to town. It looked as if he were alarmed and was getting away, so we saddled up and went after him. As we neared the gulch, he came up the bank. One of the officers told him to throw up his hands. Wheeler replied that he had not done anything and would not do it, and started to step back into the gulch. When one of the officers fired at him, he disappeared and none of us were anxious to go to the rim of the gulch to see what had happened to him.*[36]

We can imagine the conversation that occurred after Grant disappeared back into the arroyo. A poll was taken to see who was the most suicidal or the most dim-witted. No one was eager to poke his head over the lip of the arroyo and have it blown off. Discussion was cut short when a shot was heard, although it still took a while before anyone wanted to look. Grant Wheeler had promised he'd never be taken alive. Legend in Willcox has it that Joe George was a bad man. He may have been angered by Grant distributing photos that made it easy for the posse to follow. On the other hand, he may have thought of a way to slow the posse down while he got away. Or the pair may have parted company days before. In any event, Grant Wheeler would not have to face the hangman.

On Sunday night, April 28, 1895, a telegram arrived in Tucson from Southern Pacific detective Breakenridge stating that Grant Wheeler the train robber had been tracked to his camp near Mancos, Colorado, about thirty miles north of the New Mexico line. There, finding escape impossible, Grant took his own life.[37]

At the coroner's inquest, it came out that Grant had told a fellow cowboy that he didn't want to kill anyone but would kill himself before he would surrender.[38]

The whereabouts of Wheeler's companion, Joe George, remained unknown. Some said he'd gone to Pueblo, Colorado, where he was known and had friends.[39] Billy Breakenridge said he knew George's location. "Detective Breakenridge of the S.P. is in Tucson. He is said to have a good idea of the whereabouts of George, the companion of Wheeler, the dead train robber."[40] A more dubious tale claimed he was leading a gang:

It is now positively known that the leader of the Nogales bandits who were near the New Mexico line is Joe George, who planned and executed the robbery of the Southern Pacific passenger train at Steins Pass, in the territory, about eighteen months ago, and whose companion, Wheelock, was killed by Colorado authorities shortly afterward, George escaping during the fight. The robbers say they are going to live on the ranches until they make a raise. There are nine of them. They will probably rob a train or a bank.[41]

The Nogales Gang was the Black Jack Christian band, known also as the High Fives. They bungled the bank robbery in Nogales and were pursued across Cochise County into Grant County. They fought it out with a posse in Skeleton Canyon, where Geronimo had surrendered ten years before, and then went on to hold up the entire railroad town of Separ twice. As far as we know, Joe George was not a member of the High Fives and was never identified in another holdup. He disappeared from history. Perhaps he settled down near Pueblo and changed his name to escape notice. Perhaps, he died somewhere on the trail to Durango or disappeared into Mexico, where the two thousand dollars, never recovered, would have gone a long way. He may even have returned to Cochise County, where the ranchers are still helping him to hide from the dreaded SP and the law.

Breakenridge got a lead from a nurse in Tombstone. George had spent some time in hospital where a letter came for him from his sister in Beebe, Arkansas. From the local sheriff, Billy learned that Joe had gone to Livingston in the Texas panhandle. He never got clearance from his employer to hunt George down, and the outlaw was never captured.[42]

Perhaps we should trust the folks who knew them best. In Willcox, legend has it Grant's partner, Joe George, passed away soon after the rodeo hero. He was shot, they say, down in Mexico with only twenty dollars in his pocket, outliving Wheeler by only two weeks.

At the same time Grant and Joe were riding around the county enjoying the hospitality of farms and ranches, two other gangs were forming in the county. In 1882, the Earps with a federal posse had tried to clean out the Cow Boys only to find the Cow Boy posse with county warrants in pursuit. The Earps and their posse, armed with warrants for the arrest of the Cow Boys, were run off to Colorado by a sheriff's posse composed of Cow Boys holding territorial warrants for the Earp posse's arrest. Sheriff John Slaughter rounded them up and brought the Cow Boys to the Tombstone Courthouse only to find Cow Boys and their friends on the jury letting the outlaws go. It didn't help that federal standards of "proof beyond a reasonable doubt," as applied in the Territory of Arizona, made it almost impossible to convict anyone of anything. Despite these efforts, the outlaws still ruled Cochise County. In 1903, the Arizona Rangers became the famed twenty-six men. Twenty-four

Deming, where the engineer accidentally scared off the robbers.
COURTESY OF THE SOUTHERN ARIZONA TRANSPORTATION MUSEUM

of them were assigned to Cochise County to end lawlessness so Arizona could become a state. The twenty-seventh ranger was a train robber and an outlaw on the run, but that's a story for another chapter. In 1896, outlaw gangs were forming.

On November 4, 1896, the *Eagle*, a Silver City newspaper, reported:

> *Last Saturday evening the Southern Pacific train going west from Deming had some undesirable passengers on board. Before the lights of Deming had been left behind, the engineer looked back and saw two armed men on the front end of the baggage car and immediately concluded that it would be better for him to take them back to Deming. He reversed his engine and went back, but when he arrived at the station his passengers were not to be found.*[43]

As the engineer stared out toward Gage, rubbing his chin, he mumbled, "Who were those masked men?"

CHAPTER SEVEN

Black Jack and the High Five Gang

THE DEATH OF SHOOT 'EM UP DICK

Steins, New Mexico, 1897

IN 1910, THE PHOENIX NEWSPAPER *ARIZONA REPUBLIC* RECALLED, PER-
haps incorrectly:

> *About 16 years ago a train on the main line of the Southern Pacific*
> *was held up in approved style a short distance east of Maricopa and*
> *thereafter within two years robberies were frequent in the eastern*
> *part of the territory. About the same time there were a couple of train*
> *robberies on the Santa Fe. But with the breaking up of the Bill Smith*
> *and the Black Jack gangs, the holdups ceased. But there was never*
> *before such a robbery in Arizona as the one that took place yesterday*
> *evening.*[1]

Although the reporter tried hard not to, he succeeded in correctly record-
ing some elements of the story. The train had been held up the night
before at Maricopa, and sixteen years before, there had been quite a few
train robberies in the eastern, specifically southeastern, part of the territory. In 1910, it would still be two years before Arizona was admitted to
the union. However, the 1910 holdup was definitely not done in any of
the approved styles, other than those seen in movies. We'll discuss the
1910 robbery in another chapter. Black Jack and his gang didn't rob a
train in southeastern Arizona, though as it turns out, this area was their

114

home country and where they started out. In fact, in 1896, soon after the train robbery on the Willcox Playa, they got their start in the San Simon Valley, where Curly Bill Brocius, Johnny Ringo, and Ike Clanton had once had ranches near Galeyville. In 1897, an entirely different gang of outlaws stole a train at Steins Pass and rode it into the San Simon Valley. The reporter's confusion might be understood, even forgiven.

Once an outlaw becomes infamous, every crime imaginable attaches to his name. We soon find him committing crimes at the same day and hour in places one thousand miles apart. It seems that folks figured that if they had to be shot or robbed, it might as well be by someone famous. In 1897, that's the way it was with Black Jack. Part of becoming famous, or infamous, is having a catchy name. Wimpy names, such as Sleepy or Dopey, Sneezy or Grumpy, Happy or Bashful, just don't make it, although a few badmen managed with Doc. Frequently, it's the newspapers who assigned the name, and they could destroy an honest outlaw's entire career with a poor choice.

In December 1882, Shoot 'em Up Dick stole a horse.[2] The name carries more derision than threat. It appears he was apprehended in Globe, and "Shoot 'em Up Dick skipped out on his bondsmen, while Attorney McGabe [was] going to make them [the bondsmen] pony up."[3] Shoot 'em Up remained absent from the press for the next fifteen years, perhaps taking a lengthy vacation in Yuma or just hiding in shame. Skipping over the 1897 event for just a moment, we find the next mention at El Paso in 1900:

One day a braggart named "Shoot 'em Up Dick" wearing two six-guns, a big Bowie knife and fringed buckskins, stormed into Jim Sam chop house and ordered the most expensive meal on the menu.

When he had finished the huge meal, he ordered the best cigar in the house, lit up and started to walk out without paying.

"Hey, fliend, you fogettum somesing, yes?" Jim Sam sang out.

"No, you damned yellow heathen," said the badman. "I didn't forget nawthing. I was your guest. I'm Shoot 'em Up Dick."

"Oh, so?" said Jim Sam with a smile, pulling out his own six-gun from beneath the counter. "So you Shoot 'em Up Dick. I

Shoot-em-down Sam. You pay pletty damn soon or Shoot-em-up
Dick be pletty damn dead."
    Dick paid.[4]

In all probability, the 1897 "Shoot 'em Up Dick" is not the 1882 Dick or
any other Dick, nor even a member of Black Jack's gang. He was just a poor
sod, a Cochise County cowboy doing what Cochise County cowboys do.

With a poorly chosen moniker, an outlaw just didn't get any respect.
Black Jack got respect, and his gang was everywhere. He was wanted
for a double homicide in Camp Verde though I can find no evidence
he was ever there.[5] On November 13, 1897, Burt Alvord, Texas John
Slaughter's sometime posseman and snitch, the newly appointed constable
of Willcox, shot and killed Billy King, an Erie Cattle Company cowboy.
Reasons behind the shooting, apart from sheer meanness, were unclear, and
Burt faced an attempted indictment.[6] Perhaps of more concern to Alvord
was a news item appearing Christmas Day. The Associated Press reported
that Black Jack had a list of three men who "must die." At the top of the
list was Constable Burt Alvord.[7] With his excellent, threatening moniker,
Black Jack was getting lots of respect, and his name was constantly being
mentioned as operating in and around Cochise County.

It's hard to say if Black Jack had the best or worst outlaw name ever.
In the movie *Shanghai Noon* (2000, starring Jackie Chan and Owen
Wilson), we are transported back to 1881 and watch as Chon Wang (a
homophone for John Wayne) tells Roy, who has just revealed that his
real name is Wyatt Earp, "That's terrible cowboy name." Or consider
Captain Jack Sparrow being told that he is the worst pirate anyone has
ever heard of replying with the immortal words, "Ah but you have heard
of me!" Everyone had heard of Black Jack, and many borrowed his name.
Eventually, it got the wrong man hanged. "Ah, but you have heard of me.
I'm Black Jack." On December 10, 1897, it came as no surprise that Black
Jack's gang held up train No. 20 on the Southern Pacific Road at Steins
Pass and rode it into the San Simon Valley to complete the robbery.
According to the *Arizona Republic*: "Four men rode up to the station a
short time before the train was due and after robbing Agent St. John and
Section Foreman McMullen, they cut the telegraph wires and waited for
the train. When the passenger train pulled into the station one of the

bandits covered the engineer and fireman with a Winchester rifle, while the others prepared to attack the express car."[8]

Four masked men, one about six feet in height and the others a bit shorter, ordered the train moved across the line into the San Simon Valley, where they had it stopped by two waiting bonfires. While one of the bandits covered the fireman and engineer, two proceeded to the express car, where, well warned, express messengers Jennings and Thatcher awaited them. As the door was opened from outside, the pair opened fire, putting a bullet through the brain of the leader and wounding another. The startled bandits mounted waiting horses and galloped away to the south post haste.[9] Shoot 'em Up Dick lay dead.[10] A posse followed in hot pursuit.

Meanwhile, eight members of Black Jack's gang were down on the Mexican border, perhaps one hundred miles away, in a shoot-out with Mexican border guards. The Mexicans attacked, and Black Jack's gang fled, all except for Frank Ophallard, who dismounted and, drawing his trusty Winchester, shot and killed three of the guards before they killed him. Ophallard, who had terrorized the border country for thirteen years, was the last of the Sam Bass Gang and a brother to two of the men who rode with Billy the Kid.[11] Black Jack's gang was in two places, one hundred miles apart, at the same time!

One of the passengers on the train, A. E. Stoeger of St. Louis, was duly impressed with the prowess of the gang: "Tucson parties state that A.E. Stoeger, of St. Louis, who has been posing as a hero and claiming credit for having prevented a collision between the Limited and Train 20 at Steins Pass on the night of the hold up, exhibited the reverse of bravery on that occasion. He ran back and forth through the car imploring the ladies to lie down on the floor to escape being killed and made himself generally ridiculous."[12]

An explanation for part of the mystery was soon forthcoming from the *Santa Fe New Mexican* by way of the *Lordsburg Liberal*, a newspaper only twelve miles from the scene of the railway robbery:

A wild correspondent for the Associated Press sent out from Silver City last Thursday an account of a fight on the border between Arizona and Old Mexico, between some Mexican guards and a section of the "Black Jack" gang, in which three of the Mexicans were killed, as was one of the gang, named Frank Ophallard.

Ophallard was said to have had two brothers in the old Billy the Kid gang, and was the last of the Sam Bass gang. The entire dispatch was the result of a pipe dream in which the Associated Press correspondent had indulged. There was no such scrap and no such a killing as that described. The dispatch was entirely too vivid to have been produced by Silver City Whisky, only opium could have caused it. Lordsburg Liberal.[13]

The robbery and death at San Simon were real enough, but the border incident was a pipe dream. The *Albuquerque Journal* clarified further that it wasn't Black Jack's Gang.[14] In fact, Cochise County residents had known this for some time. The dead man was a local cowboy, Ed Cullen.

"The dead robber, from a letter found on his person, was believed to be Edward H. Cullen, who is known to have been in Bisbee not long ago. Some are of the opinion that the men were a part of Black Jack's gang, while others claim that it was only a party of inexperienced cowboys from San Simon valley."[15]

The posse followed a trail that led to the Cush ranch at the southern end of the Chiricahua Mountains, where between the named mountains and the Peloncillo Range[16] the San Simon Valley merges into the San Bernardino Valley, home to John Slaughter's ranch. The *Florence Tribune* reported,

The capture was made in Texas canyon, about fifty miles south of the Southern Pacific railroad and not far from the Sonora line. . . . [The posse] came to a ranch house in Texas canyon, surrounded it, and found three of their birds, who under cover of rifles surrendered. The posse learning that the other two had not arrived awaited their coming, and took them in also by surprise. The five taken, were the four who escaped from the train, after their partner Cullen was shot, and the other was in charge of the horses. One of the captured bandits was wounded; it is supposed he was shot in the fight at the train.[17]

Ed Cullen, a Cochise County cowboy, was called "Shoot 'em Up Dick" by the press.
COURTESY OF SULPHUR SPRINGS VALLEY HISTORICAL SOCIETY

The *Tribune* went on to state that while the captured men were not the Black Jack Gang, Black Jack was thought to be cooperating with them. The men had a surprising amount of ammunition and explosives.[18] One had a gunshot wound, and the trail led to the ranch. The robbers were the now deceased local cowboy Ed Cullen, featured in the newspapers as Shoot 'em Up Dick, while those captured were Walter Hoffman, F. L. Capehart, Henry Marshall, William Warderman, and Leonard Alverson. The *Arizona Range News* boldly proclaimed that these were not Black Jack's gang.[19]

At trial the defendants protested that Ed Cullen was about to join the "Black Jack gang of border bandits" and that the robbery was attempted by members of that band. That they were preparing to become outlaws also served as explanation for the ammunition, explosives, and fuses found at the Cush ranch: it served as a rendezvous for the notorious gang. Naturally, the defendants, peaceful cowboys one and all, were afraid to offend the Black Jack Gang and kept quiet.[20] Who had done what to whom and when was sorted out at trial. Some had robbed the post office in Steins Pass, some had taken the train, and some, to quote the poet, also served by only standing and waiting while holding the horses. These confused relations, degrees of participation, and the particulars of who was in possession of what gave way to a complexity of verdicts, as the *Western Liberal* reported,

> *At the trial of the men arrested for robbing the Steins Pass post office and the Southern Pacific passenger train, at Las Cruces last week, Hoffman and Alverson were convicted as told in the last LIBERAL. Warderman was also convicted and the other men were acquitted, but were not turned loose, as they are under indictment from the territorial court for holding up the train, and will be tried at the next term of court. The convicted men were sentenced to ten years each in the penitentiary, and are now safe at Santa Fe. Lawyer Fielder will appeal the case.[21]*

Incredibly, although the newspapers often disputed the issue, Black Jack was probably not the leader of the Black Jack Gang, which was also known as the High Fives. He was a bronco buster who earned his name training horses among the black jack oak of the Peloncillo Range.[22] His name may have been Jack McChristian, Ed Williams, or William Christian, this latter perhaps the most likely as Bob Christian, a brother, may have been part of the gang. Others of the gang styled the High Fives included Bob Hayes or Hays; George Musgrave, alias Jesse Williams, alias Jeff Davis; Cole Young or Cole Estes; and Tom Anderson.[23] Of Black Jack the *Arizona Republic* said, "The difficulty in the identification of Black Jack has been the finding of anybody on the side of law and order that knew him. There was even a doubt regarding his real name. It was believed to be either George Musgrave, Tom Williams or Tom Ketchum. Ketchum was killed near Clifton more than two years ago, and Williams was killed near Silver City."[24]

In 1899, apparently, in Phoenix, there was reasonable doubt as to whether Black Jack was still alive. Authoritative historian Dan L. Thrapp believed that Black Jack was William T. Christian, who later died near Clifton, Arizona, on April 28, 1897, in a shoot-out.[25]

Black Jack and the High Fives first came to folk's attention about 9 p.m. on July 20, 1896, when they took over Weems's store and post office at the whistle-stop known as Separ, New Mexico. The *Deming Headlight* reported,

The leader of the gang was tall and slim; had a thin, dark mustache; wore a brown hat; light brown and white shirt; a new double cartridge belt—upper row rifle cartridges and carried a revolver. Another with a rifle, guarding the outside of the building, was of medium size, with mustache; wore black hat, coat and vest and light shirt. A good description of the third man was not obtained but enough was seen of him to recognize him if caught. They rode a dark dun and two bay or brown horses.[26]

The town consisted of three buildings, and in addition to cleaning out the safe and cash drawer of about thirty dollars, the outlaws took everything that wasn't nailed down: a Navajo blanket, two more pairs of blankets, a demijohn of whiskey, sacks of provisions, and cigars.

The outlaws were identified as Jesse Miller, alias Jesse Williams, alias Jeff Davis; Cole Young, alias Cole Estes; and a fellow known as "Black Jack."[27] Black Jack didn't get top billing. Cole Young seemed to be the leader.

About noon on August 6, 1896, in Nogales, Pima County,[28] the High Five or Black Jack Gang attempted to rob the International Bank. Three men entered the bank, two brandishing a Colt revolver in each hand and one armed with a Winchester rifle. One with a brace of revolvers covered the cashier, Fred Herrera; another covered the bank president with his rifle, while the third tried to get to the vault. Encountering men meeting in a back room, he demanded that they throw up their hands. This activity distracted the man covering Herrera, who drew his pistol and opened fire. With one man wounded, the High Fives fled with a posse in pursuit. The reporter neglected to mention the make and model of Herrera's pistol.[29]

The would-be robbers headed west across Cochise County, passing Fort Huachuca, Bisbee, and Tombstone to Skeleton Canyon, where ten years before Geronimo had surrendered. The High Fives did not. They lay in ambush. As Deputy Sheriff Burt Alvord, accompanied by line rider Robson, Sheriff Leatherwood of Pima County, John Slaughter, Sheriff C. S. Fly of Cochise County, and others, approached, the gang opened fire, killing Robson in the first volley. His horse carried the dead man to the outlaws, who found it useful because the exchange of fire slew Black Jack's horse.[30] The outlaws' hidden position was impregnable, and they escaped up the canyon into New Mexico. Robson was the gang's first murder.

In the evening of October 2, 1896, at the Rio Puerco Station (the name in Spanish means "filthy river"), about thirty-four miles west of Albuquerque, six men of the High Five Gang attempted to rob the Atlantic & Pacific No. 2 train. On board was Chief Deputy US Marshal H. W. Loomis, who might well have warned Black Jack that you do not mess with the US mail. It was a federal offense.

"[Loomis] happened to be on the train at the time. Single-handed and alone he stood off the desperadoes, killed the leader, Cole Young, and set to flight the whole party. . . . It must have given Deputy Loomis

extreme pleasure to have encountered so unexpectedly this crowd of desperadoes. He has been after them for four weeks."[31]

In November 1896, the High Fives returned to Separ.

"Last Tuesday evening, about 6 o'clock, two men held up the entire
population at Separ, this county, and took every available thing in sight.
One of the men was recognized as 'Black Jack,' and the other, it is said,
was none other than Jeff Davis, both of whom belong to the famous
Nogales and Separ gang of Bandits."[32]

Bit by bit, the gang was whittled down; outlaws did not live long.
On November 24, 1896, Robert Hayes was shot and killed by a pursuing posse.[33] William T. Christian, Black Jack, lasted a few more months
until April 1897. But his sobriquet would live on, and Black Jack and his
gang continued to strike terror in hearts across the Southwest and to be
blamed for myriad crimes until Tom Ketchum was hanged in 1901. By
1900, the sole surviving member of the High Fives was digitally chal-
lenged Jesse "Three-Finger Jack" Dunlap.

Tom and his brother Sam Ketchum were bad outlaws who each held
up at least one train. It is unclear if they ever did more than that. Dubious
claims linked them to many robberies and murders going back at least to
1896 and possibly earlier. Consider that their operational area was in the
extreme northeast corner of New Mexico, while Black Jack Christian and
the High Fives had operated in Cochise County, Arizona, and neighboring
Grant County, New Mexico, in the bootheel, the extreme southwest of
New Mexico Territory. For those readers on the East Coast, the distance is
similar to that between New York City and Georgia.

In a letter to President McKinley, Tom Ketchum claimed that his gang
consisted of Atkins, Ed Cullin (deceased at San Simon), Will Carver, Sam
Ketchum, Broncho Bill (probably William H. McGinnis),[34] and himself.[35]
We'll overlook for a moment the fact that Tom had no gang and was a
soul with scant association with the truth, and note that the "one and only
original High Fives gang" of Black Jack Christian consisted of "Black
Jack," who may have been Jack McChristian; George Musgrave, alias Jesse
Williams, alias Jeff Davis; Cole Young or Cole Estes; Bob Hayes; and
Tom (or Frank) Anderson.[36] There are no common members. With the
exception of Ed "Shoot 'em Up Dick" Cullin, the gang that bungled the

Steins Pass/San Simon robbery on December 10, 1897, in which "Shoot 'em Up" was shot up, held no members in common with either Tom's list or the High Fives. The gang that rode with Ed Cullin were Walter Hoffman, F. L. Capehart, Henry Marshall, William Warderman, and Leonard Alverson. Of the members of this gang who were serving hard time, Tom Ketchum, on his last morning, wrote to the president: "There are three men in the Santa Fe penitentiary serving a sentence for the robbery of the US mail at Steins Pass, N.M., in 1897, vis: Leonard Albertson, Walter Huffman and Bill Waterson. They are innocent of the crime as an unborn babe."[37]

Folsom was a tiny hamlet in northeastern New Mexico on the Colorado and Southern Railroad, part of the Santa Fe system, between Denver and Fort Worth. At about 10:30 p.m. on July 11, 1899, four masked men stopped the southbound passenger No. 1 train about five miles south of Folsom.[38] Sam Ketchum, William H. McGinnis, and Franks, first name unknown, were later identified as the outlaws.[39] The fourth man was assumed to have been holding the horses and may not have existed at all.[40] The *New Mexican Review* reported, "Only three men rode away, two men riding one horse." It seems unlikely that the robbers would stage a robbery with two men on one horse. In the next two days, they covered over one hundred miles, riding west, passing Springer, and going on beyond Cimarron into the Sangre de Cristo Mountains. The *Review* went on to state that the robbery occurred "at the same point at which the passenger train was held up last September."

> *After the train had been brought to a standstill tonight, and the train crew had been intimidated by guns, the robbers used dynamite with good effect blowing open the sides of the express car.*
>
> *Their work was in vain, however, as there were no valuable or money in the express safe.*
>
> *Superintendent Webb and the Wells-Fargo express agent, Blover, both state positively that nothing was secured by the robbers.*[41]

Other parties, seemingly in the know, believed that a large amount of money was taken. Sheriff Fred Higgins of Roswell was a passenger on the train. He observed only three outlaws but noted that they departed with a great many packages.[42] The railroads and Wells, Fargo and Company seldom admitted to any losses because such an admission would have encouraged robbers and been bad for business. On the other hand, outlaws never seemed to have had much money.

A posse formed in Colorado from the closest points by train. Officers of the law were still allowed to collect bounties to supplement their pay. Special Officer W. H. Reno of the railroad recruited a posse at Trinidad. He was joined by Wells, Fargo and Company detective John Thacker; United States Marshal Foraker; Sheriff Farr of Wickenburg, Colorado; Deputy H. M. Love; and F. Hopkinson Smith, the celebrated author who happened to be in the vicinity and joined the posse through love of adventure.[43] The posse divided over leadership, with five more men under Marshals Elliott and Foraker acting independently of Sheriff Farr.

On July 16, 1899, the outlaws were cornered in a rugged canyon ten miles west of Cimarron. Sheriff Farr's posse got the worst of the confrontation, suffering numerous casualties. Outlaws Sam Ketchum and McGinnis were both wounded. Farr was shot dead, and Deputy Love died shortly afterward of his wounds. Reno rolled the dead sheriff off of wounded author Smith, panicked, and ran for Cimarron. The *Las Vegas Daily Optic* reported, "Reno . . . denies that he left the scene of the battle in precipitate haste and arrived at Cimarron in a panic stricken condition. . . . He does not attempt to explain, however, the misstatement that he made regarding the killing of one of the outlaws, which, in itself, is a strong indication that he was badly rattled and was at the time unable to give a straight report of the fight."[44]

Gravely wounded, Sam Ketchum made his way to the ranch of Henry Lambert, who claimed to have been the chef for President Lincoln and who was the owner of the St. James Hotel and Saloon in Cimarron, the scene of many gunfights.[45] After patching him up, Henry notified the authorities. "Although Special Officer Reno is credited with having figured in his capture, Ketchum was apprehended by Mr. Lambert."[46] McGinnis was captured shortly afterward, and Franks got clean away, which may account for why we don't know his given name.

To the *Optic's* reporter, Sam Ketchum said that he was a brother of Tom Ketchum, the original Black Jack. Captain Thacker said, "That is he. We have him at last." W. H. Reno believed Sam was the original Black Jack. Sam Ketchum, however, was not Black Jack, and neither was his brother Tom, as we've shown above. The brothers may have been bad outlaws, but at this juncture, I find no evidence that they committed any crimes other than those mentioned here, and searching for that evidence goes beyond our scope. They were not the Cochise County gang, nor did they rob trains on the Southern Corridor.

Sam Ketchum, a muscular-looking fellow, heavily built, nearly six feet in height, wore a blond mustache and passed away in his cell in Santa Fe on July 24, 1899, of blood poisoning from the wound he had incurred. McGinnis was convicted. Sam's body was shipped to relatives in San Angelo, Texas.[47] After death, he was photographed in his cell where he had been found.

"The picture is a most excellent one, plainly showing the stubby beard of a week's growth covering his face. Ketchum's countenance demonstrates that he was a vigorous, coarse grained man, possessed of considerable stubbornness and animal courage."[48]

On August 16, 1899, Tom Ketchum held up the Colorado and Southern train about five miles south of Folsom, New Mexico, seemingly unaware that his brother, Sam, had attempted to rob the train only a month before at almost the same spot. The *Holbrook Argus* wrote:

One night as the express was puffing laboriously up grade the engineer saw a light ahead giving the signal to stop. When the train slowed down Tom Ketchum jumped into the cab and, carelessly swinging a 45 Colt near the engineer's nose, told him to obey all orders given during the next few minutes. This, Tom said, would save heartaches in the engineer's home and the intrusion of an undertaker in the family circle. Then he jumped off and tried to uncouple the engine, which was made impossible by the steep grade. Failing in this, Tom walked back to the Wells-Fargo express car and, thumping the door with the butt of his Colt, demanded admittance. The messenger opened the door and poked the muzzle of a Winchester out into the dark and pulled the trigger. That put an end to the hold-up that night.[49]

Having twice been robbed on this spot, the Colorado and Southern Railway now showed considerable prescience in arming its trainmen against road agents and by having them stand ready on high alert. Unaware of these precautions, this lone gunman proceeded with this mad attempt. At the same time the express agent opened fire, the conductor, armed with a double-barreled shotgun, opened fire on the shadowy figure near the car. The shadow disappeared into the night, and the conductor ordered the train onward.[50]

"He was severely shot by conductor Harrington, and was found next morning lying in a pool of blood in the shelter of an embankment near the railroad track, too weak to move. He, like all his ilk, played the game too long, and will now pay the penalty."[51]

This appeared to be the work of an amateur and not that of an experienced outlaw, although one newspaper account portrayed Tom as a regular Jesse James:

> *He received the contents of a double-barreled shot gun in his right arm, but quickly changing the rifle to his left shoulder, he succeeded in wounding both the conductor and mail agent. He then escaped in the darkness, but was found the next day by a freight crew about one hundred yards from the scene of the battle. He was weak from the loss of blood, yet on their approach he reached for his gun and held them at bay until at last he grew so faint that he dropped his rifle and was captured.*[52]

In truth, the entire escapade ended with more of a whimper than a roar. Tom was wounded, but the trainmen were not.

Initially, Ketchum claimed to be Thomas Stevens but was soon identified incorrectly as Black Jack by lawmen anxious for a score and correctly as Tom Ketchum. He was told that he must lose his arm or die. He declined to have it taken off. Convinced that he was dying, Tom Ketchum confessed to being the notorious Black Jack. By this confession, he would die an important and respected outlaw. Oddly, he did not confess to his long list of presumed crimes, thus clearing the books.[53] He only mentioned the two most recent train robberies, and these may have been his complete criminal history. He confessed thinking himself dying. His tune would change when it became clear that he was not.

> *Trinidad, Colo., Aug. 26—Ketchum, alias Black Jack, has confessed his identity to Sheriff Stewart of Eddy County, N.M. He says he planned the Folsom train robbery, but was not there, and received his share of the booty from a member of the gang. He was about to leave for South America when captured. Ketchum has been identified by the officer of Yavapai county as the Camp Verde murderer, and a requisition was made to-day for his return to Arizona. Black Jack is now in the hands of the United States officers at Santa Fe, N.M. The officers are certain that they have the sure enough Ketchum this time.*[54]

On Sunday evening, July 5, 1899, R. M. Rodgers and Clinton D. Wingfield were murdered at their mercantile in Camp Verde, Arizona, a few miles from Prescott.[55] Posses searched for the culprit through the mountains between Camp Verde and Prescott and farther afield, searching caves and canyons without success.[56] Somehow, they arrived at the conclusion that the killer must be Black Jack despite the fact that Black Jack Christian or McChristian, the Cochise County outlaw, had been killed some years before. They focused on Tom Ketchum, the New Mexico outlaw who claimed to be "the one and only original Black Jack." The *Journal-Miner* wrote, "The belief that the person captured is none other than the notorious Black Jack, does not seem to be well founded. A gentleman who was personally acquainted with the above outlaw, informed us that Black Jack was killed three years ago at Blue River, in the eastern part of Arizona by a posse under a United States marshal, and the gang of which this bandit was at the head was broken up."[57]

A photograph seemed to link Tom Ketchum to the Arizona crime.[58] Undaunted and not being of faint heart, the Arizona authorities persisted in requisitioning Black Jack Ketchum from New Mexico. Perhaps, unconvinced of Tom's guilt in the Arizona crime, Governor Otero continued to resist the requisition.[59]

In early October 1899, while in the penitentiary at Santa Fe, the only jail in New Mexico secure enough to contain the notorious Black Jack, Tom Ketchum was quoted as saying, "I am getting fat, so when they hang me they can eat me if they want to." Tom's weight would be an issue later on. Meanwhile, the authorities grew suspicious. A search showed that he'd made a saw from a clock spring, and in the water closet he had concealed a wooden gun. He was still convalescing from his wounded arm but had recovered enough that he no longer believed he was going to die, and with that change, his attitude evolved. He wanted out and did not want to hang. When his bold attempted escape failed, he broke down with emotion and was promptly removed from the hospital ward to a proper cell.[60] Eventually, infection set in again, and he lost the arm.

On September 8, 1900, Tom Ketchum was convicted of train robbery, a hanging offense in New Mexico.[61] Prior to this trial, he had pled guilty in December of 1899 to holding up the United States mail. The *Holbrook Argus* wrote, "It is thought that by his action in pleading guilty to the United States offense he will prevent his neck from coming into fatal proximity with a hempen collar."[62] The laws that made train robbery a capital offense in Arizona and New Mexico were not popular. Governor Otero was not eager for Ketchum to hang, nor was he ready to see the outlaw sent to Arizona to hang for the Camp Verde murders. The Arizona newspapers raged at the delay.

> *Tom Ketchum, the man who is believed to have murdered Rogers and Winfield at Camp Verde, last July, it is stated, has not yet had his trial in New Mexico, but is simply being held in jail there. Governor Otero persists in refusing to allow him to be extradited for trial in this county on the charge of murder, but says if he is not hanged in New Mexico he will permit the courts here to have him. Inasmuch as he is not even brought to trial there, the action of Governor Otero is enexplicable [sic].—Journal-Miner* [63]

Confusion surrounded Black Jack. No one was sure of his real name. Some thought it George Musgrave. Others thought he was Tom Williams or even Tom Ketchum, but they also thought Ketchum had been killed near Clifton in 1897 and Williams killed at Silver City.[64] Ketchum even attempted an appeal to the Supreme Court of the United States, but the effort seems to have borne fruit a few days too late for Tom. According to the *Silver Belt*, Tom won a stay until the Supreme Court would convene in January 1901.[65]

A Fine End to a Bad Outlaw

Clayton, New Mexico, 1901

Clayton, in the distant northeast corner of New Mexico, is the county seat of Union County, formed in 1894. Hangings were usually done by the sheriff at the county seat. There are three important points to recall about Clayton: (1) Socially and geographically, the railroad line put it closer to Denver than to Santa Fe. (2) There had never been occasion to hang anyone in Clayton. And (3) Folsom was in Union County. And so it was that an item appeared in the Denver newspaper: "Denver, Colo., April 23.—The *Times* today says: It is said that 'Black Jack' Ketchum, is being removed today by a special train from Santa Fe to Clayton, N.M., where he will be executed on Friday, for the double crime of train robbery and murder."[66]

According to the newspapers, Tom Ketchum "passed a quiet night, ate a hearty breakfast, took a bath and put on a new suit of clothes." He wrote a letter to President McKinley taking credit for crimes he hadn't committed and exonerating those who had. Tom sent a message to the conductor who had shot him and caused the amputation of his arm: "Hey, tell Harrington I'll meet him in Hell for breakfast." He asked that Sheriff Garcia hurry on with the hanging so he could get to Hell in time for dinner. Tom dearly liked food and gained weight in jail. Ketchum claimed he'd never killed a man and only wounded three.[67] For once, he was probably telling the truth. We know that a priest visited him. Perhaps the holy man read to him a passage from the book of Mark: "And when [Salome] the daughter of the said Herodias came in, and danced, and pleased Herod and them that sat with him, the king said unto the damsel, Ask of me whatsoever thou wilt, and I will give it thee. And she went forth, and said unto her mother, What shall I ask? And she said, The head of John the Baptist."[68]

On April 26 at 1:17 p.m., Tom ascended the scaffold with the priest at his side. His final words were "Goodbye, please dig my grave very deep. . . . All right, hurry up!" The trap was sprung, and Tom descended a bit too far perhaps. The rope went taut and snapped, but so did Tom's neck, and his head popped off. "His body pitched forward, the blood spurting forth [from] the headless trunk. Many spectators turned away in horror."[69] Imagine the front row at a Gallagher concert when he strikes the watermelon with a mallet.

Clayton and Sheriff Garcia were embarrassed. Hangings are supposed to be solemn and dignified. Everyone comes in for the entertainment and the morality lesson: "Sonny, keep on like ya are, and ya'll end up like this!" But they don't want their clothing ruined with bloodstains! Thus, Sheriff Garcia, ever the politician, wrote an apology that admitted nothing.

"Clayton, N.M. April 27—Denver Post: Tom Ketchum's head being severed from the body was caused by his being a very heavy man. Nothing out of the ordinary happened. There were no bungles whatever. Everything worked nicely and in perfect order. (signed) Salome Garcia, Sheriff"[70]

And thus, we might conclude that Tom Ketchum, ever the man to violate the Ten Commandments, in a reversal of Holy Writ, danced for Salome and lost his head.

CHAPTER EIGHT

Lawmen Burt Alvord and Billy Stiles Rob a Train

A CLEVER PLAN

Cochise, Arizona, 1899

WHILE RESEARCHING THE 1916 TRAIN ROBBERY AT APACHE, I SHARED the first article I found with Kathy Klump, who advised that the robbery had probably never occurred because the writer had made a total mess of the then recent history he included. She is correct. Mrs. Klump's family has been responsible for a great deal of Cochise County history. This bit of "history" is a complete mess; however, it was the source of the first versions of the story of the Cochise and Fairbank robberies that I encountered in secondary sources. The writer conflated several events, and if he got anything right, it was only by mistake. *Be warned, this version of the story is not true.*

From the *Bisbee Daily Review*, 8 September 1916:

> *The robbery of Wednesday night was the first to take place in Cochise county in many years. Its object, in all probability, was a supposed shipment of money with which to pay off the soldiers at Douglas.*
>
> *The first train robbery which occurred in Cochise county was at Steins Pass, about thirty years ago. This attracted much attention and some of the trainmen were accused of complicity and arrested. They were tried in Tucson and acquitted. Another robbery of a train in*

this county occurred near Cochise station. The train was held up in the usual way and something like $80,000 taken from the express car. It is said that Grant Wheeler and Joseph George were the men who did this robbery, but it was afterward shown that Bert Alvord and a constable in Pearce were implicated in the job. Alvord was arrested and lodged at Tombstone. Friends on the outside slipped him a gun and he held up George Bravin, the jailer, and made his escape. Then Alvord became an outlaw and defied the authorities for more than a year. Afterward he was caught in Mexico and finally got free from the charge and went to South America. That robbery occurred in the early nineties. The Pearce constable was tried and served a term in the penitentiary and was killed in Willcox after he returned to this county.

Capital Offense

Not long after this there was an attempt made to hold up the train on the Nogales branch of the Southern Pacific at Fort Huachuca Siding. Railroad officials had been notified of this proposed robbery and Jeff Milton, now immigration inspector at Ajo, then a special officer, boarded the train at Nogales. When the robbers appeared Milton opened fire on them with a shotgun and wounded "Three-Fingered Jack," a noted outlaw, so badly that he was next day captured and died at Tombstone. Milton was shot by the bandits and had his arm broken. In this robbery besides "Three-Fingered Jack" were Bravo Juan and the Owens boys. The Owens boys were captured, tried and executed at Tombstone.

After the first train robbery in Arizona the next session of the legislature passed a law making train robbery a capital offense and it was under this law that the Owens boys were hung.[1]

The Owens boys weren't hanged, railroad officials weren't warned, and the robbery attempt occurred at Fairbank not Huachuca Siding. The first train robbery in Cochise County, Arizona, might have been at Steins Pass in Grant County, New Mexico. They stole the train at Steins and took it to Cochise County to rob. The

Cochise Depot, where the most successful robbery took place.
COURTESY OF SULPHUR SPRINGS VALLEY HISTORICAL SOCIETY

first Cochise County robbery was at Willcox and they didn't get eighty thousand dollars. Journalistic standards haven't changed. This story has more mythology attached to it than even the story of Pearl Hart.

Legend has it, for I cannot locate a primary source, that when Three-Fingered Jack Dunlap informed Sheriff Scott White that Burt Alvord and Billy Stiles had planned the Fairbank robbery, the sheriff exclaimed, "Those two idiots, they couldn't plan anything!" It was only thus exposed that Billy Stiles turned himself over to the law as state's witness. Without evidence from Jack, the outlaws should have been free and clear as in the Cochise robbery. Billy's record is nothing short of astonishing. I think it's the result of cowardice and idiotic blunders. Author David Grassé, on the other hand, calls Stiles "undoubtedly one of the shrewdest outlaws to ever grace the territory."[2] Genius is often mistaken for madness. In Stiles's case, being consistently underestimated as an idiot may have opened the door to inspired blundering. Others have said of Stiles that he was the "most cowardly stool-pigeon that ever tried crime."[3]

There has always been much speculation concerning the number of outlaws who got away with train robberies. Wells, Fargo and

Company and the railroads were always reticent about revealing the amount taken, which led to newspaper editors allowing their imagination to run wild. The companies who had been robbed had good reason to keep the amounts secret. If the amount was large, revealing it would encourage more robberies, and the loss might damage the companies' image and hurt stock prices. The amount recovered from captured outlaws was always miniscule. Outlaws who robbed again didn't do it because they had been so successful. They did it because they were broke.

There is a question of what the outlaws were after. Once the railroad and the express companies got things figured out, they secured the large transfers in the through safe. The express agent didn't have access to this safe. It would have to be blown. Blowing the safe was no mean task. To blow it neatly, one would have to drill into the locking mechanism and pour in the explosive, usually nitroglycerine. Such elaborate measures would take both time and a drill. Otherwise, one could crack the safe by tamping a large explosion of sticks of dynamite on top of the safe. This process would open the safe and destroy the express car. We have seen very few instances where the express car was blown up and fewer still where the safe was expertly cracked. Safes were made of heavy material, not so much so that they would take time to open as to ensure that they could not be conveniently carried off and opened elsewhere.

The outlaws were often after payrolls for the military and for the mines, for these were large enough amounts to be interesting. The time of their transfer was always a deep, dark secret, for this cash could not be secured in the through safe. The express agent had to have access to it in order to disperse it to the proper recipients at stations between the endpoints, where the keys to the safe were kept. During the Mexican revolution and the Great War, large payrolls went to the army stationed at Douglas and Fort Huachuca. Monthly payrolls were sent to the mines at Pearce, Tombstone, and Bisbee. How the express company shipped and protected this cash was another secret. In the Cochise robbery we are about to discuss, the outlaws were probably after the Commonwealth Mine payroll on its way to Pearce. It has been speculated that the payroll had been shipped days before, unloaded at Willcox, not Cochise, and transferred as part of a wagon load of groceries and supplies. Lynn R. Bailey wrote that they got off with $1,700, a much more reasonable figure than the five to thirty thousand dollars some newspaper editors wrote at the time.[4] And much less than the eighty thousand dollars reported in the newspaper story that opened this chapter.

William "Billy" Larkin Stiles, a native of Casa Grande, had come to Cochise County, where he worked at various jobs, including prospecting. In an earlier chapter, he served on a posse as a deputy constable with Billy Breakenridge. In Pearce, he worked as a deputy under Constable George Bravin. In the late 1890s, he married a Mexican woman named Maria. Her best friend was Lola Ochoa.[5]

Albert "Burt" Wright Alvord was born in Susanville, Lassen County, California, on September 11, 1867. In 1881, at age thirteen, he came to Tombstone, where his father worked as justice of the peace. As we've already seen, by the time he was nineteen in 1886, he was working as a deputy for Sheriff John Slaughter, though the sheriff later claimed that Burt "had not at any time been a regular appointed deputy, except in special cases and for a short period."[6] Slaughter had hired Burt because he knew Burt was well informed on outlaw activities, and he knew that Alvord would sell his best friend down the line for a fee.[7] In 1896, he married Lola Ochoa and lived at Pearce, where he was a deputy constable under George Bravin. Lola was a good friend of Maria Stiles. In 1897, Burt Alvord moved to Willcox, where he had been hired to clean up the town.[8]

In 1902, cattleman L. J. Overlock, who probably knew Alvord better than anyone, talked to the newspapers. Alvord worked on John Slaughter's San Bernardino ranch, which straddled the border, and Overlock thought Slaughter had employed Burt as a deputy. In 1894, Burt Alvord was employed by Overlock on his ranch at the same time that Grant Wheeler worked there, before he left off cowboying and rodeoing and took up train robbing. The two did not like each other. Burt served on the posse that went after Grant. For a while, Burt worked driving a stage for Arizona's outlaw justice of the peace, Jim Burnett. Alvord was working at Pearce when Andy Darnell and his gang of cowboys started terrorizing Willcox, turning it into the toughest town in the West.[9]

Billy Stiles was a deputy, Arizona Ranger, and train robber. Was he the stupidest or the cleverest outlaw in Arizona history?
COURTESY OF SULPHUR SPRINGS VALLEY HISTORICAL SOCIETY

On November 13, 1897, Andy Darnell, a tough hombre from the Erie Cattle Company, and his sidekick, Billy King, made their way into George Raum's saloon in Willcox.[10] Billy was wayward and as "variable as the whirlwind." They drank deeply of Raum's stock. Burt Alvord happened by to show off his shiny new constable's star, and the boys, full of firewater, tried to bully him just for fun. Apparently, Andy got it into his head to show the "bad" constable and his two deputies, Billy Stiles and William Downing, how harmless the Willcox law was. Drawing his revolver, he covered Burt and his deputies and escorted them down the ladder to the cellar where George stored his stock and then locked the trap door to seal them in. Later, the constables were ignominiously liberated by friends. Not one to take this insult lightly, Burt sought out Billy King, found him at Kasper Hauser's saloon, and invited King out back, where Alvord promptly blew off King's head. "Two witnesses testified to having heard King threaten to kill Mr. Alvord." The shooting was ruled self-defense.[11] Two witnesses? Stiles and Downing?

On May 13, 1898, while the Spanish-American War was raging in other quarters, a drunken Mexican in the Headquarters Saloon at Willcox made the mistake of arming himself with a long knife and proclaiming himself for Spain while hunting Americans to kill. Alvord shot him dead. Black Jack, outlaw, cowboy, and friend of cowboys, proclaimed that Burt must die, but by this time, it was unclear which of the many Black Jacks this culprit was or even if Black Jack was still alive.[12] Willcox was left to ponder its fate. Which was worse, the cowboy toughs or the constable cure?

The train robbery at Cochise has grown to be interwoven with legend. At the time, the *Arizona Republic* in Phoenix seems to have gotten the most reliable account by talking to the train crew the next day. The southern Arizona papers turned a quiet adventure into a flaming shoot-out.[13] Among other important facts, the *Arizona Republic* reported, "It is not customary to send any great amount of money by rail through the southwestern states. The Wells, Fargo and Company has sustained various losses by train robberies, and it is the policy now to carry drafts instead of coin, if possible. Then if there was any great amount of money it is probable that a guard would accompany it, and there was no guard in this instance."[14]

William Downing, former deputy constable, did hard time for his role in the train robbery.

COURTESY OF SULPHUR SPRINGS VALLEY HISTORICAL SOCIETY

Looking back, the record shows that the Southern Pacific and Wells, Fargo and Company did their best to foil robberies, so we need to understand what Cochise was and where it stood in relation to the rest of the world. Located eleven miles across the Willcox Playa, often dry though a lake in summer, from the town of Willcox, Cochise had a mercantile store, a train station, a telegraph office, and a hotel where "Big Nose Kate" Elder, Doc Holliday's main squeeze, no longer in her prime, worked as a housekeeper. It was the gateway to the Ghost Town Trail, when the ghost towns were the then thriving mining communities of Pearce, Courtland, and Gleeson. Eventually, a railroad spur would run all the way to Gleeson. In 1895, shipments for these communities, including payrolls, moved through Cochise. The robbery, as it turned out, was as nearly perfect as any on the Southern Corridor. It went off without a hitch, and the perpetrators wouldn't have been caught if they hadn't been so successful that they tried it again in February 1900. They tried again because Billy Stiles's share came to only $480.[15]

On February 28, 1900, in testimony given at a pretrial hearing in Tombstone, Billy Stiles and Matt Burts confessed, and Billy provided the following information: "The witness stated the matter had been considered between the four—Downing, Alvord, Burts and himself for two months. Downing was to furnish the horses. Alvord's duty was to provide men to swear to alibis if the two robbers were caught and Burts and himself were to 'hold up' the train which they did, the two doing the work alone, the horses being provided for by Downing."[16]

Another presumed confederate, Felix Mayhew, confessed to having been in on the early planning although he dropped out before execution. He testified that early on they had scouted Benson as a possible site for the robbery but decided that it was not suitable. To this statement, William Downing protested, "That's a lie!" He was gaveled to silence. Benson, once again, lost its chance to make history.[17]

Stiles went on to state that Alvord had forced the door at the Soto Brothers powder house, located behind the store, and secured giant powder and fuse. The boys took blasting caps from a mine at Dos Cabezas.[18]

Burt Alvord's role was to provide alibis for the others. How he did this is open to speculation and a lie or two. It is told that he and his deputies went into the back room of a saloon to "play cards."[19] Burts and Stiles went out the window, mounted their waiting horses, rode to a spot a mile and a half west of Cochise, and then walked back to the station to await the train. Meanwhile, Burt and Downing whooped it up, drinking for four, and ordering more drinks throughout the night. With the deed done, Burts and Stiles returned through the window, alibi established. One version of the story states that the bartender grew suspicious and finally caught on but was threatened to silence. In the following months, at least one "detective" thought he scented the trail and had the bartender ready to break when the bartender, fearing for his life, suddenly left town. Sources in Willcox swear this account isn't so because the bartender in question never left town.[20] In any event, it is very hard to know what a witness is about to say. Burt Alvord did something to secure ironclad alibis for the gang.

After midnight on September 9, 1899, Matt Burts and Billy Stiles walked casually into Cochise from the west just as the westbound passenger train was heaving to a stop at the station. Express Messenger Charles Adair slid open the door of his car and threw out the mailbox. Out in the dark, he saw two men covering him with pistols. One called out, "Come down, you ——- ——-." That wasn't his name, but he didn't care to argue a case of mistaken identity. One account, probably mistaken, said he'd been robbed the previous spring and had killed his assailant. Perhaps. In any event, they had Adair cold, so he climbed down and was escorted quietly to the locomotive. The affair was handled so quietly that passengers asleep in the sleeper and day coach were unaware that anything untoward was happening. The three passed the freight car ahead of the express and arriving at the engine took control of the engineer and fireman Gray. The fireman was ordered back to unhook the passenger cars. He informed his captors that he was unfamiliar with the duties of a brakeman, but a .44 caliber Colt interceded and won the argument. Fireman Gray undertook the task.

With the passenger cars left behind, the gunmen ordered the engineer to move the train a mile and a half up the track to the west. Once there, the taller outlaw took charge of the three trainmen and had them sit alongside the tracks. He was chatting with them in a jocular way when they heard a small explosion and bit of cussing. Billy Stiles, the shorter outlaw, was busy in the express car putting the lessons he'd learned while prospecting to use. Failing to open the safe on the first try, he employed a much larger charge and succeeded in cracking the safe, destroying the express car, and waking the passengers left back in Cochise. Billy emerged with a sack of gold coins and paper money. It was said he left behind the silver. Matt told his prisoners, "You needn't be in a big hurry about running back to the train. You'd better wait fifteen minutes anyhow."[21]

Matt and Billy walked away into the dark night. After a while, the train crew backed the train to Cochise, where a tenderfoot among the passengers emerged and began firing his brand-new six-shooter into the dark after the robbers. He was soon subdued. Stiles and Burts found their horses and rode back to Willcox. The money was taken to Alvord's house, and later it was carried to Downing's house. After a time, it was divided among the three.[22]

The telegraph in Cochise was found to be in order, and word went out to Willcox, Tucson, and Tombstone. There was some early confusion concerning two loafers who had been seen around Cochise in the days before the robbery. A passenger reported three suspicious men who had been on the train since Albuquerque dressed as cowboys and carrying telescope valises. The passenger became acquainted with them and reported that they were still on at Deming but were not seen after the robbery although they had claimed to be heading for a ranch south of Benson.[23] Posses were soon hot on the trail, following clear tracks from Cochise to the edge of Willcox, where the trail was lost among a multitude of hoof prints. The *Epitaph* carried the tale: "A posse followed the trail of the robbers to one-half mile from Willcox, a distance of thirteen miles, where the trail came to an abrupt end apparently as though the men and horses had gone up into the air."[24]

More likely the outlaws had gone in through a window rather than up into the air, then out the front door of the saloon, and over to Burt Alvord's house. In the morning, Willcox law enforcement officers were on the job helping to locate the train robbers. The *Arizona Republic* reported: "There is a report that an hour after the robbery five men rode through the edge of Willcox going north at a rapid gait. Constable Alvord and Deputy Styles [of] Willcox left today to take the trail. Scott

White, sheriff of Cochise county, is in pursuit. George Scarborough and son, well known detectives, arrived on the scene of the robbery yesterday and are devoting their well-known energy and ability to the pursuit of the daring criminals."[25]

Pursuit continued intermittently beyond the turn of the century, which was only three months away. Sheriff Scott White sent William Downing, a cattleman, and William Stiles, a former constable who had been with him in Willcox, over to Silver City to assist Wells, Fargo and Company detective Johnny Thacker in the search, hoping to cut their trail in New Mexico.[26] Unlike sheriffs, marshals (US or city), and constables, railroad, Wells, Fargo and Company, and US postal detectives don't have other duties. They are salaried and can stay on the job indefinitely, until the next train robbery, drawing per diem and sending in reports to the company explaining how close they were to making an arrest. Thacker would later claim, "He has known for a long time that Alvord was the man who planned the robbery but was unable to prove it until the Fairbank robbery."[27] Sounds completely plausible. Matters were at an impasse until Billy Stiles decided that he needed more money.

In 1891, Jesse P. "Three-Fingered Jack" Dunlap stole a horse from John Thomas, taking the saddle and bridle as well. He was associated with other crimes, including stealing many cattle from the Erie Cattle outfit and highway robbery, but the warrant on the horse theft charge remained in effect. In July 1894, he spent some time in jail at Solomonville. His name was mentioned in connection with Black Jack Christian of the High Five Gang. If he was a member of that illustrious band of brothers, he was the last surviving member, perhaps disbarred from the gang as he lacked sufficient digits for a high five. Along with a sidekick named Moore, he'd even once held up two men between Willcox and Fort Grant. Captain Carlton Kelton (sheriff) had almost captured him in New Mexico, but he got only Dunlap's horse and blankets after a fight. In July 1899, Jack got married in Colorado. Harry Miller, a former hand with the Erie Cattle Company, positively identified Three-Fingered Jack working up by Cripple Creek, Colorado. In October 1899, eight years after the fact, Sheriff White got papers to fetch him back to Cochise County on the Thomas indictment. Dunlap had sworn to kill Sheriff White for bringing him back to Cochise County to stand trial in 1899.

Railroad Avenue in Fairbank, Arizona, where the holdup took place.
COURTESY SULPHUR SPRINGS VALLEY HISTORICAL SOCIETY

Once Jesse Dunlap arrived in the county, Thomas could not be found, and Jack was released to seek gainful employment.[28]

A NOT SO CLEVER PLAN

Fairbank, Arizona, 1900

In February 1900, the *Arizona Republic* printed a description of Jefferson Davis Milton: "Messenger J.D. Milton has the reputation of being one of the nerviest men and deadliest shots in Arizona. He was for a long time connected with the customs service at Nogales as line rider, and since then has been employed as a peace officer. He took part in the long pursuit of the Black Jack gang four years ago and soon after entered the service of Wells, Fargo and Company."[29] On February 15, 1900, Jeff Milton, one tough hombre, was employed by Wells, Fargo and Company as an express messenger on the New Mexico and Arizona Railroad for the run between Benson and Nogales. Billy Stiles was broke again. Dissatisfied with his take at Cochise, he got together with his friend Constable Burt Alvord, and they spent six weeks planning their next robbery. They recruited Three-Fingered Jack Dunlap, Bob

| New Mex. & Ariz. & Son. Ry |
| New daily Passenger Train service through between Benson and Guaymas. |

South		STATIONS.		North
5:30 P. M.	Lv.	Benson.	Ar.	8:40 A. M
6:13		Fairbank.		7:57
6:44		Huachuca.		7:31
7:54		Crittenden.		6:20
9:00	x	Nogales.	x	5:10
11:57 A. M.		Imuris.		3:00
12:20		Magdalena.		2:34
12:56		Santa Ana.		2:04
1:30		Llano.		1:30
2:25		Querobabi		12:36
3:25	x	Carbo.	x	11:30
4:20		Pesqueira.		10:35
5:15		Hermosillo		9:38
6:30		Torres.		8:53
7:57		Ortiz.		7:12
9:10	Ar.	Guaymas.	Lv.	6:00 P. M

x Dining Stations.
Pullman Sleepers are attached to these trains.
Connections made at Benson, Ariz., with the Southern Pacific Co., Southern Pacific Company's eastbound train No. 19 arrives at Benson at 3:15 a. m., and westbound train No. 20 at 12:25 a. m. Southbound passenger can take sleeper any time after it arrives from the south at 11:45 p. m. Northbound passengers are allowed to remain in the sleeper at Benson until arrival of Southern Pacific train No. 10.
Trains makes connection at Torres with Torres & Prietas Railroad, leaving at 11:30 a. m. and 7 p. m. daily for Colorado and Minas Prietas.
Close connection is made at Guaymas with Pacific Coast Steamship Company's steamer "Orizaba" sailing the 11th of each month for Altata, Mazatlan, Cape St. Lucas, Magdalen Bay and Ensenada; and with the Occidental Railroad Company's Steamship line of steamers sailing June 10th and 30th, July 20, August 10 and 30, September 20, October 10 and 30, November 20, and December 10 and 30, for La Paz, Altata, Mazatlin, San Blas, Manzanillo, Acapulco, Puerto Angel, Salina Cruz Topala, and San Benito.
For particulars address
J. A. NAUGLE,
General Pass. Ag't. Guaymas, Sonora. Mex

Schedule for the New Mexico and Arizona Railroad showing the train was headed south.
PUBLIC DOMAIN

Brown, the middle-aged and bearded brothers George and Lewis Owings (various spelled Owints, Owen, and Owings),[30] and Tom "Bravo Juan" Yoas to conduct the actual robbery using the same technique employed at Cochise. The boys had heard the train would be carrying a load of Mexican gold and coin or possibly the payroll for Fort Huachuca. Alvord would provide alibis while Billy Stiles, an acquaintance of Jeff Milton, was to make sure J. D. Milton was not in the express car when they struck.[31]

The outlaws seemed to have been seriously concerned that Jeff might upset their plans. Billy arranged with Milton to introduce him to a mining man interested in Milton's mining claims in the Quijotes.[32] However, when the day came, Jeff Milton, then at Imuris, Sonora, Mexico, south of Nogales, received a telegram from W. F. Overton that messenger Jones, Milton's alternate, had fallen ill and that he should make the run from Nogales to Benson. However, he was unable to communicate this information to Billy Stiles.[33]

On February 14, 1900, the Owings brothers, Bob Brown, Bravo Juan, and Three-Fingered Jack set out from Pearce headed across the Dragoon Mountains by the Middle

Pass.[34] They camped for the night in a canyon recess, with flickering firelight throwing weird, distorted shadows. With the silent stars as witnesses, they swore a solemn oath to kill the first man who showed fear during the coming raid.[35] Alvord sought out Bravo Juan to lead the raid. His choice was now confirmed, and the gang elected Tom Yoas, Bravo Juan, as honcho. The next morning, Juan insisted that it would look strange if five men rode into Fairbank all at once.[36]

On the morning of February 15, the brothers rode some distance ahead while Brown, Juan, and Jack followed. The ride from the Dragoons to Fairbank on the San Pedro River was close to twenty miles. At 6:10 p.m., as the sun sank below the horizon, the gang arrived at the edge of the village. They were late. Train No. 1 of the New Mexico and Arizona Railroad was pulling up at the platform from Benson on its way to Nogales and Mexico, bringing mail for Tombstone.[37] The boys hastened to turn their horses over to George Owings, who would wait hidden out of sight in the thick mesquite along the river. Bob Brown and Lewis Owings hastened to the locomotive, while Three-Fingered Jack and Bravo Juan headed for the express car.

The Tombstone stage was nearby with Ed Turbell on box waiting to take passengers and the mail to town. Agent Gay had locked his post office and stood by the open door of the combined express mail car where Jeff Milton was handing out sacks of express matter. In the second compartment, postal clerk F. W. Cousins was gathering mail sacks to hand over to Gay. A crowd stood around watching the excitement of the train arriving or waiting to board. Fairbank was a tiny village where only children, the schoolteacher, and the storekeeper weren't connected to the three railroads that passed through. The plan called for the gang to hit the express car while its door was open, just as Matt and Billy had done at Cochise, but Burt hadn't considered the lingering twilight and the crowd at Fairbank.[38]

At the engine, Bob shouted through his mask for the engineer and fireman to throw up their hands and not move themselves or the train. He then ordered the trainmen down and to walk toward the express car. Spicing his command liberally with profanity, Bravo Juan ordered everyone to throw up their hands. Express messenger Milton complied, but when

NMAZ Station, Fairbank, Arizona.
COURTESY OF SOUTHERN ARIZONA TRANSPORTATION MUSEUM

his hands rose, they held a messenger's shotgun,[39] and he let fly at Three-Fingered Jack, catching him in the belly and knocking him down. The masked outlaws returned fire. A round from approaching Bob Brown took Jeff in the right arm. He remained game, switching to a pistol to keep on firing until blood loss left him unconscious.

The gang told the crowd to "bunch up." Perhaps, they hoped having the crowd in a group would inhibit Jeff's fire. Among those bunched were Ed Turbell, agent Gay, and the engineer and fireman. The horses, frightened by all the firing, started the stage in motion. Three-Fingered Jack called out for the driver to stop the stage, but Ed was with those bunched and not at the reins. Jack solved the problem by shooting at the horses, eventually hitting one in the leg, crippling the animal.[40]

Jeff had stopped firing. As shooting from the outlaws ceased, Cousins emerged from the car and Brown and Bravo Juan, apparently assuming Milton dead, entered, stealing Jeff's gun and rummaging about for anything of value. Eventually, they turned up forty-two dollars in Mexican money. The express agent was unable to open the safe for them, and for some reason, they hadn't brought, or chose not to use, giant powder as Billy had done at Cochise.[41]

Annoyed, Bravo Juan headed for the post office, which he found locked. He demanded to know where the postal agent was. In the bunched-up crowd, agent Gay said nothing, and no one pointed him out. Juan kicked in the door but found the safes and drawers inside locked. Picking up their fallen comrade, the gang walked out of town to the east to their waiting horses. Everyone assumed they'd head south for Mexico. Instead, the boys continued to the east, back the way they'd come through Middle Pass to Pearce. Nine miles from Tombstone, they stopped at Sycamore Spring. Three-Fingered Jack was slowing them down. They left him damning them and promising vengeance.[42]

The engineer backed the train to Benson, where a special train was assembled to carry Jeff Milton to Tucson for medical care. He would eventually, after much suffering, lose the arm. Meanwhile, Sheriff Dell White assembled a posse. Among those who served were Deputy George Bravin, the jailer under whom Billy Stiles had served in Pearce as a deputy constable, and Deputy Sheriff Sid Mullen.[43]

Matt Burts, top left.
COURTESY OF SOUTHERN ARIZONA TRANSPORTATION MUSEUM

Bravin and Mullen found Three-Fingered Jack and took him to Tombstone by wagon. Jack was angry and made a dying declaration concerning every single one of his pals who'd been in on the deal. Legend has it that when Sheriff White heard that Stiles and Alvord had done the planning, he was incredulous. He is supposed to have said something like, "Those two dummies? They couldn't plan a two-man parade!" Mullen also found a hot trail to Pearce and followed it. The entire gang was soon rounded up, except for Bob Brown and Matt Burts, who had conducted the Cochise robbery. Matt had left the territory. Nailed with his fingers in the cookie jar, Billy Stiles decided to become "state's evidence." Alarmed, Felix Mayhew was afraid that his name might come up. He claimed to have been in on the early planning and also wanted to make himself "state's evidence" before he got in real trouble. Billy Stiles would later claim that Felix had no part in planning, but this may have been twistedly self-serving. With Jack dead and Billy giving evidence against the others, only Felix could testify against Billy.[44]

With things looking altogether silly, Wells, Fargo and Company chose April 1, 1900, to announce a reward of five hundred dollars each for the arrest and conviction of Matt Burts and R. C. Brown. Perhaps the company thought it might be able to rescind the reward if anyone tried to collect by claiming it was a jest. Wells, Fargo and Company detective J. H. Thacker didn't think so and on April 8 set out in a special train with Sheriff Lyman Wakefield of Pima County, George Oakes, Nabor Pacheco, and John Nelson in a caboose under charge of brakeman Porter pulled by Engine 1326. The *Arizona Daily Star* reported, "Matt Burts who had been apprehended in Wyoming by Burt Grover on the charge of being a party to the Cachise[45] station holdup. Wm. Stiles traveled with Captain Thacker and carried the shotgun that belonged to the captain, who, reposing confidence in Stiles, permitted him to retain possession of the gun as he would act as a guard at the county jail."[46]

Train robber Billy Stiles was out of jail as state's evidence and was also one of the arresting officers with Thacker to get Matt Burts. Thacker gave Billy a shotgun. While bringing Matt in, on the way back to Tombstone, it became clear that Matt planned to go state's evidence. In Tombstone, Thacker took Matt to dinner to talk over his evidence while Stiles, still armed, was left on his own. Billy now had his freedom, a gun, and a problem. Matt Burts had decided to become state's evidence, and he could testify against Stiles.

On April 14, the day they arrived in Tombstone, while Matt was at dinner with the officers talking over his plea agreement, Billy Stiles went to the jail and ordered his old friend and boss, jailer George Bravin, to hand over the keys. George tried to knock Billy's gun aside and got shot in the leg for his trouble. Stiles grabbed the keys and opened the cells. George, bleeding badly, pleaded with the prisoners to remain, telling them they would soon be recaptured. Burt Alvord and Bravo Juan departed with Stiles.[47]

Among those who stayed behind to tend Bravin's wounds were the Halderman brothers, William and Thomas. They stood accused of murdering eighteen-year-old Teddy Moore and Constable Ainsworth of Pearce, who were serving a warrant for cattle stealing. The constable treated them decently, letting them breakfast and get dressed. Once dressed, they emerged shooting and killed the constable in the first volley. Teddy was shot in the back but escaped to his home and told the tale before dying. Once Deputy Sheriff Sid Mullen arrested them, folks in Tombstone talked of borrowing them from the jail for a lynching. They couldn't have been more guilty, but perhaps they thought that their kindness to Bravin might get them some consideration. It didn't. In July 1900, they were convicted and sentenced to be hanged. Several pleas were made to the governor, which bought them only a temporary reprieve. On November 18, 1900, in Tombstone, the brothers were hanged.[48]

Meanwhile, Burt Alvord, Billy Stiles, and Bravo Juan were on the loose somewhere in Arizona with the keys to the Tombstone courthouse jail. These were returned with a letter published in the papers.

ON THE ROAD
  Friday, April 20, 1900.
  SCOTT WHITE, Esq.—We send you the keys; we would have given them to Sid Mullen but he was too fast for us, we could not overtake them. We met the Mexicans that killed that gambler in John-son camp but as we had no warrants we did not arrest them—and then we were afraid they would shoot, and we had no warrant and were afraid that we couldn't collect the mileage—Tell the boys that we are well and eating regular. Tell the man we got the Studebaker saddle from, will send it home soon.

Yours truly.
JUAN BRAVO
STILES,
ALVORD[49]

In June, a newspaper reporter for the *Arizona Daily Star* claimed Alvord and his pals had given him an interview in the dark of a moonless night somewhere in the Santa Catalina or Tortolita Mountains of Arizona. Burt Alvord protested his innocence, something he would continue to do for many years. But he also said, according to John T. Hughes, "We have not been out of Arizona once and are not going till we get ready." Alvord told the reporter that he'd kill any officer who came within range or anyone he didn't know who approached as well.

Billy Stiles is then supposed to have said, "Yes, there is one man that I would like to kill. He is a treacherous —— ——. He caused me to turn state's evidence, promising me a big reward and then fell down on me. He promised to give me a good job and then went back on me. Yes, I let the boys out of the jail to even up with him and I got even all right."[50]

According to the reporter, Billy then fell to sobbing and shedding tears. "I wish you could see my mother and wife. I would like to have you take a message to them." He then broke down completely and cried for several minutes.[51] In September, Billy denied this interview ever took place. "I was 400 miles away." It sounds oddly like him, accusing others, feeling sorry for himself, looking for a reward and a job. One of the stranger things to show up in the press was the story of Burt Alvord's skull. A human skull, apparently fresh, was found near Casa Grande, Billy's hometown. Folks who knew Billy thought he'd turned on Burt and killed him for getting Stiles into his current fix. The only reason for thinking this was Burt's skull was that he hadn't been seen in a while, and they knew Billy was a dirty rat.[52]

On July 1, 1900, Billy Stiles surrendered again. In the process of getting a deal to turn state's evidence, apparently the prosecutor implied that Stiles wouldn't be prosecuted for shooting George Bravin. There were territorial charges against him for two railroad robberies (Cochise and Fairbank), both of which required hanging. He also faced federal charges for both robberies, which included interfering with the mail, and there were territorial charges for jailbreak and for assault with a deadly weapon on George Bravin, a peace officer. He was probably also wanted for jumping bail. In any event, the county DA at Tombstone could promise immunity from territorial charges, but the federal charges could only be waived by the federal DA in Tucson. Who was making what promises was not always clear in the newspapers. We can, perhaps, partially infer by whom the promises were being made. Pending charges for which they thought they had immunity would come back to haunt both Billy and Matt Burts. At this time, it was unclear if Stiles was let out on his own recognizance again. He probably was. After all, he'd turned himself in and could be trusted.

Stiles and Alvord had separated from Bravo Juan some time before, and Billy had parted company with Burt three or four days before coming in.[53] Bravo Juan is mentioned again and again in newspaper stories, in which he's usually sighted in Sonora, often in company with Burt Alvord, and just as often having recently parted company with Burt. It is not clear what became of him. He'll show up time and again in the story, like Elvis pumping gas at the Circle K.

With trials approaching, George Owings surprised everyone by confessing and offering himself as state's evidence. His brother Lewis joined him the next day. Robert E. "Bob" Brown managed a hung jury at his first trial. The jury was apparently suspicious of a dead witness and coconspirators providing state's evidence. He was convicted at his second trial, the only outlaw to tough it out. The judge sentenced him to ten years in Yuma Territorial Prison. The Owings got four years each. The trio departed for Yuma.[54] That took care of the Fairbank train robbery for the time being. Jack Dunlap was dead, Bravo Juan and Burt Alvord were nowhere to be found, Billy Stiles was state's evidence, and the Owings brothers and Bob Brown were on their way to prison, while William Downing had charges pending.

The court now took up the Cochise train robbery. The court had a very hard time coming up with a jury. Nobody wanted to hang a man for a robbery where no one had been killed. Eventually, they found twelve men who said they would uphold the law. On December 9, 1900, Matt Burts walked into the courtroom smiling. He'd cut a deal and was now state's evidence. Matt and Billy, the two gentlemen who had physically robbed the train at Cochise on September 9, 1899, testified against William Downing, who had provided the horses and an alibi. If convicted, William Downing must hang. That was the law for train robbery. There was some disagreement in testimony. Downing said he wasn't in on the planning but allowed that he was an accessory after the fact. Downing's wife testified for him, saying Matt Burts had never come to the Downing home, let alone slept there.[55] Billy Stiles testified that the district attorney had offered him total immunity if he would return from Mexico and testify. Moreover, Charly Hood, an employee of Wells, Fargo and Company, had promised him enough money to leave the country afterward. Billy would turn on anyone for a buck. The jury didn't like this confusing evidence from men more guilty than the defendant, and they acquitted Downing and set him free. The jury didn't like the idea that the two who had done the robbery were testifying against a fellow on the sidelines. Matt Burts, with a plea deal, was sentenced to five years for what was otherwise a hanging offense, and Billy Stiles was set free.[56] The newspapers called for the law to be changed.[57] Jury nullification, a refusal to enforce an unpopular law, had cleared Downing on the territorial charges. Billy and Matt had their plea agreements. The federal charges were about to come back to haunt them. The newspapers wrote: "Stiles and Burts states evidence against Wm. Downing. Two who did the crime get off, unwilling to hang without murder. It was evident from the verdict in the Downing case that the jury didn't put much faith in the evidence of Matt Burts and Billy Stiles, the self-confessed train robbers."[58]

Not at all happy about having his deputy, George Bravin, shot and the man who shot him set free, Sheriff Del Lewis got a warrant for Stiles's arrest. Word came down that Stiles was in Casa Grande and would surrender. The sheriff headed for Casa Grande. On January 26, 1901, Del Lewis found Stiles drinking in a saloon and soon had him in handcuffs. He had started to shackle Billy when the local constable said the handcuffs wouldn't be necessary, for he would help out. Billy made a break for freedom, and, helping out, the constable tripped Sheriff Lewis. Billy disappeared into the night. According to the *Cochise Review*, the *Arizona Republican* wrote: "The train robber seemed to have nothing but friends at that place, and the people laughed at the efforts of the officer

Burt Alvord—deputy, constable, killer, and train robber.
COURTESY OF SULPHUR SPRINGS VALLEY HISTORICAL SOCIETY

who attempted to discharge his duty. Lewis searched faithfully, but could not again trap his quarry."[59]

In April 1901, Billy Stiles resurfaced in Tucson to testify against Downing. On April 6, 1901, William Downing was tried in Tucson on the federal charges for tampering with the mail. Billy and Matt testified against him, while Mrs. Downing testified for him. On April 14, 1901, Downing was convicted and sentenced to ten years in Yuma Territorial Prison, where Matt Burts, when not testifying in court, had been serving time since December 1900. Matt and Billy had done their duty and kept their promises to the courts. On April 17, 1901, Governor Murphy, at the request of the district attorney, pardoned Matt Burts.[60] Billy was already out of jail with no convictions, as of yet, and promised immunity by various district attorneys.

Notwithstanding the apparent plea bargain, Sheriff Del Lewis wanted Billy Stiles for shooting his deputy while breaking men out of the Tombstone jail, but nobody else seemed to want to see Billy Stiles behind bars. Perhaps the federal prosecutor at Tucson just wasn't concerned with territorial charges pending in Tombstone and didn't think to have Billy detained. Stiles had just helped him win a conviction in a much-publicized case. During the late winter and spring of 1901, Billy arranged to depart from Arizona and head for Mexico into the Yaqui country to prospect.[61] By the end of April 1901, after giving his testimony in Tucson, Billy was gone, presumably with charges still pending against him. Less than a year later, Captain Burt Mossman hired Billy as a private in the newly formed Arizona Rangers.

Stiles crossed into Arizona from Sonora at will and visited his two-hundred-pound Mexican wife at their ranch a dozen miles west of Naco. Billy worked off and on driving an ore wagon at the Puertacitas Mine. In January 1902, Ranger Captain Burt Mossman approached Billy, offering him wages as an Arizona Ranger and reward money if he would help bring in Augustin Chacón. Alvord was also a wanted man, and it was believed that Billy knew where to find him. Newspaper stories had Alvord traveling with Chacón, so Mossman might capture both wanted men. For many months, Billy Stiles did little except complain that he wasn't getting paid as much as other rangers. He also carried messages from Alvord, who wanted his wife to drop divorce proceedings.[62]

Burt Alvord was a man-killer, having slain at least two men, and so was Augustin Chacón, or at least that was what the newspapers wrote. He may have been an innocent bystander to the crime of which he was accused. Nonetheless, he ranked as Arizona's most wanted man, followed closely by Burt Alvord. Both had escaped from jail. Both faced the noose, and Augustin had already been convicted. Contrary to the movies and dime novels, man-killers were feared in the West, where it's believed there were fewer per capita murders than in the eastern cities. If the newspapers of the day had maintained morgues, editors and reporters either feared them or were too lazy to visit them. For anything that had occurred longer ago than last week, they relied on memory and fantasy.

Travelers brought in fanciful stories as well. And so it was that both Burt and Augustin grew in legend and added multitudes to the ranks of those they had slain. Recall the reading of Tuco the Rat's crimes in the hanging scene from *The Good, the Bad, and the Ugly.* The list was probably inspired by Chacón's fancied crimes. David Grassé has deconstructed Augustin's legend, so I won't go into it here.[63] It is enough to say that Burt Alvord and Augustin Chacón became the most wanted and feared men along the border and became Ranger Captain Burt Mossman's highest priority. So high, in fact, that he actually recruited treacherous Billy Stiles as a Ranger private.

Burt Alvord was seen everywhere. In March, most of the newspapers in the territory carried the story of how Alvord had gone to the Warren Ranch near Pearce, a ranch Alvord used to own, and demanded dinner from Frank Swink. He sat with a rifle across his knees throughout the meal and was accompanied by a Mexican. The pair returned for dinner again the next night, assuring Swink that they would treat him right. In the morning, Swink discovered they'd departed with five of his horses. He went in pursuit and was soon joined by a posse from Tombstone. The press began to speculate. The man with Burt must be Bravo Juan. Then word came that the pair had parted company a year prior. It was then that the Mexican became Augustin Chacón.[64]

In May it was rumored that Alvord might turn himself in.[65] He might have done so if the territory had allowed him to collect the reward on himself and plea-bargain for going state's evidence against himself. On July 14, 1901, he was in Sonora heavily armed with a Winchester, pistols, and crossed cartridge belts.[66] In December, down Mexico way, he fought and lost in a three-cornered duel. His death went unconfirmed.[67] In February 1902, the Rurales, a Mexican militia-police force reporting to the governor of Sonora, arrested Burt and Bravo Juan. Sheriff Del Lewis hastened to Sonora to collect the outlaws. As it turned out, the *rurales* thought they had the boys surrounded, but they didn't have them in custody. Unaware that he was surrounded, Burt Alvord made a daring escape, and Del Lewis was disappointed again. Bravo Juan wasn't there, so it might have been Chacón who was almost captured.[68] Both the Mexican and the Arizona outlaw were rumored to be running bandit gangs, crossing the border at will, and terrorizing people and the Arizona banks.

There were bank robberies, murders, and cattle rustling and more often than not rumors of the same. As it were, wars and rumors of wars. Their legends grew. On Sunday, August 31, 1902, Alvord and Bravo Juan were seen near Hermosillo. Finally, at least one newspaper thought the report doubtful.[69]

At least three divergent accounts exist of the events of September 10, 1902, and what led up to the confrontation between lawmen and outlaws. The reasons that Burt Mossman and Burt Alvord told different stories, with Mossman telling more than one version, are easy to discern, and we can guess at what really happened. Informants needed to be protected from both the possibility of a Chacón escape and from whatever henchmen he may have left behind. Stiles cheated Alvord, and Alvord in turn cheated Mossman. Mossman needed to protect his reputation.

The general outline of events is that in all probability Billy Stiles knew where to find Burt Alvord in Sonora. Billy offered to split the reward for Chacón's capture with Burt if Burt could lure the outlaw into Arizona. Alvord found the outlaw and lured him north to join with two of his gang, Billy and Mossman, to steal some horses. Although nervous, the Mexican came alone without henchman to meet with Alvord's friends. They met south of the border on the night of September 9, and they decided to wait until morning to cross to the north and take the horses. Sometime during the night, Alvord left camp, perhaps with the excuse to do some scouting. Mossman was hesitant to mention his name or give him credit since when the arrest was made, Alvord wasn't there to be arrested. Billy had short-changed him on the reward, giving him only forty dollars. According to Sheriff Lewis, "When I saw Alvord later he said that he came there to give himself up to me but it was on Stiles' account that he did not. I had given Stiles the $450 reward for the capture of Chacon. $225 of which was to go to Alvord, but Stiles gave him $40 and blew the rest in gambling, and I have receipts for this amount in my safe."[70]

On September 10, 1902, over breakfast in Sonora, Mossman and Stiles outmaneuvered and arrested Augustin and then escorted their captive north of the border. Mossman's commission had expired a day or two prior to the arrest, which was made with doubtful legality in Mexico. Alvord had slipped through the net. The former Ranger captain walked gently around a few technicalities in talking to the newspapers. No matter. All Arizona was delighted. The terror was over. The legendary outlaw had been caught and was soon sent for execution of sentence.[71]

On September 10, 1902, Burt Alvord surrendered to Sheriff Del Lewis. He continued to protest his total innocence:

> *"I feel relieved that this moving around is over with," said Alvord, "and made up my mind to surrender to Sheriff Lewis, come back to jail and stay here until I am turned loose by the court. I am not guilty of train robbing, or obstructing the mails, or helping to, for which I am indicted, and they can't convict an innocent man."*
>
> *The reporter referred to the jail break, which in the light of his remarks, might leave his action open to comment. "Why shouldn't I leave the jail?" promptly said Alvord, who previously had not lain any claim to being a humorist. "The jail was open and I walked out and stayed out until now."*[72]

Burt surprised the people of Tombstone by appearing armed and without handcuffs or shackles. Likewise, Billy was seen with a pistol stuffed in his pants. The courts now moved slowly. In December, at Tombstone, the district attorney moved to dismiss the 1899 Cochise train robbery charge against Alvord. The case against Downing had fallen apart, and fewer witnesses were available. Burt was still faced with charges relating to assault and jailbreaking.[73] Stiles had disappeared into Mexico. Although the papers didn't mention it, there were still those pesky federal mail robbery charges and possibly some charge left over from Fairbank. In July 1903, perhaps having waited for Stiles to turn himself in again, Alvord was indicted and his old buddies then residing in Yuma were brought over to Tombstone to testify.[74] A charge of interfering with the mails at Fairbank went to court that month, and charges of the same at Cochise went to court the next day.[75] Alvord and Stiles were plotting more deals. On December 12, 1903, Stiles's attorney argued in court that the court didn't have the right to try him since he'd been promised immunity. The argument failed.[76]

On December 8, 1903, Burt Alvord withdrew his plea of innocence, finally admitting his role in mayhem, and in return was awarded two years in Yuma Territorial Prison. Other indictments against him were still pending. Billy also had a few pending, and as noted things weren't going his way.[77] So the pair did what came naturally to them: they broke jail. They had friends smuggle in saws and chisels. Using blankets to muffle the sound, they cut through the bars and made an opening in the second-floor wall of the courthouse. Eleven other prisoners, thirteen in all, went with them. Among these were James Bennett, held for smuggling Chinese into the country; Tom Pries for highway robbery; Dave O'Brien for sodomy; "Sailor" Brown, who was held on a peace bond; and Johnny James, who was charged with murder.[78] Burt and Billy got clean away and escaped into Mexico.

Early in February 1904, the boys robbed J. F. Tener, a resident of Magdelena, Sonora, of eight thousand dollars' worth of gold bullion he was transporting from a mine.[79] The Arizona Rangers went after the two former lawmen. On February 18, 1904, Tom Rynning, the new captain of the Arizona Rangers, along with Sam Hayhurst, returned from Sonora without finding Billy Stiles or Burt Alvord.[80] In March, Bob Hilburn located the stolen bullion near Naco.[81] Billy and Burt had taken the bullion there and hidden it as they ran from Mexican *rurales*. Convinced they were about to be caught by the Mexicans, who captured their horses, putting the outlaws afoot, they crossed the border near Naco.

They sought shelter at the Young Ranch one mile west of Naco. There, Sheriff Lewis and Arizona Ranger J. J. Brooks and a small posse surrounded them, approaching the house in the dark from two sides. As Brooks and Lewis came over a hill, Alvord and Stiles called out "Hello!" Stiles then jumped up. "Is that you, Skeet?" At the same time, he raised his weapon to his shoulder. The officers opened fire, and Alvord was caught in the first volley, falling to the ground.

He wasn't game. Burt cried out, "Don't shoot!" More shots were exchanged, but Stiles and another man ran away, escaping into the night.[82]

Burt Alvord survived and was sent to Yuma to serve his time. A Mexican warrant was outstanding against him over the Tener affair. Alvord got eighty-seven days off his two-year sentence, six days for every month served for good behavior. The superintendent of the prison miscalculated, basing the start of Burt's time at the date of his sentencing in December 1903 instead of on the day he began serving the sentence in March 1904. The miscalculation gave Burt a break in two ways. He served a lot less than two years. When the federal marshal arrived to serve the Mexican warrant after Burt's release, the jailbird had already flown.[83] Where Alvord went and what became of him after his release from prison is unknown. It's rumored that within a few years, he died of fever somewhere in Central America. His wife had divorced him.

William Stiles disappeared although he managed periodic sightings. In April 1904, Arizona Ranger Brooks caught sight of him in Agua Verde Canyon in the San Jose Mountains near Naco. Brooks captured Billy's horse and camp equipment. With Stiles afoot and without gear, the Ranger was certain he'd make the capture soon.[84] In November, there was a report that Billy visited the home of his niece, Juanita Sanchez, near Douglas, giving her a letter for his wife.[85] Perhaps the letter contained information that Billy planned to flee to China. In December 1904, the US marshal for Arizona Territory claimed to be in possession of information that the "Artful Dodger" had shanghaied himself and taken passage for the Far East.[86] The sightings stopped. The US marshal and the Arizona Rangers had taken themselves off the hook. Of course, they couldn't catch Billy, not because he was too slick for them, but rather because he was far away in Hong Kong or Shanghai where they couldn't touch him.

Billy was a supremely self-centered confidence trickster who would sell out anyone, except his wife, for a few dollars and then complain that his share was too small. Was he the greatest outlaw ever to roam the Wild West? Or was he so immature and plain dumb that folks repeatedly underestimated him and trusted him? He had to have presented himself as nonthreatening and sincere. He was definitely untrustworthy, and his stunts, rather than being clever, tended to leave him worse off than before.

A writer for the *Arizona Daily Star* claimed to have been acquainted with Billy Stiles since childhood. His mother had been married to a man named Bible and had one son, Ben. Widowed, she married Stiles's father, and in a family difficulty the stepson murdered Billy's father.

Ben Bible ran away and became a locomotive engineer, which may explain Billy's hostility to railroads. Billy, fatherless and of a wild disposition, grew up in Casa Grande. He opened a butcher shop in Casa Grande and with plenty of "loose" cattle on the range, the necessity of paying for those he slaughtered never occurred to him. His neighbors objected, and Billy headed south to Cochise County. The writer went on: "When arrested he shirked the responsibility of the crime by turning state's evidence. Because of doing this he was pampered and made much of by the Wells-Fargo company official. He was sent to Yuma for safekeeping and was 'kept safe' for six or more months, pending the trial of his associates."[87]

In December 1908, Billy's wife received word that Deputy Sheriff William Larkin, while serving a warrant, had been killed by a rancher named Barr at Kings River in Humboldt County, Nevada. William Larkin was the alias William Larkin Stiles used to conceal his identity. As an alias goes, it wasn't particularly imaginative. Billy Stiles, aka Deputy Sheriff William Larkin, was dead.[88]

In October 1903, having completed their terms at Yuma with time off for good behavior, George and Lewis Owings returned to Cochise County and went to work for Mr. Johnson at his ranch near Pearce. The former outlaws concocted a plan to steal Johnson's horses and sell them in Mexico, but he got wind of the plot and, as they prepared to leave, confronted them. The Owings drew their six-shooters and opened fire. Unarmed cowboys dashed for cover as Johnson returned fire and hit Lewis, who dropped from the fight. Running out of ammunition, George and Johnson confronted each other hand to hand, mano a mano. Grasping a branding iron, Johnson struck George in the head. Undaunted, George overpowered his soon-to-be-former employer and tied him up. He then helped his brother to his horse and the two rode away to Willcox, where George, nearly overcome with blood loss from the gash in his head, was taken to hospital. Owing to their enfeebled conditions, neither brother was arrested.[89]

Had this been 2003 and not 1903, surely the Owings brothers would have filed for workman's comp over their multiple injuries. OSHA might have stepped in, requiring new warning labels on branding irons and possibly monthly safety briefings on the proper employment of hot irons. There might have been action taken over a toxic workplace environment.

But this was 1903, and soon the Bisbee newspaper took the Owings brothers' side.

On November 29, the *Bisbee Daily Review* published "the facts." The Owings brothers had made their new home at the Johnson Ranch and appreciated how their new employer had taken them in despite their criminal records. However, after a few weeks, Johnson became abusive and overbearing. When the boys had had enough, they packed up their things and were loading them onto their horses when Johnson intervened, striking George Owings in the head from behind with a branding iron and knocking him to the ground. Lewis jumped into the fray, overpowering Johnson and tying him up. The boys finished packing, untied Johnson, and departed and rode to Pearce to seek a doctor. George's head took seven stitches. Constable Pruitt got word of the affray and injury and sought out the boys. They told him they didn't want any trouble with Johnson; they just wanted to leave. He got them to swear out a complaint, and Johnson was arrested for assault with a deadly weapon.[90] Afterward, the newspapers seem to have lost sight of the story, which probably means that the charges were eventually dropped and the Owings brothers, like Matt Burts before them, quietly left the county.

William Downing was an entirely different matter. On April 8, 1901, he was sentenced to ten years in Yuma and broke down in court as the gavel knocked out his time. He was credited with time served since February 1900, and in September 1907, he was released with time off for good behavior.[91] Unfortunately, in February 1902, while Downing was serving time, his wife, who had stood by her man and testified for him, died suddenly.[92] Downing returned to Willcox, where he operated a saloon that soon came to be considered something of a public nuisance, which in Willcox took a real effort. In 1908, the new captain of Arizona Rangers, Harry Wheeler, hearing the complaints, sent Lieutenant Olds to Willcox to have a talk with Downing, who promised to do better. The *Arizona Republic*, which referred to Downing as an old-time outlaw and cattle rustler, wrote: "Complaints were received from time to time of his lawless conduct there. He set out to terrorize the town and the community. He wore his gun as in the old times and now and then he rounded up a peaceful citizen."[93]

Way back in May 1899, Downing had been involved in a shooting scrape in Willcox in which he killed William Traynor, a well-liked former Rough Rider who had served with Teddy Roosevelt. Traynor had also ridden as a cowboy for former sheriff John Slaughter. In 1899, Downing's friend, Burt Alvord, was the constable at Willcox. Sheriff Scott White pursued Downing and captured him. The coroner's inquest called the shooting justified, for Traynor had reportedly made threats on Downing's life, and Downing told friends he was in fear for his life. Among his friends were Matt Burts and Burt Alvord. Traynor came into a saloon where Downing was drinking with Matt Burts. Traynor and Downing were both wearing guns. Traynor stood with his hands on the bar. Their attention was called to each other. Traynor's hands dropped to his side, and Downing shot him dead. Did Traynor go for his gun? No one could say for sure. On May 28, 1899, at a preliminary hearing in Tombstone, District Attorney Land, after hearing witnesses, asked Judge Schuster to dismiss the charges. The only witnesses were friends of Downing, and it was rumored that Traynor was a stock detective.[94]

On August 6, 1908, although promising to do better, Downing had "spent nearly half a century of lawless years and he would now turn over a new leaf. In the meantime, he was running a tough saloon in the tenderloin district and was constantly surrounded by persons as lawless as himself. It was generally predicted that Downing would shortly find an excuse for killing somebody."[95]

Ranger William Speed was sent to Willcox to serve Downing with a warrant for his arrest over Traynor's killing. The old outlaw displayed a gun, and Speed shot him dead. On the other hand, kinfolk of Traynor say that this shooting didn't have anything to do with his eventual demise.[96] In Willcox, Downing's death is remembered differently and probably more correctly as follows.

After his release from prison, Bill Downing operated the Free and Easy Saloon, which was as tough as the name implied. Downing beat up Cuca Leal, a working girl, that is to say, one of the prostitutes in his employ. Cuca complained to the authorities. Word went around that Arizona Ranger Billy Speed was going to arrest Downing. The layabouts at the saloon convinced Downing to give himself up as Speed was one tough Ranger. "Leave your six-shooter behind at the saloon," they told him. If he went armed, Ranger Speed would surely shoot Downing for going for his gun. One assumes one of the wastrels might have been nicknamed Oracle. Bill Downing started down Maley Street toward Speed's residence with the intent, perhaps, of turning himself in. He didn't have far to go. Speed lived on Railroad Avenue, a block or so away. As Downing rounded the corner into the alley between buildings, the two men came face-to-face, Bill Downing and Ranger Speed accompanied by the town constable. Downing's hand instinctively dropped to his side, where his pistol usually hung. Speed saw the move, jerked his smoke wagon, and shot Downing dead. The next day, the *Arizona Range News* story said, "I hear Billy Speed shot Bill Downing on Wednesday. What was the complaint?" The answer, "No complaint. Everybody's satisfied."[97]

CHAPTER NINE

The Beardless Boy Bandits Making History

Maricopa, Arizona, 1910

DO YOU REMEMBER THE TV SHOW THE *BEARCATS*? IT DIDN'T LAST VERY long, but I loved it. Airing in 1971, it starred Rod Taylor and Dennis Cole as troubleshooters in the period before the American entry into World War I. The stories revolved around the heroes' use of a Stutz Bearcat sportscar to bounce across the roadless American southwestern deserts in search of villains and excitement. Turns out the show had a basis in reality with the first, we think, chase of train robbers by a petroleum-powered posse. The papers called the outlaws the Beardless Boy Bandits.

Maricopa, Arizona, was named, as was the county, after the Maricopa Indians, who still live nearby. It is surrounded by the Gila River Reservation, which the Maricopa share with the Akimel O'odham, formerly known as Pima. The town is about forty miles southwest of Phoenix at the junction of the Southern Pacific Railroad and the spur line, the Maricopa and Phoenix Railroad that runs across the Gila River to the aforementioned city. In 1857, the Overland Mail (Butterfield) had a station, Maricopa Wells, near there.

In 1909 or 1910, Ernest Woodson came to Arizona and found work on a farm. He wrote to his younger brother Oscar that he also should come, "Because there is no place on earth that a man can get rich quicker than here, by fair means or foul means."[1] Oscar came, and the two determined that they would get rich by foul means. Indeed, they broke all the rules, those of train robbery as well as those of common sense.

They staked two ponies at the Gila River bridge. These were equipped with one beer bottle filled with water, enough to last themselves and their steeds, they thought, as far as the Mexican line.[2] Because they apparently had not consulted a map, they did not realize that this was over one hundred miles away with no towns along the way. That was just as well, since outlaws avoid towns where they might be apprehended. From Oklahoma, the pair did not comprehend that in Arizona the merry month of May was the second-hottest month of the year, surpassed only by June in ferocity. Arizonans take bets on the day and hour that the temperature will first exceed 100 degrees Fahrenheit. They take no bets on humidity because there is none. Jerky was invented in Arizona by a fellow who didn't get his two-inch-thick steak on the barbeque fast enough. These outlaws had no regard for the laws of man or nature.

Ignoring the rules and methods of train robbery, they boarded the train in Maricopa as passengers. So as not to alarm anyone, they did not wear masks, which is how the press discovered that they were beardless boys. It is not clear if they purchased tickets at the station or intended to get them from Conductor Woodcock on board. On May 11, 1910, at 7:30 in the evening, the Maricopa and Phoenix train pulled out of Maricopa consisting of the engine, baggage car, and two coaches, one a mixed baggage and passenger coach and the other a day coach. Shortly after leaving the station, approaching Woodcock, the Beardless Boy Bandits drew revolvers, one with trembling hand, the other boy of cooler demeanor demanding that the conductor divest himself of his wealth.[3]

They were confronted with the first great challenge of their career as outlaws. "The perpetrators were a couple of boys whose greatest difficulty was to convince their victims that they were not joking." The record doesn't say, but surely Woodcock must have responded, "Put away the guns and show me your tickets." Indeed, at first sight of the guns, the conductor supposed that the bandits were among the numerous deputy sheriffs then on board. Told to hold up his hands, Woodcock only smiled. The click of a hammer being drawn back disavowed his previous conviction, and he allowed the boys to search his pockets. In haste, they missed the pocket where he kept most of his money.

They now confronted the seated passengers, who included Territorial Attorney General Wright, sitting beside Deputy Sheriff Ralph Sturgis of Gila County, who was on his way to Florence and the new prison with a couple of convicts. His pistol lay beside him on the seat. While confronting the conductor, the outlaws had their backs to the deputy, but he saw Woodcock's smile and assumed it was all just horseplay. By the time the deputy realized that a train robbery was in progress, he also realized that if he started shooting, civilians might be injured. A bandit thrust a revolver into Ralph's face and despoiled him of seventy-seven dollars. No one was amused when the shackled prisoners were forced to raise their hands. Sleeping passenger Dick Miller failed to comprehend the order to "throw up his hands or I'll kill you." The barrel of a pistol crashed down on his head and blood spurted before he surrendered thirty-two dollars and "some old nickels." Mrs. E. Johnson, who to her regret had been visiting Benson, was robbed of thirty dollars. She didn't regret Benson so much as the loss of her money and her ticket to Phoenix. Apparently, the boys had not yet purchased their own ticket and now took hers. She arrived in town penniless.[4] The victims were robbed of $295, a princely sum in 1910, but hardly enough to live on for long even in Mexico. The contributors to this fund were AG John B. Wright, Deputy R. W. Sturgis, George M. Souter, J. C. O'Connor, R. J. Miller, Mrs. Johnson, Kerst, Jas. E. Wilson, a guard with Sturgis, Mrs. F. H. Myers, J. E. Sullivan, and S. J. Rogers. Other guards, prisoners, and passengers declined to give their support.[5]

With their beardless faces exposed to so many, law enforcement was given excellent descriptions of the miscreants: "No. 1—Four feet, seven inches, weight 140 pounds, sandy complexion, heavy jaws and prominent cheek bones, about twenty years of age, smooth face, wore grayish clothing and dark hat.

"No. 2—Five feet, seven inches, weight 150 pounds, dark curly hair, age about twenty-one, mole on side of face, dark clothes."[6]

Four foot seven inches tall? No wonder his hand trembled holding the pistol. Surely this part of the description is a misprint and the boy stood five foot seven, like his brother.

Even as the robbery progressed, Conductor Woodcock started chuckling, undoubtedly unnerving the four-foot-seven bandit with the trembling hands still further. Through the glass, the conductor saw brakeman Sharpe approaching without a care in the world from the rearward car, whistling a happy tune, and lighting the lamps. "Boy, is he in for a surprise, Woodcock thought, though at this later date we remain uncertain as to who "he" was, the outlaw or the brakeman. "Hands up!" cried the robber, spotting this new victim.

Up they went, and the brakeman replied, "Hold your hands still!" Afterward, he declared that he feared the gun might go off from all that shaking. With the passengers relieved of their wealth, the train approached Gila Crossing. The calm outlaw turned to Sharpe and told him that since his hands were already up, wouldn't he be kind enough to reach over and pull the signal cord. The brakeman complied, giving the cord two jerks. The outlaw ordered that a third jerk be given. "We want to get off right here."[7]

As they jumped off the now slowly moving train, an outlaw pointed his revolver at engineer Goodrich and told him that he needn't wait. So the train kept moving as the outlaws ran to their waiting horses. Finding their weapons, the lawmen on the train and the crew exchanged a few parting shots with the postadolescent badmen. The train halted at the distant end of the bridge, and Section Foreman Morgan set out in pursuit with four others no more than five minutes behind the outlaws. Morgan and crew may have been on foot, although a section foreman, living with his crew at the section house at the bridge, might have had horses available.

Word soon went out in all directions. Indian trackers were brought from nearby Sacaton. Before the outlaws lay the Gila River Reservation and then the Tohono O'odham Reservation. Had they been familiar with the ground, they might have plotted their course across the low desert, steering by distant mountains. Unfortunately, to this pair one desert mountain looked much like another, and they were as helpless as a sailor unfamiliar with the constellations steering by the stars. The Mexican Line was then unmarked, so they'd not have known when they reached Sonora. Water was worse than scarce, and they were avoiding the few towns, Casa Grande, Tucson, Tubac, and Nogales, where it might be found. Many Western movies are ruined for the author when fleeing outlaws in Texas, Kansas, and Montana gallop through a forest of towering saguaro cactus. Such was not the case for the Beardless Boy Bandits. They were fleeing through the saguaros and through mesquite, Spanish bayonet, and palo verde, all of which would have ripped at their clothing and none of which would have provided a drop of water.

A posse, formed under Sheriff Carl Hayden of Maricopa County, included Deputies Adams and Woolf and Billy Wilson, Constable Murphy and Deputy Sheriff Sturgis of Globe, Marion McCann, Officer Sullivan, Superintendent Scott, and Sheriff Nelson of Pima County. Before embarking on the adventures of the posse, we need to consider for a moment Carl Hayden. He would become Arizona's first representative in Congress, serving eight terms before entering the Senate. He would then go on to serve seven terms there, setting a record for longest-serving member of Congress and finishing his career in 1969, having served as Dean of the United States Senate and president pro tempore. He started out as a sheriff armed with a six-shooter on horseback in the Arizona Territory, not yet a state.[8] He lived from traveling on horseback to witnessing a lunar landing.

Meanwhile, the newspaper recorded the arrival of the train in Phoenix:

THE ARRIVAL OF THE "BROKE"

On the arrival of the trainload of plundered passengers, Superintendent Scott made arrangements to relieve them from the embarrassment which always attends a financial stringency. He took the names of the losers and those of them who were in immediate need were supplied.

The passengers, or most of them, still regarded their experiences lightly. The audacity of it appealed to them and they did not generally speak unkindly of the robbers. But one of them, R.J. Miller, harbored resentment. His head was still sore and his shirt front was smeared with blood from the wound the robber had inflicted upon his head with the gun barrel. Mr. Miller found some relief in profanity. When asked to what extent he had suffered financially, he replied, "I'm left destitute; not a damned cent."[9]

The newspaper declined to stoop so low as to refer to Mr. Miller as a "sore head." Conductor Woodcock complimented the behavior of the women.

Stoddard-Dayton MODEL 9 A
CAPE TOP

FIVE passenger Touring Car, having all the quality and finish of the larger car. ❦ The only difference is in the size and price. Plenty of power to go anywhere. ❦ 35 Horse Power Touring Car. Price $2000, without Top. ❦ ❦ ❦ ❦ ❦

Ad for Stoddard-Dayton Touring Car.

PUBLIC DOMAIN

THE WOMEN WERE COOL

Conductor Woodcock said that the conduct of the women on the train was admirable. There was no screaming or hysterics. After the first surprise, following the discovery that a robbery was in progress the thing was accepted as a part of a traveler's life.[10]

The women of the Territory of Arizona were made of stern stuff. According to the paper, the Beardless Boys had conducted the first train robbery in sixteen years. Actually, it had only been ten. It was also the first train robbery since the "Arizona Rangers . . . were disbanded by the last legislature."[11] This was cause and effect although the Rangers had employed, albeit briefly, at least one train robber, Billy Stiles, as a ranger.

History was being made as Sheriff Hayden set out after the young outlaws. He asked Mr. J. F. McCarthy if he were game to pursue the lads across the desert in his $3,900 Stoddard-Dayton Touring Car. Shades of the *Bearcats!* Thus, Hayden came to lead, by all accounts, the first ever motorized posse to pursue robbers, particularly train robbers. There were no paved roads where they were going. The first paved road in Arizona can still be seen in Bisbee. In 1910, it had only recently been completed, bringing the total paved road surface in Arizona to one hundred yards. To say that a $3,900 car was expensive in 1910 is like saying that Jay Leno has one or two nice cars in his garage—an understatement. McCarthy was game! Long before *Star Trek*, the posse was boldly going where no man had gone before. Mrs. McCarthy was not pleased. "Mrs. McCarthy came out to give a parting warning. She was not afraid her husband would be killed by bandits but she feared that he would kill himself and his companions by his reckless driving. That fear was subsequently shared by Sheriff Hayden after they had got started. He never before rode so fast."[12]

They took along Inspector Cronin, who although loath to leave his post went anyway. As a former line rider, he knew the waterholes in a land without roads and with few trails. They couldn't follow the tracks left by the horses directly. Arroyos, dry streambeds, crossed and crisscrossed their way. They bounced over rocks and cacti, making frequent pit stops to repair damage and to add water to the radiator in 100-plus-degree heat. For each flat, and thorns may have caused many, there was an innertube patch kit and a bicycle pump. Automobiles came with tools, and early owners had to know how to make repairs.

"The automobile could not follow the trail which led through a country broken by arroyos. It swung around below Casa Grande and striking the road to Vekol flew in that direction. There were many minor mishaps and Mr. McCarthy spent much time under the machine with the thermometer far above 100. But the time thus lost was made up in the ensuing flight."[13]

The sheriff had spread a wide net, but the desert was even wider. Nonetheless, there were but few places where water could be obtained. Unfortunately, the Woodsons were unaware of any of them. About two o'clock, after a bone-jarring ride at frightening speeds that might have reached twenty miles per hour, Hayden came upon a posse on horseback. The posse had turned back to the Papago village of Cockleburr for water. The tiny village was still seven miles distant. The "automobilists" provided the horsemen with all the water they had and then sped on after the Beardless Boy Bandits. The motorists came upon Deputy Sheriff Wilson, whose horse had given out, and they took him aboard for he was able to show them the trail so that they soon encountered the outlaw boys, now so thirsty they were thankful to be saved. The party turned back for Maricopa, and shortly thereafter, the automobile gave out. Trudging to Sandhill, the sheriff hired an Indian to take them by wagon.

Speaking of the automobiles as train robber chasers, Sheriff Hayden said that the result in this case must be attributed in great measure to good luck. If they had not encountered the horsemen when they did they would not have known which way to go and would have missed the fugitives. Or, if the bandits had moved back from the road a hundred yards they would not have seen one of their horses. If the breakdown of the machine had occurred on the way out instead of on the way back, the pursuit would have been useless.

But as things turned out the automobile saved the horsemen a ride of forty miles. In that distance counting their ride back for water they would have overhauled the robbers anyway. But if they had

missed them, the boys by this time would have been dead on the desert.
There was beside the Vekol [Wash]—only place where they could have
found water—[water available] at Ajo but the chances are many to
one that they would have missed it.[14]

When captured, the Woodsons had only seventy-six dollars on them.
Of the $295 the passengers claimed the Woodsons had taken, that was
all they had, and they'd had nowhere nor time to spend any of the loot.
Perhaps, like pirates, they'd buried the rest. Deputy Sheriff Adams
discovered the purse belonging to Deputy Sheriff Sturgis containing
sixty-five dollars. It had fallen through a hole in one of the Woodsons'
pockets. Straightaway, the deputy lost it again. It was found by one of the
Indians and was turned over to Sheriff Hayden, "who took a strangle hold
upon it determined to bring it to Phoenix or die in a mighty effort."[15]

When the youth of the bandits was discovered, a strange switch
occurred. They went from being villains to being lionized in the press. The
newspapers noted that the American Robin Hood, Jesse Woodson James,
shared a name in common with the brothers. Perhaps they were related
and had come to distribute stolen wealth to the poor and oppressed.
The elder brother was held in especially high esteem. On January 10,
1910, Ernest had come to Arizona and worked for Lee Walker and
Mahlon Brown, who lived near Tempe. Seeing the boy in his cell, Brown
exclaimed, "I can't believe it!" Mr. Brown told the press that Ernest
Woodson was the best and the most industrious boy he had ever seen.
He would have trusted him with anything, as he was absolutely truthful
and clean minded.

The Arizona legislature had rescinded the law that required capital
punishment for train robbery. On November 15, 1910, nonetheless the
boys were charged by grand jury.[16] And on November 18, they were
convicted and sent to prison for ten years.[17] The boys enjoyed public
sympathy. "Because of their youth, and the sincere efforts of their father,
who came here from Oklahoma to work in their behalf, the young men
won much sympathy." On March 31, 1914, they were given parole and
released from the federal prison at Leavenworth, Kansas.[18] They returned
to Oklahoma, which may be presumed punishment enough.

The Beardless Boy Bandits broke all the rules of train robbery. They molested the passengers instead of robbing the express car. They boarded the train and acquired tickets instead of using one of the approved methods of stopping the train. They did not separate the cars from the locomotive in order to conduct mayhem in privacy and without getting fired upon. They failed to wear masks. Their escape plan went beyond reason.

Nonetheless, they go down in history as the first train robbers pursued by "automobilists."

CHAPTER TEN

Matt Dillon Makes an Arrest

Author's note: I have to thank Chuck Smith of Safford for this one. Every search had missed it. No one else was aware of it. Cochise County historians denied it had happened.

Apache, Arizona, 1916

APACHE, ARIZONA, WAS A WHISTLE-STOP ON THE TRACKS OF THE EL Paso and Southwestern Railroad. There was a water tank, a corral, and a general store, and a school may have already been operating. The school, still there, is one of four remaining one-room schools in the state. It provides K–8 education to the children of ranchers, farmers, and others.[1]

The El Paso and Southwestern Railroad started its corporate life as a project of the Copper Queen Mine and Phelps Dodge Corporation as the El Paso and Southeastern Railroad (EPSE) on May 24, 1888. The people of Tombstone had high hopes that the train would run through their fair city, but those hopes were dashed, and the thirty-six-mile run, completed in January of 1889, went from Bisbee along the foot of the Mule Mountains to the San Pedro River and on to Fairbank, where it met the Santa Fe. It was built to haul copper ore to the smelters. On September 26, 1894, an additional nineteen miles of track linked the EPSE to Benson. On October 19, 1900, through a complicated series of short-line construction projects and subsequent sales and purchases, the EPSE became the El Paso and Southwestern (EPSW), still apparently owned and operated by Phelps Dodge through one or another of its subsidiaries. In 1902, the tracks ran 155 miles east to Douglas and then northeast to Deming, New Mexico, where it met the Santa Fe and the Southern Pacific Railroad.² It was not yet connected to El Paso, but one day would be, making it possible, on March 9, 1916, for Pancho Villa to cross the tracks, not to mention the border, and kill nineteen Americans at Columbus, New Mexico. During the summer of 1917, the International Workers of the World imported strikers, folks who weren't on the mines' payrolls, to Bisbee demanding worker ownership of the mines and an end to the Great War. On July 12, 1917, Sheriff Harry Wheeler deported 1,300 of the Wobblies, as they were known, to Columbus in cattle cars on the EPSW, but they never got there. Columbus expressed its adamant desire not to entertain these unwanted guests, and the train was stopped eight miles west of town.

The tracks linked the mines to Douglas, where there were two smelters, one of which was operated by Phelps Dodge. Douglas may be said to have begun its corporate life in 1902. It soon became the commercial hub of southeast Arizona with influence extending across the Peloncillo Mountains into New Mexico's Animas Valley. Douglas was conceived as one of the earliest projects of urban engineering, with a fancy hotel, the Gadsden, a wide commercial street, a fancy train station,

The train station as it stands today in Apache, Arizona. The railroad ran behind the building.
AUTHOR'S PHOTO

and parks surrounded by upscale homes, with the homes of lesser folk a bit farther out. It is a crossing point on the border with Mexico.

Apache, although tiny, is at the center of a great deal of history. It is named in honor of Geronimo's 1886 surrender to General Miles, which took place four miles to the east in Skeleton Canyon. This canyon links the San Simon Valley, home to the outlaw Cow Boy Gang of Curly Bill Brocius, Johnny Ringo, and Ike Clanton and to Black Jack Christian's High Five Gang, to the Animas Valley of New Mexico. Skeleton Canyon is the route of smugglers and rustlers between Arizona–New Mexico and Chihuahua and Sonora. Legend has it that in 1879, the Clanton Gang ambushed a Mexican gang led by Jose Estrada. In reality, there was no Clanton Gang. Those so called were Curly Bill's Cow Boy Gang, and the Clantons were not the leaders; they were more like cattle launderers working much as money launderers, and Old Man Clanton was the gang's camp cook. The Mexican smugglers had sacked several banks and cathedrals in Monterrey and were taking gold, silver bullion, and diamonds north. The Cow Boys killed them all, leaving the bones of the Mexicans, their horses, and their mules to bleach in the Arizona sun, hence the name Skeleton Canyon.[3] They then buried the treasure somewhere in the canyon. For this reason, strangers are no longer allowed in the canyon. Not because treasure is to be found there, but rather because folks looking for it keep digging holes.

It is certain that both Apaches and rustlers used the canyon as a conduit. In July 1881, the abovementioned Cow Boys were ambushed by a party of Mexicans. The Cow Boys were either leading a stolen herd north after attacking a rancho and killing the inhabitants and were pursued by *rurales*, or they had ambushed a party of Mexican smugglers and got off with four thousand dollars in bullion and livestock. This robbery may explain why one of the McLaury brothers had a large amount of cash on him when the Earps and Doc Holliday shot him on October 26, 1881, on Fremont Street near the O.K. Corral. Mexican bones were left to bleach.[4]

On September 8, 1916, the *Bisbee Daily Review* expressed astonishment that a horse-mounted posse led by Sheriff Harry Wheeler was on the trail of "the seven men who held up the Golden State Limited

Wednesday night [September 6, 1916], west of Apache. Cochise county opened its eyes to the fact that the old Arizona has not entirely passed to the limbo."[5]

It's unclear why eyes would ever have been shut. Folks in Cochise County still aren't sure the Wild West is over and certainly wouldn't have been sure in 1916. After all, in March 1901, the Arizona Rangers had been founded to combat lawlessness.[6] Most of the ranger force was assigned to Cochise County. On October 22, 1904, Sergeant Harry Wheeler, future sheriff, was a Ranger when he shot it out with two outlaws at the Palace Saloon on Congress Street in Tucson. On February 28, 1908, a love triangle erupted in Benson, playing out its drama between the Virginia Hotel and the train depot. J. A. Tracy had been dumped by "Mrs." D. W. Silverton in favor of Mr. Silverton. Tracy figured to slay them both, but Lieutenant Wheeler intervened. Allowing Tracy the first shot, which pierced the Ranger's thigh, Wheeler commenced to put four .45 caliber holes in Tracy, who continued firing wildly. Claiming to be done in and out of ammunition, Tracy lay in the street as the Ranger lieutenant approached. Tracy waited for his moment to fire a round into Wheeler's foot. The Ranger responded by throwing rocks and then kicking the pistol out of the hand of the dying lover, apparently employing the foot that was not as yet wounded. Soon after, Wheeler was promoted to captain, the top slot in the Rangers.[7] On February 15, 1909, the Arizona legislature abruptly disbanded the highly effective Arizona Rangers. This was not because lawlessness had ceased; the legislature, after all, was still in session.

In addition, according to the *Tombstone Weekly Epitaph*, there were still Apaches on the prowl in 1916: "A detachment of cavalry went through Tombstone today mounting at daylight, bound for the Dragoons. They were from Huachuca and had been ordered to intercept the Apaches supposed to be on the way from San Carlos to the Sierra Madres in Sonora."[8]

The fellow who led the raid on the train at Apache Siding might have surprised them. Joe Davis, alias Joe L. May or Mayes, although young, was a part-Cherokee career criminal in Oklahoma. According to the *Bisbee Daily Review*:

RIDE 'EM AS THEY COME

BY RUSTY TULK

Rodeo cowboy Rusty Tulk (left) and an unknown cowboy. This photo is taken from the cover of Tulk's memoir.

COURTESY OF SULPHUR SPRINGS VALLEY HISTORICAL SOCIETY

Davis first broke into prominence several years ago when a posse of thirty-two men, headed by a sheriff, stopped at the Davis ranch to investigate. No warrant was held for Davis or any of his family and when the posse attempted to search, was held off. Davis' wife was commanded to halt in the yard when the posse rode up. She fled into the house, however, and a member of the sheriff's force opened fire. In the fight that followed a number were killed on the attacking side. Davis was exonerated from all blame in this matter as it was proved that he did not fire the first shot. It is said that the man is wanted in four different states on charges varying from train robbery to murder.[9]

He got away with the shooting of a deputy but was wanted in four states with charges ranging from train robbery to murder. He was mistaken for a cowhand and might have classified as a "saddle tramp," although he never seemed to have stayed anywhere long enough to earn a paycheck. He had plenty of money and bought a car in Douglas. He used a number of aliases and apparently had some interesting friends. One of these was rodeo champion C.W. "Doc" Pardee of Prescott, a bronco rider, movie actor, rodeo announcer, and breeder of thoroughbred horses. Pardee was inducted into the Arizona Horseman's Hall of Fame in 1965.[10] In February 1917, he was indicted for attempting to assist Joe Davis in breaking out of the Prescott jail. He was acquitted although there was a plot involving acid, hacksaws, and complicit jail trustees.[11] Among the first men arrested by Sheriff Wheeler, formerly Ranger lieutenant and captain, was another rodeo cowboy, "Rusty" Tulk. The newspapers do not make explicit what became of this attempted prosecution, but the rodeo connection is interesting. Perhaps Joe Davis worked the circuit. Tulk doesn't mention the arrest in his autobiography, but he was in Arizona at the time and although several spellings of his name appear, he's likely the man in question.[12]

Joe Davis met W. T. "Buck" Bertholf in Arizona during February 1916, and the plotting for a railroad heist seems to have begun at that time. Buck had been in Arizona for some time and had known Davis since childhood in Oklahoma. In March, while the boys were on the prowl between Prescott, Cochise County, and Deming, New Mexico, Pancho Villa raided Columbus on the EPSW line. In April and May,

Buck and Joe met at Seligman, at Prescott, and at the Boquillas Land and Cattle Company south of Benson. Jess Spurlock and Johnny Carroll joined the pair at a July meeting. On August 1, they settled in at the ranch of Clay McGonigle, where they stayed for three weeks before moving to the Henderson Ranch in New Mexico's Animas Valley across the Peloncillo Mountains from Apache, Arizona. They stayed there for ten days until September 5, 1916.

This raises questions about whether or not they stayed anywhere long enough to earn a paycheck. And it leads to questions about whether McGonigle or Henderson and their ranch hands were complicit in coming events. Henderson died in December after being injured in a car crash in September. Questions directed at his widow suggest that law enforcement officers thought he might be involved.

During late August and early September, the boys kept busy. Joe Davis found time to send a telegram from Deming to Lulu Davis at Claude, Texas, telling her to wait for word before starting out, and that he would send her money, but he couldn't just now because "Little Pants" (Carroll) had forged a check on him for seven hundred dollars.[13] On August 15, Davis bought a car at Overland Auto in Douglas from D. B. Hutchins using the name Joe L. Mayes and paying with a thousand-dollar check. Meanwhile, Bertholf was busy at the hardware store buying ten feet of fuse and blasting caps under the name of Bill Smith.[14] They used the car to scout locations along the EPSW.

During this happy summer season, Joe found time to write to his Lulu, although he may have been puzzled as to whether she was Lulu Davis, Cobb, or Mayes or even if she was actually his wife. Bertholf seemed to think so, but no one could find proof. Nonetheless, he wrote to her, and the letters were later found by the law in a trunk the pair left behind at the Henderson ranch in Animas Valley. At trial, Davis's lawyer, Judge W. L. Barnum, in a carnival atmosphere of numerous objections, claimed that reading these "private" letters in court was a violation of the defendant's Fourth and Fifth Amendment rights. Davis wrote:

(Written from Douglas to Lulu Davis at Claude, Texas.)
My Dear One,

I have bought a car and will leave for you about the 3rd of Sept., if I am alive and get by with the deal. I feel pretty good. I will leave a letter at the place where I start from. If I am killed it will be mailed to you. If I am not, it will not be mailed. This letter will tell you where my stuff is. Don't let anyone know when I am coming back. I have been in Old Mexico. Buck is backing up on everything and had to get another man. When I get through here, we will be together and stay that way. Be a good girl . . . Be good, darling, and have a good time for us both. Joe.

(Second Letter—A registered letter mailed from Deming by Joe Davis to Lulu Davis at Claude, Texas.)
My Dear Lulu,

The range is pretty bad and there is much mud. Come to Douglas and stay at the Gadsden. Get there by Sept. 9. Go by the name of Mayes at Douglas. Things may be pretty hot by the 6th or 7th. If I cannot come for you myself, I will send someone. I will be an old man, about 50 years, and getting gray. We spent four hours in a mudhole today. Maybe we will take a trip in the car. Will send you some money as a woman sometimes goes broke. I heard "money" over the phone and so send you some in case you need it. Don't let any of your people know where you are going. Joe.[15]

"Come to Douglas and stay at the Gadsden." In 1916, the Gadsden Hotel with its marble pillars, grand staircase, Turkish bath, barbershop, saloon, shops, restaurants, and stained-glass windows and skylights was arguably the finest accommodation in Arizona. These outlaws knew how to live in style.

At the Henderson ranch, Carroll displayed the quart container of nitroglycerine he'd brought from Oklahoma. After securing a pint to take with them, the four outlaws buried the remainder and on September 5 took off on horseback for Rodeo, New Mexico. Mrs. Morgan, a rancher's wife, recalled Bertholf and Carroll stopping at her ranch near Rodeo to wash their feet.[16]

In accordance with the letter's instructions, Joe Davis's moll boarded the Fort Worth and Denver railway in Claude, switching later to the Santa Fe and finally at Deming to the EPSW for the ride to Apache. As the train passed through Hachita, seeing "Steamboat" and other hobos riding the blind baggage, Private William Hynes of Troop K, Fourth Cavalry, was suddenly taken with an overwhelming romantic desire to take "French leave" and join the hobos.

At Rodeo, on September 6, Bertholf and Carroll stayed in town, waiting for the EPSW train that carried Hynes, Steamboat, and Mrs. Lulu Davis. On board, Conductor George Davy punched Lulu's ticket, as he later recalled in court.[17] Meanwhile, Joe Davis and Jess Spurlock continued their ride, going south another fifteen miles to Apache and then proceeding a mile farther, where they tied up their stock and lighted signal fires.

When the train arrived in Rodeo, it was already a dark evening. Bertholf and Carroll joined several hobos and Private Hynes in the blind baggage. It must have been crowded and may explain why later on Hynes couldn't identify either of them. As they boarded, they may have already been wearing masks. Given the cloud of hot soot and cinders that hovered over them in the blind baggage right behind the tender and locomotive, wearing a mask wouldn't have struck anyone as strange. Cowhands wore neckerchiefs over their faces as a shield against dust. Shortly after leaving the station, the two outlaws began the climb over the tender toward the cab. The hobos and the soldier would have reacted in one of two ways. Either they'd have thought it was none of their business and they didn't want to be involved, or they'd have thought the newcomers were just seeking a more comfortable spot.

The outlaws surprised engineer Allen Lovett and fireman W. E. Jones and ordered them to stop the train at Apache. There the criminal duo ordered the passenger cars disconnected, leaving only the mail and express cars to continue the journey. Davis and Spurlock boarded the train while it was stopped at Apache. Brakeman John Graham, eating his dinner in the dining car of the fancy Golden State Limited, was surprised by the unscheduled stop and hurried outside to see what was wrong. A man with a gun ordered him to give the order to start the train. There was some confusion as the train departed, which may have included a shot fired over Jones's shoulder. One of the outlaws told a train crewman that he better get on and then, running to catch the train himself, called out, "Too late. You've missed it."

The passenger cars and passengers were left behind unmolested. Nonetheless, there was panic. The *Bisbee Daily Review* reported, "One woman, it is said, hid a diamond ring so well that she was nearly an hour finding it after the scare was over and the train on its way to Douglas."[18]

The dining car conductor hid all the money he'd taken in from passengers paying for dinner. And then, thinking that the outlaws might think it strange that he had no money on him, dug out fifteen dollars, which he said he intended on handing to the robbers willingly to show "that there was much sympathy between members of the profession." (This comment seems to be a reference to solidarity between members of the proletariat, union men and outlaws. He said it, not this author, who merely quotes him, and would never suggest that the unions are run by crooks and socialists.) While some passengers were on the verge of hysteria, others sat on the observation platform sipping lemonade. Half a mile down the track toward Douglas and Bisbee, the outlaws were about to provide a show.[19]

Outlaws, soldier, hobos, and some of the train crew crowded into the blind baggage and the locomotive's cab. Joe Davis stood beside Private Hynes, and although the bandit was masked, Hynes was later able to identify the man who stood beside him for the court although he was unable to pick out any of the others. At the signal fires, the outlaws had the train stop, and everyone was escorted to the middle express car, which Davis ordered the brakeman to open. It was locked from the inside, and he could not. A pick was soon found, and Hynes and the tramps put to work cracking the door.

Realizing that the express agent or mail clerk might be waiting within with a loaded weapon prepared to go postal, the bandits selected a hobo to enter and ensure that the car was safe for them. R. M. Collier of the Post Office waited within. According to Steamboat, the man selected for this task, he cried out, pleading, "I'm only a poor hobo, if you kill me, you will kill a good man."[20]

Assured that the car was safe, two outlaws entered. Confronting Collier, they told him that they would now proceed to the mail car to get the registered mail. Collier replied, "Partner, you have selected the wrong day." He explained how the mail was "Sunday out of New York and Labor Day out of Chicago." He said that the man said they would look anyhow, that when they got down he saw the man making an effort to shove the two registered pieces of mail either into his pocket or inside his shirt.[21]

Taking the registered mail was a mistake. They had now committed a federal crime, and the records kept allowed the officers of the court later to identify the mail wrappers and tie the men conclusively to the crime.

The bandits now commenced the comedic grand finale as they attempted to blow the express safe. Those with seats and lemonade on the observation platform looked on as the badmen made six attempts to blow the express safe. They only managed to get the top door open and found nothing of use within. Frustrated, the outlaws collected their horses and rode away into the night.

Pursuit followed swiftly as Sheriff Harry Wheeler of Cochise County went after them assisted by Constable Sam Hayhurst of Douglas. Sam was running against Harry for sheriff, and both had to make trips to town to vote. Tension in the posse must have rivaled an episode of *Longmire*. Like Longmire, Harry Wheeler prevailed. Within a few days, the sheriff succeeded in in arresting Flin "Rusty" Tulk, who at a hearing on September 20 was held over on twenty-five thousand dollars' bond on a charge of robbing the United States mails.[22]

By September 27, Rusty Felk (Tulk) had a Bisbee defense team, who may have gotten the bond reduced to ten thousand dollars. There are several possibilities here. There may have been two Cochise County cowhands named "Rusty" in 1916 who were both arrested for robbing the mail, Rusty may have changed his name from Tulk to Felk, or the *Epitaph* may have reported the name and bail incorrectly. The latter is most likely because John Clum was no longer the editor. Here is where Rusty Tulk fades from the story. He may have been a cowhand at one of the ranches the bandits frequented who ratted out his buddies in exchange for his release, or may have known them from the rodeo circuit, or he may have been innocent. He isn't mentioned in court during the trial of Spurlock and Davis.[23]

The four outlaws and Mrs. Davis drove away in their new car, first stopping briefly at the Henderson ranch in the Animas Valley, where Mr. and Mrs. Davis left behind a trunk containing the incriminating letters quoted above. Two days after the robbery, Mr. Henderson went to Douglas, where A. T. Prather cashed a check for him. The check was signed by Joe Davis. The outlaws drove on to Oklahoma, where the gang split up. The nitroglycerine was still buried at the Henderson ranch in the Animas Valley.[24]

At this point, Sheriff Wheeler drops from the picture, and pursuit is handed off to Marshal Joe Dillon and Post Office Inspector Thomas Butler. Butler testified that he had been present at both arrests of Jess Spurlock, one at Sioux City, Iowa, and the other at Purcell, Oklahoma, where Spurlock was using the name Tom Miles. Butler was assisted by Sheriff Dillon during one of the arrests. At court, on cross-examination, Butler mentioned a Deputy Sheriff Dillon. Assistant US Attorney Flynn asked, "It wasn't our Dillon (meaning Joe)?" To this Butler replied, "No." Undoubtedly, the surfeit of lawmen named Dillon gave rise to years of debate about whether Dillon's name was Joe or Matt and whether he was a US or Dodge City marshal or possibly a county sheriff.[25] By December 12, 1916, most of the gang was in custody of the United States district court. Johnny Carroll drops precipitously from the story. Perhaps he got clean away and went straight the rest of his life under an assumed name, or perhaps, like so many of his kind, he was shot soon after in an aborted holdup. The *Arizona Daily Star* wrote: "Joe Davis, Alias Joe L. May, accused of being the ring leader in the hold-up of the west-bound Golden State Limited on the night of September 6, at a point near Apache, Arizona, was brought to Phoenix Sunday night from Purcell, Oklahoma. Davis was indicted by the federal grand jury in Tucson for the crime. He will be tried at Tucson later in the session."[26]

It was at about this time that convicted felon Buck Bertholf decided that he was in real trouble as a repeat offender and went state's evidence against Joe Davis and Jess Spurlock. Judge W. L. Barnum, attorney for Jess

Spurlock, objected strenuously to his testimony. "W.T. Bertholf was then called as the prosecution's first witness. Before he began his testimony, Judge W.L. Barnum, counsel for Jess Spurlock, objected to the witness on the ground that he was a co-defendant. The objection was over-ruled."[27]

Subsequently, Barnum would object to Bertholf's testimony on the grounds that Buck was a convicted felon whose civil rights had not been restored. Counsels for the defense also asked for a severance of the cases of Joe and Jess.

> In asking for a severance for Davis, his counsel stated that his client is without funds to secure witnesses from Oklahoma, who, the attorney said, would be necessary for the defense in case Davis were tried jointly with Spurlock. The motion in behalf of Spurlock was made on similar grounds. The court, in denying these motions, announced that if it were shown certain witnesses were necessary to the defense, they would be subpoenaed at the government's expense.[28]

The trial went forward. Ultimately, the defense offered no witnesses, relying on an appeal to the jury that Bertholf's testimony must be corroborated by other evidence and had not been. They also prepared several appeals on grounds that the "private letters" should not have been admitted and that Bertholf's testimony should not have been allowed. The jury's verdict was guilty on all counts.[29] Joe Davis and Spurlock were sentenced to twenty-five years each in the federal penitentiary and were shipped off to McNeill's Island in custody of Marshal Dillon.[30]

CHAPTER ELEVEN

You'd Better Not Mess with the US Mail

WHEN THE LAW IS ON YOUR SIDE

Guthrie, Arizona, 1922

WHEN I STARTED THIS BOOK, I KNEW TO A MORAL CERTAINTY THAT IF I named some holdup the *last* that one of two things would happen. Someone, determined to prove me wrong, would go out and hold up a train. It hasn't happened yet, but I'm waiting. The other possibility was that someone would find an obscure robbery and say, "Aha!" It was bound to be a break-in of a boxcar parked on a siding and a case of stolen Spam. This did happen, but fortunately they couldn't turn up a copy of the alleged news story giving the newspaper banner, and when we straightened out the clipping, the burglary turned out to have occurred in 1918.

Another latent train robbery appeared. On March 29, 1922, at Anapara, New Mexico, robbers stole a case of shoes. It was decided that these were probably Mexican bandits or revolutionaries; it was hard to tell the difference.[1] They had broken into a boxcar parked on a siding.

Subsequently, the story of a 1926 conviction for train robbery involving a real robbery at an obscure town was found. Researching the story, I learned the robbery had actually taken place on May 12, 1922. The robbery I had named as last occurred on May 15, 1922, in Tucson, so by three full days, it was the last!

Why did outlaws stop robbing trains? Communications had improved. It seems likely that less money was traveling by train as wire transfers and travelers' checks made the physical movement of cash less important. Although paved roads outside of towns were still almost unknown, the railroads ran to almost every town, and there were more miles of track than paved roads although stagecoaches still carried passengers on short runs in the hinterland. While in 1881 Wyatt Earp had been able to place telephone calls to the mines a mile and more away, and a little later Sheriff Texas John Slaughter had telephone line strung from sagebrush to mesquite from Tombstone all the way to his ranch, the phone lines now connected towns and railroad whistle-stops, making the communication about robberies almost instantaneous. In Tucson there were more than twenty dude ranches, a sure sign that the Wild West was dying. Although Tucson and Phoenix waited to grow until air-conditioning became affordable after World War II, the Apache were on reservations, and travel between towns was relatively safe. Prohibition was on, and Cochise County was alive with "importers."

Not everyone enjoyed "cactus juice," and a few miles north of Tucson, near a place the railroad called Jaynes, a goat herder ran a still as a sideline.

Meanwhile, farther north and east near Guthrie, Arizona, two cowboys, perhaps trying to revive the dying Wild West, hatched a half-baked plan to rob the El Paso and Southwestern Railroad. Since 1888, James Douglas of the Phelps Dodge Mining Company had been working on a different scheme. To service extensive mining interests and to defend against high shipping rates on the Southern Pacific, Douglas envisioned the Arizona and Southeastern Railroad, which ran from Tucson to Bisbee. The system grew and prospered. In the early twentieth century, Bisbee was connected to El Paso, and the railroad became the El Paso and Southwestern Railroad. Eventually, the railroad owned 1,200 miles of track. One line connected the mines at Morenci, north of the Gila River along the San Francisco River, by way of Duncan and Lordsburg, to the Bisbee–El Paso line at Hachita near the Mexican line in the bootheel of New Mexico.[2] Clifton, the seat of Greenlee County, is near neighbor to Morenci, which is slowly disappearing into an open-pit copper mine. Greenlee County is tiny by Arizona standards and hugs the border with New Mexico. Its only real town was the mining center at Clifton-Morenci, while Guthrie was a collection of buildings on the Gila River.

On May 12, 1922, on a dangerous curve three miles south of Guthrie, the outlaws, more energetic than most, piled ties across the track. There was speculation that the intent was to derail the train. As it was, the locomotive crashed into the pile at twenty miles per hour and pushed the ties seven car lengths along the tracks before the brakes took hold. Twenty miles per hour doesn't sound like much today, but in 1922 on a curving mountain line, that was fast, perhaps double the speed of a horse-drawn wagon.[3]

Leveling their weapons on the engineer and fireman, the outlaws escorted the pair to the express car. They ordered the express messenger to open the door only to learn that there was no express messenger on board. The bandits called for Conductor Malone and brakeman Spaw. Upon their arrival, the outlaws ordered the car opened and the registered mail and valuable express produced forthwith. They reassured the crew that as long as they did not resist, no one would get hurt. The train crew opened the car door, and looking inside, the outlaws decided they might do better to rob the passengers. The badmen looked into the coach and changed their minds without molesting anyone. At this late date, we do not know which of the passengers looked too dangerous or too poor to be worthwhile.

The bandits made off with a few locked mail pouches. One of the outlaws remarked that there was very little of value on this train, but where he came from the express cars always had money. After telling the crew not to move the train for at least twenty minutes—they'd be watching—the outlaws walked off down the tracks and out of sight around a curve.

The outlaws got away with four sacks of mail and a package of eggs marked "E. J. Malone, personal property." In Guthrie, a call was placed to Clifton, and Sheriff Bradberry was on the trail that same night with a posse.[4]

On May 19, 1922, a week after the holdup, the following item appeared in the newspaper: "Deputy Sheriff, Johnnie Fulcher, has this week filed his resignation with the Clerk of the Board of Supervisors to take effect July 1st. Mr. Fulcher has made an efficient and fearless officer while serving under Sheriff Bradberry and his many friends regret seeing him leave the force. Mr. Fulcher has not made known his plans for the future."[5]

On Tuesday, July 11, at 10:15, there was a shoot-out just over the line in Grant County, New Mexico. Johnny Fulcher, former deputy sheriff, lay dead while his brother Sidney was severely wounded, his right arm shattered above the elbow. Bate Bradberry lay dead as well, while his brother, Mart, emptying his six-shooter at his assailants, escaped injury and rode off to find his remaining brother, Sheriff John Bradberry, and a young man named Jordan. Sid somehow rode to the Rayburn ranch, where he requested and received first aid.[6]

Johnny Fulcher lay dead, his rifle under him, his hand still clutching the lever with a cartridge thrown halfway into the breech. Four empty cartridges lay beside the body. Bate Bradberry, too, lay atop his rifle, clutching it in death, the magazine empty. There were empty shell casings beside the body. Although stories conflicted as to what had occurred, both survivors agreed that Bate had slain Johnny and wounded Sid. Sid, his right arm hanging limp at his side, jerked out his revolver and slew Bate.

Sid claimed the Bradberrys were the aggressors, while Mart claimed the Fulchers had waited in ambush. The Bradberry ranch was nearby, and the Fulchers had been camped in the area for several days. There was bad feeling between the two sets of brothers over a horse sale gone wrong. Sid claimed that Johnny had called Sheriff John Bradberry to come out and keep down trouble, "as Mart and Bate Bradberry were burning brands on horses in that section. Another version of the telephone conversation is that Fulcher invited John Bradberry, sheriff, to come to Carlisle as he wanted to make a horse trade with him, and that he could not deal with Bate or Mart Bradberry."[7]

They were to meet the next day. Mart, Bate, John, and Jordan rode out toward the appointed meeting place, and Mart and Bate stopped to drink at a spring while John and Jordan rode on. The Fulcher brothers arrived from a side canyon and the shooting started.[8]

On July 28, 1922, although a preliminary hearing was postponed until August 7, the *Deming Headlight* had the story. Sheriff John Bradberry, brother of deceased Bate Bradberry, stated that the Fulchers had ambushed his party. After the train robbery of May 19, he had strong suspicions that Sidney Fulcher and his father knew something, so he fired his deputy Johnny Fulcher for cause. Bate had trailed the horses used by the train robbers and had evidence that might be used against the Fulchers, but this evidence had not been communicated to the railroad officials.[9] Discussion between the sheriff and the Fulchers the night before the shootings convinced him, in retrospect, that the Fulchers were planning an ambush.

That same day, July 28, Thomas H. Fulcher, a cattleman, was arrested in Lordsburg, New Mexico, by Deputy US Marshal J. J. Curnutt of Globe and Sheriff Oscar Allen of Hidalgo County, New Mexico. The charge was that he and his son, Syd, had robbed the El Paso and Southwestern in May. Syd Fulcher was not arrested. He was in the hospital at Lordsburg recovering from the wounded arm sustained in the gunfight.

Deputy sheriffs had followed the trail of two horses leading from the scene of the holdup. They discovered where the mailbags had been destroyed and found the locks in the ashes of the campfire. Also found were pieces of an overcoat worn by one of the robbers and a mask hanging in a bush well above the ground as if thrown there by a man on horseback. There were no tracks of men on the ground, furthering the idea of a horseman passing by. They did not disclose how these bits of evidence tied the Fulchers to the robbery.[10] During the trial, it was revealed that the tracks led to the home of Emma and Gilbert Stockton, Tom Fulcher's daughter and son-in-law.[11] On August 25, 1922, Syd was charged with the murder of Bate Bradberry, and the case against Mart was dropped.[12]

There is no record in the newspapers of the murder case against Syd ever going to trial. While it was pretty clear who shot John, the why and who fired first were not clear. The state's attorney may have considered it difficult to demonstrate that the Fulchers intended an ambush. After a delay of four years, Tom and Syd Fulcher went to trial on federal charges of train robbery and interfering with the mail. The record does not address the reasons for the lengthy delay in coming to court. The newspapers describe the case as sensational and the Fulchers as having many friends throughout Arizona. More than one hundred witnesses were notified although only a few were placed on the stand.[13] The government asked for and received special guards in the courtroom.[14]

We note a four-year delay in coming to a trial in a difficult-to-prove case, based completely on circumstantial evidence, of a crime where no one was hurt and nothing of value taken, could only have made the case more difficult to prove. Why did the government bother and not plead it down to some lesser offense? Why the massive public interest and fear of armed interference from friends on behalf of the Fulchers? There is no direct evidence to offer, but we can note that this is the part of Arizona that was home to misbehavior by Mormon officials leading to miscarriages of justice as in the case of the Wham Payroll Robbery (1889) and the Power's Cabin Shootout (1918), which bore similarities to the more recent Ruby Ridge shootings. Did the Fulchers receive justice? We can only say they received a sentence of twenty-five years in the federal penitentiary at Leavenworth, Kansas, while of the fellows who robbed the trains three days later at Jaynes, near Tucson, only one did jail time.

The fingerprints of Syd Fulcher, confirmed through army records from the Great War, appeared on a medicine bottle found near the trail of a horse with a peculiar, injured hoof, along with the torn end of a cigarette paper and other detritus of items from the robbery. The defense claimed all cowboys tore of the ends of their cigarette papers and that it wasn't Fulcher's unique habit.[15] The judge admonished the jurors not to read anything other than local newspapers, who were cooperating with the court. The *Citizen* wrote, "In the week's time that the trial progressed, the government built up a net of circumstantial evidence that pointed to Tom and Syd Fulcher, and then capped the case with the expert testimony on signatures and the finger print. Just how this net will stand to hold the two defendants remains to be seen."[16]

The net held.

FINAL CHAPTER
Tucson, Arizona, 1922

I mentioned in the opening passages that the Phoenix newspapers were more apt to say "hang 'em high!" while the Tucson newspapers would hope to see the poor boy get a break. Just after midnight on Monday, May 15, 1922, between Jaynes, a flag stop about eight miles northwest of Tucson, and Cortaro, a red fusee and three track torpedoes were used to bring the Golden State Limited (Chicago, Rock Island, and Pacific Train No. 1) from Chicago to Los Angeles to a halt for the purpose of robbery and mayhem. Of Tom Dugat, goat rancher, an outlaw killed while firing on Conductor D. M. Madigan, the *Arizona Daily Star* wrote that Mrs. Dugat said,

> *Six months ago Mr. Dugat found it hard to sell his stock, and to tide us over the hard times I have been working as a nurse. He had a proud spirit, and it broke his heart to see me have to do this. I didn't mind it, and I told him so, but he wasn't satisfied.*
>
> *A month ago he wrote me that it was driving him mad to thing [sic] that he could not make enough to support me and our little baby, Corinne. He said he was prepared to make the supreme sacrifice so that I could quit the work. I couldn't imagine what he meant, but I see it now.*[17]

He had a hard time selling his stock, which seems to have left him a great deal of time to hang out in pool halls.[18] Perhaps the habitué of the pool halls was only there on business hawking his moonshine. Sheriff Ben F. Daniels discovered five barrels filled with mash in a tunnel under a creek one hundred yards from Dugat's goat ranch on Silver Bell Road. Cornmeal, sugar, and other "makin's of whisky" were also found.[19] Although Prohibition had driven up the demand, Dugat's must not have been selling well as he was still a poor boy with financial troubles who forced his wife to take on a nursing job, leaving him to hang his head in shame. Times were tough, and they were about to get tougher.

His wife told the *Arizona Daily Star* about his activities on Sunday, May 15:

> *I'm sure he hadn't thought of this awful business until late Sunday night, for he acted perfectly natural all day. He came in from the ranch to spend the day. At 6 o'clock we had a tea. Afterwards he took little Corinne to the junior class at the Baptist church, and later he went back after her.*
>
> *He was a good husband and father. He loved little Corinne more than anything on earth. He had not a single bad habit—I know he*

hadn't. He never drank, he never gambled, and he never stayed out late at night.[20]

Dugat returned to the goat ranch on Silver Bell late in the evening and there soon went to bed, telling his hired hand he was turning in for the night at 9 p.m. The Mexican hired man was sure he'd have heard the noise if Tom had gotten out of bed.[21]

Young Charley Bailey of Covington, Kentucky, barely out of his teens, had started out from his eastern home sometime before riding "the blind" as a deadhead,[22] looking for adventure, romance, and possibly a job. He was on his way to Los Angeles but thought he might stop at Maricopa since there was work there, he thought. That Sunday night, May 15, he lay down on a park bench and fell asleep, waking to the sound of two trains leaving the station. One was the Golden State Limited, and the other a slower freight that would make more stops. Wishing to travel in a bit more style, he hopped into the "blind" behind the tender of the moving Golden State.[23]

The Golden State Limited was a named passenger train that ran from 1902 to 1968 between Chicago and Los Angeles on the Chicago, Rock Island, and Pacific Railroad and the Southern Pacific. At 2,340 miles, it was one of the longest continuous passenger railroad routes in the United States.[24] Bailey chose to ride the "blind" in luxury.

At 1:10 a.m. on Monday, May 15, the train was only ten miles out from the Tucson yards up between Jaynes on Silver Bell Road and Cortaro. Express messenger Harry Stewart turned out the lights and was already dozing, safe inside his car. In the chair or passenger car directly behind the express car, D. Michael Madagan, conductor, was still collecting tickets when he heard the explosions of three track torpedoes and felt the lurch as the engineer braked in response.[25] In the locomotive, engineer George L. Reid and fireman Maurice F. Ingham heard the same small explosions and saw a red fusee lying by the track ahead. Reid braked the train to a halt.

As he did so, three masked, armed men boarded the locomotive. Their leader barked orders in a voice Ingham would later recall as sounding a lot like that of a man named Frank W. Jirou.[26] The trainmen watched as a fourth shadowy figure made his way toward the passenger car, presumably to guard the people there. Charley Bailey, "beating his way" westward riding the "blind" as a "dead head," heard voices in the cab tell the engineer and fireman to "line up and be good!" And then a shot was fired, rupturing the still of the night. Afraid he'd been detected, Bailey cried out, "I'm in here, brother." A tall, thin holdup man, who Charley thought must be the leader, cussed at him and told him to get out of there and line up with the others. "For God's sake, don't shoot!" Bailey cried, throwing up his hands. He and the crew were escorted out into the field, Charley certain they were about to be shot. On his first trip west, Charley Bailey's wildest dreams of the "wild and wooly west" had been surpassed. It was a night to remember.[27]

Seeming to change their minds about execution, the bandits, poking a gun in his face, asked Bailey if he knew how to disconnect the cars. Ready to agree to anything, Charley said he did. Escorted to the space between the express and passenger cars, an outlaw barked, "Cut her quick!" as Bailey, crawling under the car, fumbled at the unfamiliar task.

Above him, seeing that the train had stopped, Conductor Madagan began to open the vestibule to climb out when he heard a voice shouting, "Keep back!" From beside the express car, good provider, loving father, goat rancher, and moonshiner turned outlaw Thomas Dugat fired twice with deadly intent at the figure emerging from the car behind. One shot shattered the window beside Madagan's head, and the splintered glass cut his face deeply, the bullet exiting through the roof of the car. The other went through the bumpers, or shock absorbers, between the cars. Sensing his chance, Charley Bailey, sliding under the car and out the other side, took off, running back along the tracks toward the freight train he knew couldn't be far behind.[28]

Finishing the job of unfastening the passenger cars from the express car, the outlaws had the train pulled forward five or six car lengths, just enough so that they'd have warning of anyone trying to interfere with them. Inside the express car, Harry Stewart was awakened by the noise and lurching of the train. His first thought was that the train crew was having trouble with hobos. He got out his sawed-off shotgun and checked his revolver, glad that he had the former. Harry was getting older, his eyesight dimming, and he was thinking about retiring. He wondered how the fight with the "dead heads" was proceeding. After he stood by the door a while, he heard steps coming from the direction of the engine and looked out his window. He saw Charley Bailey go by with his hands in the air, and Harry expected to see a man with a drawn weapon following but, in the dark, saw no one. Moments later he heard the unmistakable sound of someone fooling with the chains under the car and heard a man call out, "For Christ's sake, can't you make the cut? Go ahead! Go ahead!" It occurred to him that this wasn't a problem with hobos. He heard more shots, and someone cried out, "Come on out, or we'll blow you up!" Unknown to Stewart, Charley had made his break for freedom while Madagan nursed his wound.[29]

Stewart said that a man came from the direction of the engine, and he could tell by his actions that this man was one of the robbers. Harry opened his door and fired at him, and the man disappeared into the night. The expressman closed his door again. Someone pounded on it demanding that it be opened. Someone tried to open the door on the other side. Harry made some noise, unintentionally getting the man's attention. The outlaw looked up. The figure in the night went a few steps and then came back. As he passed the door, Harry opened it and fired the shotgun. "I fired and the man fell. He crawled toward the bushes." Later that morning, Sheriff Ben F. Daniels and his posse would find Tom Dugat's dead body.[30]

Hobo Bailey ran back toward Jaynes, where there was a phone as well as an approaching freight train. He approached a man standing by the train, probably one of the brakemen, W. Clyde Brainard or William M. Tucker, and asked him if he was the conductor. The hobo said he had a lump in his throat so big he could hardly talk. The man responded that he'd been shot at six times. Bailey responded, "That's nothing. I've been shot at three times myself."[31]

The train crew suspected that someone familiar with railway operations had been involved in the robbery. The outlaws knew how to signal the train to stop. Upon return to the cab, the engineer discovered that the fires had been quenched and it would take them hours to bring up steam.

Extra Freight No. 2702, in charge of Conductor D. S. Montgomery, approached from the direction of Tucson. The remaining robbers scattered into the night, mounting two waiting automobiles, one of which was the property of Tom Dugat, who had been left lying by the tracks, his black mask and spectacles still obscuring his face. Montgomery had his train backed to Jaynes, where there was a phone, and the robbery was reported to the sheriff and railroad officials, who arrived within twenty-five minutes. The outlaws and the posse must have passed each other in the night bound in opposite directions.[32]

At the scene of the crime, Undersheriff Charles H. Pogue identified the body of Tom Dugat, a man he had known for twenty years. The Southern Pacific posted a three-hundred-dollar reward for arrest and conviction of each bandit.[33]

Mr. Drachman, the manager of the Tucson Opera House, waxed philosophical, telling the *Daily Star*: "If the eight men who were in the hold-up Monday morning of the Rock Island train had seen *Turn to the Right*, that is showing at the Opera House tonight for the last two, there probably would have been no hold-up. The moral taught and the scene shown in this picture is without question the greatest lesson for a prevention of crime that has been shown on the screen for many a year."[34]

Undoubtedly, Drachman's motives were pure and in the public interest, with no hint that he wished to pack the theater. This 1922 silent comedy drama film starred Alice Terry and was probably worth viewing.

The sheriff found the tracks of two automobiles that had headed toward Tucson. On May 19, Richard Star, a pipe fitter for the Southern Pacific Railroad, was arrested.[35] Sheriff Daniels alleged that Star knew who the bandits were and that a neighbor had seen them leaving Star's premises before and returning after the holdup.[36] Although this was undoubtedly a step toward identifying the outlaws, Star would sue the sheriff for false arrest, asking $10,250 in compensation for damage to his reputation. He claimed that the officer had proceeded without an order, warrant, or process of any court authorizing him to make the arrest and imprison Star. Richard Star swore that while Dugat's car had been at his establishment the day before the robbery, it was only there for repairs. In February 1923, the court awarded Star $750 in compensation.[37]

With Dugat positively identified, along with the men who had gone with him to Star's to get the car repaired, it wasn't long before the sheriff worked through a list of known associates, and on May 22, he arrested Frank W. Jirou. Fireman J. A. Ingham swore that he recognized the voice of George Winkler, while hobo Charles Baily swore that possibly, maybe Jirou's voice sounded a bit like that of one of the men who had held them at gunpoint while barking orders. It was enough to convince Jirou to go state's evidence on a promise of leniency in sentencing. He gave up the names of George W. Winkler, George Winkler Jr., and Edward Winkler, a father and two sons, and of Santiago Valdez, a Mexican goat herder, now missing, who had worked for Tom Dugat. George Jr. was a juvenile.[38]

On July 30, Edward Winkler and Santiago Valdez were both missing. They were reported by reliable sources to be in company on the West Coast, at Mazatlan, Sinaloa, perhaps enjoying the sun and sand. Santiago was said to have a known alias, Pedro Valenzuela. On September 8, it was reported that Ed might be in Hutchison, Kansas. By this time, Santiago or Pedro had disappeared into the murky mists of Mexico, never to be seen again north of the border, at least not under those names. On September 18, Edward was captured in Albuquerque, where he had been working in the Santa Fe railway shops since Labor Day under the name E. F. Barthels. He told of his flight from arrest and of having gone from Tucson to El Paso and then to Kansas City, Minneapolis, Denver, and finally Albuquerque. Perhaps he'd have had better luck if he'd gone to Mazatlan with Santiago.[39]

The case of George Jr. was transferred to juvenile court, where he was given supervised probation. George Sr. and Edward pled not guilty, and on November 23, their trial along with that of Frank Jirou began in Tucson. The Winklers' attorneys fought to have Jirou's evidence excluded as the criminal code allowed that the evidence of an accomplice was valueless. The attorneys also tried to have the voice identification of George Winkler Sr. given by fireman Ingham excluded. They stressed that Jirou's evidence had been obtained under a promise of leniency, while the confession of Edward Winkler, they argued, should be excluded because it was obtained under duress. Attorney Van Buskirk also objected to the evidence of Mrs. Frank Jirou, wife of the defendant, as Jirou had only told his wife of the whole affair after its failure, making her an accessory after the fact. The objections were overruled.[40]

Outside the courtroom another fight was being waged in the press and in the streets. A petition was raised in support of Edward Winkler. Ex-Private Harold L. Henry wrote to the newspapers, begging clemency for Edward, who was a good boy who had only fallen in with bad companions, namely, his drunken father. In 1918, Edward had enlisted in the army while he was still underage and had served in the trenches of the Great War with Company F, 138th Infantry Regiment of the 32nd Infantry Division. Henry wrote that Winkler had been cited for gallantry on two occasions, and there was a silver star on his discharge papers: "This star indicates a citation for gallantry in action and the citation papers recite that this recognition was gained through distinguished service while on patrol duty on the front lines near St. Giles, France."[41]

Edward Winkler, while underage, had been gassed in the Meuse-Argonne campaign and had suffered both "gas and cooties." The citation referred to evolved into what today we call the Silver Star, the nation's second highest award for bravery in combat, ranking only behind the Medal of Honor.[42]

The courts found Jirou and the two Winklers guilty as charged. The judge in sentencing was faced with a dilemma. The minimum sentence for train robbery was ten years in the state penitentiary, but Jirou had been promised a lighter sentence for his cooperation, while Edward had garnered a great deal of public sympathy, and it didn't seem fitting that all should suffer the same fate as moonshine-guzzling George Sr., who had lured them into an evil plan. All were given the ten-year minimum sentence, but Jirou's sentence was suspended for twenty-five years on condition that he leave the state within twenty-four hours. He was banished from the state for that period. Edward Winkler's sentence was suspended for ten years. He was compelled to report at regular intervals to the probation officer and would need the court's permission if he wanted to leave Arizona. Only George Winkler Sr. served hard time.[43]

Tom Dugat, a good provider, loving father, moonshiner, and goat rancher, lay dead. He and his gang had fired on Conductor Madagan and hobo Charley Bailey with the intent to do grievous bodily harm. Tom was willing to kill rather than suffer the embarrassment of being so unable to provide enough for his family that his wife had to work as a nurse. Jirou cut a deal. Edward Winkler was a poor young man and war hero, easily led by his drunken father. Public sympathy was with them. Being a war hero counted for more in 1922 than it does today. Only George Winkler Sr. was really to be blamed and forced to serve time. If they could have found him, public sympathy might have fallen on Santiago as well since he'd been forced into a life of crime by his employer.

It would be four more years before the Fulchers were tried for the crime they had committed three days prior to the Jaynes robbery. For some reason the public feared the unrepentant outlaws, known locally as tough guys, and sympathy was not with them. They were sentenced to twenty-five years each, and railroad robberies on the Southern Corridor came to an end.

Epilogue

THE ERA OF TRAIN ROBBERIES CAME TO A SCREECHING HALT IN 1922. I refuse to consider the 1940s theft of a case of Spam off a boxcar on a siding in Benson a true train robbery. As thrilling as this might have been to the people of Benson, counting it would have meant the era died with a whimper rather than a roar. How many train robberies were there? Sixteen, I think, but to tell you the truth, like Dirty Harry, I've lost count.

Why did the era end? The railroads had another thirty good years ahead of them supplying mail, express, and passenger service before they faded into the stuff that dreams are made of, the romance of the clickitty-clacking rails and Pullman cars rocking you to sleep, of dining cars with first-class monogrammed China, excellent food, and superior service provided by liveried waiters. It was the 1950s before air passenger service and airmail took over from the rails. Airplanes were faster, and the nation was in a hurry.

Train robberies passed into history long before transcontinental air transport made passenger rail a romantic luxury. People started carrying travelers checks, which meant they didn't carry nearly as much cash, but passengers had almost never been the target of highwaymen. Wire transfers and coordination between banks made it less necessary to ship large quantities of cash by rail. The nation transitioned to paper money and got away from needing coins. Paper money, when it traveled, came packeted with serial numbers recorded, making it more difficult for small-time operators to spend. Identifiable money made it difficult for a couple of Cochise County cowboys to get drunk and decide to hold up a train. Someone would have to invent money laundering so they could rid themselves of the tainted stuff. Unlike cattle, where they could just alter the brand, serial numbers were difficult to change. They needed an organization.

More important, communications had improved. While it was still a long-distance phone call from Jaynes to the sheriff's office in Tucson eight miles away, the phone did provide instant, two-way communication, making the information flow much more swiftly than it had by telegraph.

Newspaper stories referred to Jaynes as being on the Tucson to Casa Grande Highway, which would get a new name in 1926. Thereafter, it would be Highway 80, America's Broadway, and her first transcontinental, all-weather highway. I don't care where you get your kicks, Route 66, which opened the same year, ran only from Chicago to Los Angeles, while Highway 80 stretched from Los Angeles on the Pacific coast to Savanah, Georgia, on the Atlantic coast. It ran, and still does, through Benson, Tombstone, Bisbee, Douglas, and Apache to Lordsburg and Deming. It crossed the Great or Continental Divide at Old Divide Road in the Mule Mountains near Bisbee. New Mexico, hungry for glory, has put up signs saying the divide is crossed by I-10 east of Lordsburg, in the middle of a huge, flat prairie. How likely is that? Besides, the government put up signs on Old Divide Road saying that the Continental Divide was in Arizona at Bisbee. Of course, we must trust the government. You can go and see the monument at Bisbee any time you like.

All this aside, roads and automobiles changed America. You can still go to Bisbee and see the first paved road in Arizona. It's a block or so from the Old High School, four stories high, with a street-level entrance on every floor. The high-speed chase had been born. Cars could achieve speeds as fast as thirty miles per hour. Cars, although they broke down regularly, didn't get tired like horses, and they didn't need to be fed and watered. They took up less space than horses, weren't as smelly, and didn't draw flies, so it was relatively easy to keep one in town. The police and the sheriffs had them. With high-speed automobiles and high-speed telephonic communications, outlaws didn't stand a chance. Within a few years, police cars would even have two-way radios.

The speed at which trains traveled increased. The advent, in the 1920s, of diesel-electric locomotives led to trains traveling even faster and making fewer stops. The beautiful diamond and shotgun stacks soon disappeared. Improved communications meant that engineers and conductors had current information concerning hazards on the tracks ahead, which meant that they would be highly suspicious of signals indicating a hazard for which they must stop. Wells, Fargo and Company was nationalized during the Great War, the War to End All Wars, whose name had to be modified to World War I when it was realized that it had only been the opening round. Although the express company was privatized after the war, banking had changed, and with it the manner in which money was transferred. Federal policing efforts became more professional, and "don't mess with the US Mail" became a watchword. Law enforcement coordination across the country and across state and county borders improved. Train robbing the express car or the mail car, even if you could predict when it would be carrying something of high value, was no longer a casual enterprise.

Paved roads, interstate highways (even in Hawaii, though we have to wonder how that works), and tractor trailers have supplanted the railroads. The main roads remain, but the spur lines that once bound the nation together like some huge spiderweb are gone, along with the narrow-gauge lines and steam engines. Gone is the "mellow sound of a steam locomotive whistle" and the days when "the American railroads were a vital link in our economy. The farmer, cattleman, merchant, miner, were absolutely dependent upon the flanged wheels that ran on steel rails. Most businesses hinged upon the transportation furnished by railroads. Highways, trucks, autos, and busses did not exist then and if you wished to travel or to ship goods or products from one place to another, you had to use the railroads."[1]

Appendix

A Roster of Lawmen

SHERIFFS
Cochise County Sheriffs (Prior to 1881 This Was Pima County)

Johnny Behan   1881–1882
Jerome Ward   1883–1884
Robert Hatch   1885–1886
John Slaughter   1887–1890
Carlton Kelton   1891–1892
Scott White   1893–1894
Camilus "C. S." Fly
  (photographer)   1895–1897
Scott White   1897–1900
Adelbert "Dell" Lewis
  1901–1904
Stewart Hunt   1905–1906
John F. White   1907–1912
Harry Wheeler   1913–1918
Guy Welch   1918–1925

Pima County Sheriffs

Charles Alexander
  Shibell   1877–1880
Robert H. Paul   1881–1886
Eugene O. Shaw   1885–1887
Matthew F. Shaw Sr.   1887–
  1890
James K. Brown   1891–1892
Joseph B. Scott   1893–1894
Robert Nelson
  Leatherwood   1895–1898
Lyman Willis
  Wakefield   1899–1900
Frank E. Murphy   1901–1904
Nabor Pacheco   1905–1908
John Nelson   1909–1914
Albert W. Forbes   1915–1916
J. T. "Rye" Miles   1917–1920
Benjamin Franklin
  Daniels   1921–1922

Santa Cruz County Sheriffs (Prior to 1899 This Was Pima County)

William H. Barnett
1899–1899
Thomas F. Brodrick
1899–1900
Thomas Turner   1901–1904
Charles Fowler   1905–1906

Harry J. Jackson   1907–1910
William S. McKnight
1911–1916
Raymond R. Earhardt
1917–1920
George J. White   1921–1922

ARIZONA RANGER CAPTAINS

Burton C. Mossman
1901–1902
Thomas H. Rynning
1902–1907

Harry C. Wheeler
1907–1909

US MARSHALS

Arizona Territory (Prior to 1863 This Was New Mexico)

Milton D. Duffield   1863–
1866
George Tyng   1874
Francis H. Goodwin   1874–
1876
Wyley W. Standefer   1876–
1878
Crawley P. Dake   1878–1882
Zan L. Tidball   1882–1885
William Kidder Meade
1885–1890

Robert H. Paul   1890–1893
William Kidder Meade
1893–1897
William M. Griffith
1897–1901
Myron H. McCord
1901–1905
Benjamin F. Daniels
1905–1909
Charles A. Overlock
1909–1914

New Mexico Territory

Charles P. Clever   1858–1862
Albert W. Archibald   1861
(did not serve)
Abraham Cutler   1862–1866

John Pratt   1866–1876
John E. Sherman Jr.   1876–
1882

Alexander L. Morrison
Sr.   1882–1886
Don Romulo
Martinez   1886–1889
Trinidad Romero   1889–1893

Edward L. Hall   1893–1897
Creighton M. Foraker
1897–1912
Secundino Romero
1912, 1921–1926

WELLS, FARGO AND COMPANY DETECTIVES

James B. Hume   1871–1904   John N. Thacker   1875–1907

Bibliography

NEWSPAPERS

Albuquerque Evening Democrat, Albuquerque, NM
Albuquerque Journal, Albuquerque, NM
Albuquerque Weekly Citizen, Albuquerque, NM
Arizona Daily Star, Tucson, AZ
Arizona Range News, Willcox, AZ (aka *Sulphur Valley News*)
Arizona Republic, Phoenix, AZ
Arizona Republican, Phoenix, AZ
Arizona Sentinel, Yuma, AZ
Arizona Silver Belt, Globe, AZ
Arizona Weekly Citizen, Tucson, AZ
Arizona Weekly Enterprise, Florence, AZ
Arizona Weekly Journal-Miner, Prescott, AZ
Arizona Weekly Miner, Prescott, AZ
Arizona Weekly Star, Tucson, AZ
Baltimore Sun, Baltimore, MD
Bisbee Daily Review, Bisbee, AZ
Black Range, Robinson, NM
Border Vidette, Nogales, AZ
Clifton Clarion, Clifton, AZ
Cochise Review, Bisbee, AZ
Coconino Sun, Flagstaff, AZ
Copper Era and Morenci Leader, Morenci, AZ
Daily Herald, Los Angeles, CA
Daily Sentinel, Grand Junction, CO
Deming Headlight, Deming, NM
Eagle, Silver City, NM
El Paso Tribune, El Paso, TX
Examiner, San Francisco, CA
Florence Tribune, Florence, AZ
Holbrook Argus, Holbrook, AZ

Iowa City Press-Citizen, Iowa City, IA
Las Cruces Sun-News, Las Cruces, NM
Las Vegas Gazette, Las Vegas, NM
Las Vegas Optic, Las Vegas, NM
Mohave County Miner, Mineral Park, AZ
National Police Gazette
New Mexican Review, Santa Fe, NM
Oasis, Arizola, AZ
Pecos Valley Argus, Carlsbad, NM
San Francisco Examiner, San Francisco, CA
Santa Fe New Mexican, Santa Fe, NM
Sierra County Advocate, Kingston, NM
Silver City Enterprise, Silver City, NM
Southwest Sentinel, Silver City, NM
St. Johns Herald, St. Johns, AZ
Sulphur Valley News, Willcox, AZ (aka *Arizona Range News*)
Sun, New York City, NY
Tombstone Daily Epitaph, Tombstone, AZ
Tombstone Epitaph, Tombstone, AZ
Tombstone Prospector, Tombstone, AZ
Tombstone Weekly Epitaph, Tombstone, AZ
Tucson Citizen, Tucson, AZ
Weekly Journal-Miner, Prescott, AZ
Western Liberal, Lordsburg, NM
White Oaks Eagle, White Oaks, NM

BOOKS AND ARTICLES

Alexander, Bob. *Lawmen, Outlaws, and S.O.B.s.* Vol. 2, *Gunfighters of the Old Southwest.* Silver City, NM: High-Lonesome Books, 2004.

———. *Lynch Ropes & Long Shots: The Story of an Old West Train Robbery.* Silver City, NM: High-Lonesome Books, 2006.

Bailey, Lynn R. *Mines, Camps, Ranches, and Characters of the Dragoon Mountains.* Tucson: Westernlore Press, 2008.

———. *The "Unwashed Crowd" Stockmen and Ranches of the San Simon and Sulphur Springs Vallys, Arizona Territory 1870 to 1900.* Tucson: Westernlore, 2014.

Ball, Larry D. *United States Marshals of New Mexico and Arizona Territories: 1846–1912.* Albuquerque: University of New Mexico Press, 1982.

Block, Eugene B. *Great Train Robberies of the West.* New York: Coward-McCann, 1959.

Boessenecker, John. *When Law Was in the Holster: The Frontier Life of Bob Paul.* Norman: University of Oklahoma Press, 2012.

Born, Dewey E. "The Bisbee Massacre Cost Five Lives—Actually 11 Lives, after the Six Men Responsible Were Punished." *Wild West* 19, no. 1 (June 2006).

Brown, Wynne. *More Than Petticoats: Remarkable Arizona Women.* Guilford, CT: TwoDot Press, 2003.

Chaput, Donald. *The Odyssey of Burt Alvord.* Tucson: Westernlore Press, 2000.

Chaput, Donald, and Lynn R. Bailey. *Cochise County Stalwarts.* 2 vols. Tucson: Westernlore, 2000.

Collias, Joe G. *The Last of Steam.* Forest Park, IL: Heimburger House, 1960.

Denfield, Thomas. *Lost Treasure Trails.* New York: Grosset & Dunlap, 1954.

Dunham, Glenn. "The Cochise Train Robbery." *Cochise County Historical Journal or Quarterly,* Summer/Fall 1972.

Erwin, Allen A. *The Southwest of John H. Slaughter, 1841–1922: Pioneer, Cattleman, and Trail-Driver of Texas, the Pecos, and Arizona and Sheriff of Tombstone.* Glendale, CA: Arthur H. Clark and Company, 1965.

Fischer, David Hackett. *Historians' Fallacies: Toward a Logic of Historical Thought.* New York: Harper Perennial, 1970.

Glasscock, C. B. *Man-Hunt: Bandits and the Southern Pacific.* New York: Grosset & Dunlap, 1929.

Grassé, David. *The True Story of Notorious Arizona Outlaw Augustine Chacón.* Charleston, SC: History Press, 2021.

Haley, J. Evetts. *Jeff Milton, a Good Man with a Gun.* Norman: University of Oklahoma Press, 1948.

Hocking, Doug. *Terror on the Santa Fe Trail: Kit Carson and the Jicarilla Apache.* Essex, CT: TwoDot, 2019.

Klugness, Elizabeth J. *Prisoners in Petticoats: The Yuma Territorial Prison and Its Women.* Yuma: Sun Graphics Printing, 2016.

Lathrop, Gilbert A. *Rio Grande Glory Days.* San Marino, CA: Golden West Books, 1976.

Lehman, Stanley A. "1884 Bisbee Massacre Trials: The Prosecution's Strategy." *Cochise County Historical Journal* 49 (Fall–Winter 2019).

McDevitt, Kevin. *History of the St. James Hotel Cimarron, New Mexico.* Colorado Springs: Cimarron Press, 2019.

McWhorter, Frankie. *Cowboy Fiddler in Bob Wills' Band.* Edited by John R. Erickson. Denton: University of North Texas Press, 1997.

Myrick, David F. *New Mexico's Railroads: A Historical Survey.* Albuquerque: University of New Mexico Press, 2003 (1970).

———. *Railroads of Arizona.* Vol. 1, *The Southern Roads.* Berkeley, CA: Howell-North Books, 1975.

O'Neal, Bill. *The Arizona Rangers.* Austin: Eakin Press, 1987.

———. *Captain Harry Wheeler: Arizona Lawman.* Austin: Eakin Press, 2003.

Osterwald, Doris B. *Ticket to Toltec: A Mile by Mile Guide for the Cumbres and Toltec Scenic Railroad.* Lakewood, CO: Western Guideways, 1976.

Parsons, George W., and Lynn R. Bailey, eds. *The Devil Has Foreclosed, the Private Diary of George Whitwell Parsons: The Concluding Arizona Years, 1882–87.* Tucson: Westernlore, 1997.

Pumpelly, Raphael. *Across America and Asia.* New York: Leypoldt & Holt, 1870.

———. *A Journey by Stage Coach to Arizona.* New York: Henry Holt & Company, 1918.

Smith, Brad. *Fun on the Run: The Alvord-Stiles Gang of Cochise County.* Cochise, AZ: Brad Smith, 1999.

Traywick, Ben. *That Wicked Little Gringo: Story of Tombstone's John Slaughter.* Tombstone: Traywick, 2001.

Trimble, Marshall. "The Mysterious Case of the Vanishing Train Robbers." *True West,* November 2019.

Tulk, John "Rusty." *Ride 'em as They Come: The Life of John "Rusty" Tulk.* Deming, NM: NWJ, 2005.

Wheeler, Keith, and Ezra Bowen, eds. *The Railroaders.* New York: Time-Life Books, 1973.

Notes

INTRODUCTION

1. Gilbert A. Lathrop, *Rio Grande Glory Days* (San Marino, CA: Golden West Books, 1976), 344.
2. Ibid., 21 and 23.
3. "Passenger Train Wrecked Near Benson," *Tombstone Daily Epitaph*, August 15, 1889.
4. "Virgil W. Earp," *San Francisco Examiner*, May 27, 1882.
5. Kathy Klump of the Sulphur Valley Historical Society and the Chiricahua Regional Museum in Willcox, Arizona, informs me that although my source lists this as the *Sulphur Valley News* it is more correctly known as the *Arizona Range News*. She's almost always correct about such things.
6. "A.E. Stoeger, Hero," *Arizona Range News*, December 21, 1897.
7. "Another Daring Robbery," *Arizona Weekly Citizen*, February 25, 1888.
8. The town was named for Major Enoch Steen, who passed that way in 1856 with four companies of the First Regiment of US Dragoons on his way to Tucson to take formal possession of the Gadsden Purchase. The Southern Pacific Railroad, which named the town, was no better at getting names correctly spelled than was the *Tombstone Prospector*.

CHAPTER ONE

1. San Simon is pronounced "san see-moan."
2. Lathrop, *Rio Grande Glory Days*, 23.
3. Ibid., 27.
4. "The S.P. Train Robbery," *Black Range*, December 7, 1883.
5. Bob Alexander, *Lynch Ropes & Long Shots: The Story of an Old West Train Robbery* (Silver City: High Lonesome Books, 2006), 68–69.
6. Ibid., 14–15.
7. In some reports he is T. J. Hodgkin. Bob Alexander, who has studied the matter deeply, makes it George Hodgkins.
8. "The S.P. Train Robbery," *Black Range*, December 7, 1883; "Raid on a Railroad," *New Mexican Review*, December 6, 1883.
9. Alexander, *Lynch Ropes*, 16–18; "Train Robbers' Blood," *New Mexican Review*, March 13, 1884; "Lake Valley Waves," *Las Cruces Sun-News*, November 29, 1884.
10. "S.P. Train Robbery," *Black Range*, December 7, 1883.

11. *Santa Fe New Mexican*, November 27, 1883; Alexander, *Lynch Ropes*, 56; "Train Robbers' Blood," *New Mexican Review*, March 13, 1884; "Lake Valley Waves," *Las Cruces Sun-News*, November 29, 1884.

12. Lathrop, *Rio Grande Glory Days*, 28.

13. "The S.P. Train Robbery," *Black Range*, December 7, 1883.

14. CPI Inflation Calculator, https://www.officialdata.org/us/inflation/1883?amount=8800.

15. Alexander, *Lynch Ropes*, 21. In June 1883, Spence was working as a deputy sheriff in Georgetown, New Mexico, when he severely pistol-whipped Rodney O'Hara, killing him. He was convicted of manslaughter and sentenced to a five-year term in the Arizona Territorial Penitentiary. Less than eighteen months later he was granted a full pardon by the territorial governor. "Pete Spence," Wikipedia, https://en.wikipedia.org/wiki/Pete_Spence. If he killed the man in New Mexico, why did he end up in the Arizona Territorial Prison at Yuma? Was he not yet in prison in December 1883?

16. Senator Barry Goldwater's uncle.

17. *New Mexican Review*, December 20, 1883.

18. Stanley A. Lehman, "1884 Bisbee Massacre Trials: The Prosecution's Strategy." *Cochise County Historical Journal* 49 (Fall–Winter 2019): 16–37; Dewey E. Born, "The Bisbee Massacre Cost Five Lives—Actually 11 Lives, after the Six Men Responsible Were Punished," *Wild West* 19, no. 1 (June 2006): 60–61; George W. Parsons and Lynn R. Bailey, eds., *The Devil Has Foreclosed, the Private Diary of George Whitwell Parsons: The Concluding Arizona Years, 1882–87* (Tucson: Westernlore, 1997); Alexander, *Lynch Ropes*, 36–48.

19. "Train Robbers' Blood," *New Mexican Review*, March 13, 1884

20. "Mitch Lee Captured," *Las Vegas Gazette*, January 23, 1884.

21. "Train Robbers' Blood," *New Mexican Review*, March 13, 1884; "Frank Taggert in Irons," *Albuquerque Journal*, January 15, 1884.

22. "Cleveland Captured," *New Mexican Review*, January 3, 1884; "Cleveland Captured," *Las Vegas Gazette*, January 3, 1884.

23. Frankie McWhorter, *Cowboy Fiddler in Bob Wills' Band*, ed. John R. Erickson (Denton: University of North Texas Press, 1997), 109.

24. "Frank Taggert in Irons," *Albuquerque Journal*, January 15, 1884; "Cleveland Captured," *Las Vegas Gazette*, January 3, 1884; "George Cleveland," *New Mexican Review*, January 3, 1884; "Captures of 1883 Outlaws," *Black Range*, January 18, 1884; "George Cleveland," *Black Range*, January 18, 1884; *New Mexican Review*, January 10, 1884; "Kid Joy," *Albuquerque Journal*, January 23, 1884.

25. Alexander, *Lynch Ropes*, 75.

26. Ibid., 76.

27. Ibid., 84.

28. "Frank Taggert in Irons," *Albuquerque Journal*, January 15, 1884.

29. Ibid.

30. Ibid.

31. "Train Robbers' Blood," *New Mexican Review*, March 13, 1884.

32. Ibid.

33. "Kit Joy Captured," *New Mexican Review*, March 27, 1884.

34. Alexander, *Lynch Ropes*, 123.

35. Ibid., 132–35; "Kit Joy Captured," *New Mexican Review*, March 27, 1884.

36. *Las Cruces Sun-News*, November 15, 1884.

37. "Lake Valley Waves," *Las Cruces Sun-News*, November 29, 1884.

38. Alexander, *Lynch Ropes*, 167. Obviously, the time line just doesn't work. Perhaps the Pete Spence who beat a man to death in New Mexico in June 1883 was a different man from the one serving time in Yuma Penitentiary in December 1883, though he might have been the one running the dance hall in Lake Valley in November 1884.

39. *Las Cruces Sun-News*, November 29, 1884.

40. *Albuquerque Evening Democrat*, November 25, 1884.

41. "Kit Joy Released," *Sierra County Advocate*, April 3, 1896.

42. *Santa Fe New Mexican*, June 22, 1885.

43. "Pleading Guilty to Violation of Liquor Laws," *Arizona Daily Star*, May 30, 1926.

44. Eugene B. Block, *Great Train Robberies of the West* (New York: Coward-McCann, 1959).

45. "Reward Money," *Sierra County Advocate*, May 9, 1885.

CHAPTER TWO

1. David F. Myrick, *Railroads of Arizona*, vol. 1, *The Southern Roads* (Berkeley, CA: Howell-North Books, 1975), 446–48.

2. Ibid., 363–401.

3. Ibid., 449, 182.

4. "Riot at Crittenden," *Arizona Daily Star*, May 17, 1882.

5. Raphael Pumpelly, *Across America and Asia* (New York: Leypoldt & Holt, 1870); *A Journey by Stage Coach to Arizona* (New York: Henry Holt & Company, 1918).

6. Myrick, *Railroads of Arizona*, 1:286.

7. "A Frontier Pleasantry," *Weekly Arizona Miner*, May 14, 1882.

CHAPTER THREE

1. Thomas Penfield, *Lost Treasure Trails* (New York: Grosset & Dunlap, 1954), 100.

2. Ibid., 99–102.

3. "Another Express Robbery," *Arizona Weekly Citizen*, April 30, 1887. This account makes it clear that the outlaws lacked torpedoes and used cartridges instead.

4. "Another Account," *Arizona Weekly Citizen*, April 30, 1887.

5. Ibid.

6. "World News," *Daily Tombstone Epitaph*, April 29, 1887.

7. "Another Account," *Arizona Weekly Citizen*, April 30, 1887.

8. Today the tribe calls itself Tohono O'odham, the Desert People.

9. "World News," *Daily Tombstone Epitaph*, April 29, 1887.

10. *Arizona Weekly Journal-Miner*, May 4, 1887.

11. John Boessenecker, *When Law Was in the Holster: The Frontier Life of Bob Paul* (Norman: University of Oklahoma Press, 2012), 343.

12. "Robbers Captured," *Daily Tombstone Epitaph*, May 5, 1887.

13. Marshall Trimble, "The Mysterious Case of the Vanishing Train Robbers," *True West*, November 2019 (emphasis added).

14. The Gem Saloon was where John Wesley Hardin would one day be shot from behind.

15. Boessenecker, *When Law Was in the Holster*, 341–42.

16. "Train Robberies," *Tombstone Epitaph*, August 20, 1887, story copied from *Southwest Sentinel*.

17. "They Do It Again," *Tombstone Epitaph*, August 13, 1887, story copied from the *Tucson Citizen* of August 12; "A Second Hold Up," *Arizona Weekly Citizen*, August 13, 1887.

18. *Tombstone Epitaph*, August 13, 1887; "West-Bound Train Robbed Again," *Arizona Silver Belt*, August 13, 1887.

19. "Held Up Again," *Clifton Clarion*, August 17, 1887.

20. A blasting powder consisting of nitroglycerin, sodium nitrate, sulfur, rosin, and sometimes kieselguhr.

21. "West-Bound Train Robbed Again," *Arizona Silver Belt*, August 13, 1887.

22. "Held Up Again," *Clifton Clarion*, August 17, 1887; "Robbers," *Arizona Weekly Citizen*, August 20, 1887.

23. *Arizona Weekly Citizen*, August 27, 1887.

24. *Tombstone Epitaph*, August 13, 1887.

25. *Arizona Weekly Enterprise*, August 20, 1887.

26. "West-Bound Train Robbed Again," *Arizona Silver Belt*, August 13, 1887.

27. Fred Dodge with Carolyn Lake, ed., *Undercover for Wells Fargo: The Unvarnished Recollections of Fred Dodge* (New York: Ballantine Books, 1973), 83–87.

28. *St. Johns Herald*, August 25, 1887.

29. *Arizona Weekly Citizen*, September 24, 1887.

30. "The Texas Train Robbery," *Arizona Weekly Star*, October 20, 1887.

31. Ibid.

32. "He Didn't Squeal," *Tucson Citizen*, November 5, 1887.

33. *Clifton Clarion*, November 9, 1887.

34. "Another Arrest Made for Train Robbing," *Tucson Citizen*, December 10, 1887.

35. *Clifton Clarion*, November 9, 1887.

36. "Caboose 44," *Arizona Daily Star*, January 24, 1888.

37. *Arizona Weekly Star*, January 19, 1888.

38. "Train Robbery Case," *Mohave County Miner*, January 28, 1888.

39. "Caboose 44," *Arizona Daily Star*, January 24, 1888.

40. *Tombstone Prospector*, April 14, 1887; Allen A. Erwin, *The Southwest of John H. Slaughter, 1841–1922: Pioneer, Cattleman, and Trail-Driver of Texas, the Pecos, and Arizona and Sheriff of Tombstone* (Glendale, CA: Arthur H. Clark and Company, 1965), 221.

41. Erwin, *Southwest of John H. Slaughter*, 226–27.

42. "Bob Paul on the Trail," *St. Johns Herald*, March 29, 1888; Boessenecker, *When Law Was in the Holster*, 346.

43. "The Train Robbers," *Arizona Weekly Star*, March 8, 1888.

44. Boessenecker, *When Law Was in the Holster*, 346.

CHAPTER FOUR

1. "Train Thieves," *Daily Herald*, March 26, 1888.
2. "The Train Robbers," *Arizona Weekly Star*, March 8, 1888; "Train Thieves," *Daily Herald*, March 26, 1888.
3. "Worse Than Robbery," *Arizona Republican*, February 27, 1895.
4. "Engineer Harper," *Arizona Weekly Enterprise*, February 25, 1888.
5. "Trainmen a Disgrace," *Tombstone Epitaph*, March 3, 1888.
6. "Another Daring Robbery," *Tombstone Epitaph*, February 25, 1888; "Two Men Rob the West Bound Express," *Arizona Weekly Citizen*, February 25, 1888; "Held Up," *Arizona Weekly Star*, March 1, 1888.
7. "Train Thieves," *Daily Herald*, March 26, 1888.
8. Ibid.
9. "Posse in Mexican Dungeon," *St. Johns Herald*, March 15, 1888.
10. "Detective Paul," *St. Johns Herald*, April 5, 1888.
11. "Stein's Pass Train Robbers," *Arizona Weekly Citizen*, March 24, 1888.
12. "Detective Paul," *St. Johns Herald*, April 5, 1888.
13. "Stein's Pass Train Robbers," *Tombstone Epitaph*, March 24, 1888; "Stein's Pass Train Robbers," *Arizona Weekly Citizen*, March 24, 1888; "Gallant Ex-Sheriff Paul," *Tombstone Epitaph*, March 24, 1888.
14. Marshal H. J. Burns, "Robbers Roasted Out. How Sheriff Paul Cooked Three Outlaws of Stein's Pass," *Examiner*, April 22, 1888.
15. "Detective Paul," *St. Johns Herald*, April 5, 1888.

CHAPTER FIVE

1. "Railroads Ask for Authority to Cross the Border," *Tucson Citizen*, May 11, 1888.
2. Rudyard Kipling, "The Young British Soldier," in *Rudyard Kipling: Complete Verse, Definitive Edition* (New York: Random House, 1989), 415.
3. Brad Smith, *Fun on the Run: The Alvord-Stiles Gang of Cochise County* (Cochise, AZ: Brad Smith, 1999), 4; "Jean Tullier, Alias J.J. Taylor, Delivered to the Mexican Authorities at Nogales," *Arizona Weekly Star*, June 7, 1888.
4. "Confession of J.J. Taylor. Murderers of Employees of the Sonora Railroad," *Arizona Silver Belt*, May 26, 1888.
5 Boessenecker, *When Law Was in the Holster*, 366.
6. "Train Robbery," *Tucson Citizen*, May 19, 1888; "Train Robbery in Mexico," *Arizona Daily Star*, May 13, 1888; "Shot on the Rail," *San Francisco Examiner*, May 13, 1888.
7. "Sheriff Shaw," *Tucson Citizen*, May 26, 1888.
8. "Train Robbery," *Tucson Citizen*, May 19, 1888; "Train Robbery in Mexico," *Arizona Daily Star*, May 13, 1888; "Shot on the Rail," *San Francisco Examiner*, May 13, 1888.
9. "Confession of J.J. Taylor. Murderers of Employees of the Sonora Railroad," *Arizona Silver Belt*, May 26, 1888.
10. "A Train Robbery," *San Francisco Chronicle*, May 13, 1888; "Wanted to Kill Him," *Tucson Citizen*, June 20, 1888.
11. "Robbers Described," *Arizona Silver Belt*, June 2, 1888.

12. "Taylor Makes a Confession," *St. Johns Herald*, May 24, 1888; "Naming the Guilty," *San Francisco Examiner*, May 14, 1888; "Taylor's Confession," *Arizona Weekly Citizen*, May 23, 1888; "The Train Robbers," *Arizona Daily Star*, May 22, 1888.

13. Erwin, *Southwest of John H. Slaughter*, 233.

14. Smith, *Fun on the Run*, 4.

15. Available on YouTube at https://www.youtube.com/watch?v=c1Umrej7Rvg, the Walt Disney episode of *Texas John Slaughter*, "A Holster Full of Law," captured something of the real nature of Sheriff Slaughter's deputies, except that Alvord was bald and ugly.

16. "The Nogales Robbers," *Tucson Citizen*, June 16, 1888.

17. Ibid.

18. Ibid.; "The Train Robbers," *Arizona Daily Star*, June 14, 1888.

19. "Train Robbers Killed and Captured," *Arizona Weekly Citizen*, June 16, 1888.

20. "Frederico Agua Zarca Train Robber Shot," *Tombstone Weekly Epitaph*, May 24, 1893. Thanks to Kathy Klump of the Sulphur Springs Valley Historical Society and Chiricahua Museum in Willcox for this and other items related to this case.

21. *Ranger News*, May 24, 1893.

22. "Train Robber Executed in Mexico," *Arizona Weekly Star*, August 30, 1888; *Santa Fe New Mexican*, May 17, 1889; "Not Hung Yet," *Arizona Silver Belt*, May 25, 1889; "Tallier Was Shot," *Arizona Weekly Citizen*, October 5, 1889; "As Many Lives as a Cat," *Arizona Silver Belt*, October 12, 1889; "J.J. Taylor Shot," *Arizona Weekly Citizen*, January 4, 1890.

23. *Arizona Range News*, May 24, 1893.

24. "Mr. Lewis Martin's Bill," *Arizona Daily Star*, March 5, 1889.

25. "Passenger Train Wrecked near Benson," *Tombstone Daily Epitaph*, August 15, 1889.

26. "Why the Robbers Failed to Rob the Train," *Arizona Weekly Journal-Miner*, August 21, 1889.

27. "Held Up!," *Arizona Weekly Citizen*, October 6, 1894.

28. "Daring Work of Bandits," *Arizona Daily Star*, October 2, 1894.

29. Dialog has been provided from the accounts of "Held Up!," *Arizona Weekly Citizen*, October 6, 1894, and "Daring Work of Bandits," *Arizona Daily Star*, October 2, 1894.

30. "Held Up!," *Arizona Weekly Citizen*, October 6, 1894.

31. Ibid.

32. William M. Breakenridge, *Helldorado: Bringing the Law to the Mesquite*, ed. Richard Maxwell Brown (Lincoln: University of Nebraska Press, 1992), 383–85. Originally published in 1928.

33. "Daring Work of Bandits," *Arizona Daily Star*, October 2, 1894.

34. "Rogers Under Arrest," *Arizona Weekly Star*, October 11, 1894.

35. *Cocoino Sun*, October 18, 1894.

36. Breakenridge, *Helldorado*, 405–6.

37. "Rogers Sentenced to Death," *Arizona Weekly Star*, December 13, 1894.

38. "He Still Lives," *Arizona Republic*, February 9, 1895.

39. "That Other Kid," *Arizona Republic*, May 19, 1895.

40. "Rogers in Jail Awaiting Appeal," *Arizona Silver Belt*, June 15, 1895.

41. "Rogers Must Be Hanged," *Arizona Republic*, June 25, 1896.

42. "Oscar Rogers," *Arizona Republic*, August 19, 1896.

43. "Rogers Will Not Hang," *Arizona Republic*, September 5, 1896.

44. *Arizona Republic*, September 13, 1896.

45. Breakenridge, *Helldorado*, 385.

CHAPTER SIX

1. Personal communication, letter from Kathy Klump, February 25, 2021.

2. "A Disappointed Crowd," *Tombstone Weekly Epitaph*, January 14, 1894.

3. Rock and rye was a popular Old West drink consisting rock candy dissolved in rye whiskey.

4. "Grant Wheeler," *Tombstone Weekly Epitaph*, February 4, 1894.

5. Some will say Chinaman is an insult, but how can it be? Englishman, Dutchman, and Frenchman are not.

6. Personal communication, letter from Kathy Klump, February 25, 2021; "Cowboy vs. Chinaman," *Arizona Range News*, May 15, 1894, clipping courtesy of the Sulphur Springs Valley Historical Society.

7. "Burt Alvord Is in Custody," *Bisbee Daily Review*, September 12, 1902.

8. "Held Up!," *Arizona Weekly Citizen*, October 6, 1894.

9. "Train Robbery," *Tombstone Epitaph*, February 3, 1895.

10. "A Close Call," *St. Johns Herald*, November 8, 1894.

11. "A Close Call," *Arizona Weekly Star*, October 28, 1894.

12. "Grant Wheeler Turns Himself In," *Arizona Weekly Star*, November 8, 1894.

13. "The Return of Marshal Mead—Description of the Two Men and Their Probable Whereabouts," *Arizona Weekly Citizen*, February 9, 1895.

14. "Another Arizona Train Robbery," *Arizona Republic*, February 1, 1895.

15. "Left Silvery Trails," *Morning Call*, February 1, 1895.

16. "Sheriff Fly," *Arizona Weekly Citizen*, February 9, 1895. Camilus S. Fly was the famed Tombstone photographer whose studio appeared in the 1993 movie Tombstone as the backdrop to the gunfight on Fremont Street near the O.K. Corral. In 1886, Fly went along with General Crook to Mexico and photographer Geronimo and his warriors.

17. Personal communication, Kathy Klump, Chiricahua Regional Museum and Sulphur Springs Valley Historical Society.

18. *Playa* is Spanish for "beach." In the American Southwest it refers to a dry, or usually dry, lake bed. The Willcox Playa is full of beautiful, white quartz sand. It is all that remains of Lake Cochise, which filled up at the end of the last ice age. During heavy rans it fills, making a very shallow lake. Parts are always wet, and sandhill cranes nest here in the winter. The railroad runs through the northern extent of the playa.

19. "Held Up!," *Arizona Weekly Citizen*, October 6, 1894.

20. "Another Arizona Train Robbery," *Arizona Republic*, February 1, 1895.

21. *Tombstone Epitaph*, February 3, 1895.

22. Wells, Fargo and Company were not always completely forthcoming concerning their losses. "Left Silvery Trails," *Morning Call*, February 1, 1895.

23. Ibid.

24. "Sheriff Fly," *Tombstone Epitaph*, February 3, 1895.

25. *Tombstone Epitaph*, February 3, 1895.

26. "Dies to Escape Arrest," *San Francisco Call*, April 29, 1895.

27. The Tucson papers thought his name was Bruce. "He Swore Much," *Arizona Weekly Citizen*, March 16, 1895.

28. "Worse Than Robbery," *Arizona Republican*, February 27, 1895.

29. Ibid.

30. "Heroic Brakeman," *Arizona Silver Belt*, March 2, 1895.

31. "He Swore Much," *Arizona Weekly Citizen*, March 16, 1895.

32. Ibid.

33. "Green as Grass," *Arizona Republican*, February 26, 1895.

34. Breakenridge, *Helldorado*, 400.

35. Ibid.

36. Ibid., 401–4.

37. "A Dead Train Robber," *Arizona Weekly Star*, May 2, 1895.

38. Breakenridge, *Helldorado*, 404–5.

39. "Dies to Escape Arrest," *San Francisco Call*, April 29, 1895.

40. *Tombstone Epitaph*, May 12, 1895.

41. *Arizona Republic*, September 5, 1896.

42. Breakenridge, *Helldorado*, 406.

43. "Robbers Foiled," *Eagle*, November 4, 1896.

CHAPTER SEVEN

1. "Beardless Boy Bandits," *Arizona Republic*, May 12, 1910.

2. "Shoot 'em Up Dick," *Arizona Weekly Citizen*, December 10, 1882.

3. "Shoot 'em Up Dick," *Arizona Silver Belt*, May 12, 1883.

4. Robert L. Thomas, "The Forgotten Pioneers: Chinese in Early Arizona," *Arizona Republic*, May 20, 1978. The original story ran in the *El Paso Herald* of January 12, 1900.

5. "Is It Black Jack?," *Weekly Journal-Miner*, August 30, 1899; "An Atrocious Murder," *Weekly-Journal Miner*, July 5, 1899.

6. "Killing of Billy King," *Tombstone Weekly Epitaph*, November 14, 1897; *Border Vidette*, December 11, 1897; "Billy King," *Florence Tribune*, December 18, 1897.

7. "Black Jack Says Burt Must Die," *Florence Tribune*, December 25, 1897.

8. "Stein's Pass Fluke," *Arizona Republic*, December 11, 1897.

9. "Another Hold-Up," *Las Vegas Daily Optic*, 10 December 1897.

10. Bob Alexander, *Lawmen, Outlaws, and S.O.B.s*, vol. 2, *Gunfighters of the Old Southwest* (Silver City, NM: High-Lonesome Books, 2004), 71. Courtesy of the Sulphur Springs Valley Historical Society.

11. "Another Hold-Up," *Las Vegas Daily Optic*, December 10, 1897.

12. "A.E. Stoeger, Hero," *Sulphur Valley News*, December 21, 1897.

13. "A Pipe Dream," *Santa Fe New Mexican*, December 20, 1897.

14. "Not Black Jack's Gang," *Albuquerque Journal*, December 16, 1897.

15. "Attempted Hold Up at Stein's Pass," *Arizona Range News*, December 14, 1897, on file at the Sulphur Springs Valley Historical Society.

16. In 1853, Boundary Commissioner John Russell Bartlett asserted that the range was called Peloncillo, which in Spanish means "Little Baldy." He claimed that this meant "Sugar Cone" in Spanish, although a sugar cone is Piloncillo.

17. "Train Robbers Captured," *Florence Tribune*, December 18, 1897.

18. "On Trial for Train Robbery," *Albuquerque Citizen*, March 7, 1898.

19. "Capture of Stein's Pass Train Robbers," *Arizona Range News*, December 21, 1897.

20. "On Trial for Train Robbery," *Albuquerque Citizen*, March 7, 1898.

21. "Not Turned Loose," *Western Liberal*, September 30, 1898.

22. "The Black Jack Gang," *Albuquerque Weekly Citizen*, May 4, 1901.

23. "Black Jack Gang," *Eagle*, November 25, 1896; "High Fives Gang," *Wikipedia*, https://en.wikipedia.org/wiki/High_Fives_Gang; "The 'Black Jack' Gang," *Albuquerque Weekly Citizen*, May 4, 1901.

24. "Black Jack's Gang," *Arizona Republic*, May 5, 1899.

25. Dan L. Thrapp, *Encyclopedia of Frontier Biography*, vol. 1 (Spokane: Arthur H. Clark and Company, 1988).

26. "A Robbery at Separ," *Deming Headlight*, July 24, 1896.

27. "Train Robbers Frustrated," *Santa Fe New Mexican*, October 3, 1896.

28. Nogales on the Mexican border is today in Santa Cruz County. In 1896, it was still in Pima County, which borders Cochise County on the west.

29. "Attempted Bank Robbery," *Arizona Silver Belt*, August 13, 1896.

30. "Bank Robbers" and "Deputy Sheriff Alvord Gives a Detailed Account of the Chase," *Arizona Weekly Citizen*, August 22, 1896.

31. "Train Robbers Frustrated," *Santa Fe New Mexican*, October 3, 1896.

32. "Separ Robbed Again," *Santa Fe New Mexican*, November 2, 1896.

33. "One Bandit Killed," *Albuquerque Journal*, November 25, 1896.

34. "Reporter," *Albuquerque Journal*, October 1, 1899. Lynn R. Bailey wrote that McGinnis was "none other than Elzy Lay, a member of the Wild Buch of Robbers Roost," which would tie him to Butch Cassidy. Franks would have been G. W. Franks, who was probably Will Carver. It seems a bit of a stretch to this writer. Lynn R. Bailey, *The "Unwashed Crowd": Stockmen and Ranches of the San Simon and Sulphur Springs Valleys, Arizona Territory 1870 to 1900* (Tucson: Westernlore, 2014), 266.

35. "Ketchum Pays the Penalty," *Santa Fe New Mexican*, April 26, 1901.

36. "The 'Black Jack' Gang," *Albuquerque Weekly Citizen*, May 4, 1901; "Black Jack Gang," *Eagle*, November 25, 1896; "High Fives Gang," *Wikipedia*, https://en.wikipedia .org/wiki/High_Fives_Gang.

37. "Ketchum Pays the Penalty," *Santa Fe New Mexican*, April 26, 1901.

38. "Train Is Dynamited," *Daily Sentinel*, July 13, 1899.

39. "Reporter," *Albuquerque Journal*, October 1, 1899.

40. *White Oaks Eagle*, July 20, 1899.

41. "Train Is Dynamited," *Daily Sentinel*, July 13, 1899.

42. "The Train Robbery," *New Mexican Review*, July 20, 1899.

43. "McGinnis Convicted," *Arizona Republic*, October 9, 1899.

44. "Ketchum Passes Through," *Las Vegas Daily Optic*, July 21, 1899.

45. Kevin McDevitt, *History of the St. James Hotel Cimarron, New Mexico* (Colorado Springs: Cimarron Press, 2019), 6.

46. "Ketchum Passes Through," *Las Vegas Daily Optic*, July 21, 1899.

47. "Body Shipped to San Angelo," *Las Vegas Daily Optic*, July 25, 1899.

48. "Sam Ketchum's Picture," *Las Vegas Daily Optic*, August 3, 1899.

49. "Tom Ketchum," *Holbrook Argus*, January 27, 1900.

50. Ibid.

51. *Pecos Vally Argus*, September 1, 1899.

52. "Ketchum," *Arizona Daily Star*, March 31, 1901.

53. "Surely Tom Ketchum," *Las Vegas Daily Optic*, August 25, 1899.

54. "Black Jack Captured," *Florence Tribune*, September 2, 1899.

55. "An Atrocious Murder," *Weekly Journal-Miner*, July 5, 1899.

56. "Still on the Search," *Weekly Arizona Journal-Miner*, July 19, 1899.

57. "Is It Black Jack?," *Weekly Journal-Miner*, August 30, 1899.

58. "The Original Article," *Weekly Journal-Miner*, September 6, 1899.

59. "Tom Ketchum," *Arizona Silver Belt*, June 28, 1900.

60. "A Bod Attempt," *Tombstone Prospector*, October 10, 1899.

61. "Black Jack Convicted," *Albuquerque Journal*, September 9, 1900.

62. "Tom Ketchum," *Holbrook Argus*, December 2, 1899.

63. "Tom Ketchum," *Arizona Silver Belt*, June 28, 1900.

64. *Arizona Republic*, May 5, 1899.

65. *Arizona Silver Belt*, September 27, 1900.

66. "Ketchum's Journey to Death," *Arizona Republic*, April 24, 1901.

67. "Ketchum Pay the Penalty," *Santa Fe New Mexican*, April 26, 1901.

68. Mark 6:22 and 24, King James Bible.

69. "Ketchum Pays the Penalty," *Santa Fe New Mexican*, April 26, 1901.

70. "A Very Heavy Man," *Albuquerque Journal*, April 28, 1901.

Chapter Eight

1. "That Train Robbery, All for an Empty Safe Which They Couldn't Open. Many Bisbeeites Have Thrills," *Bisbee Daily Review*, September 8, 1916.

2. David Grassé, *The True Story of Notorious Arizona Outlaw Augustine Chacón* (Charleston, SC: History Press, 2021), 119.

3. Donald Chaput and Lynn R. Bailey, *Cochise County Stalwarts*, vol. 2 (Tucson: Westernlore, 2000), 140–41.

4. Lynn R. Bailey, *Mines, Camps, Ranches and Characters of the Dragoon Mountains* (Tucson: Westernlore Press, 2008), 123–24; Glenn Dunham, "The Cochise Train Robbery," *Cochise County Historical Journal or Quarterly*, Summer/Fall 1972, 3.

5. Chaput and Bailey, *Cochise County Stalwarts*, 2:140–41.

6. Donald Chaput, *The Odyssey of Burt Alvord* (Tucson: Westernlore Press, 2000), 10.

7. Erwin, *Southwest of John H. Slaughter*, 233.

8. Donald Chaput and Lynn R. Bailey, *Cochise County Stalwarts*, vol. 1 (Tucson: Westernlore, 2000), 7–8.

9. "Burt Alvord is in Custory." *Bisbee Daily Review*, 12 September 1902.

10. Kathy Klump, personal communication, June 2022. There is no better expert on Willcox than Ms. Klump. The newspapers always get the names wrong.

11. "Killing of Billy King," *Tombstone Weekly Epitaph*, November 14, 1897; "Burt Alvord—Billy King," *Border Vidette*, December 11, 1897; "Billy King," *Florence Tribune*, December 18, 1897; Erwin, *Southwest of John H. Slaughter*, 244; "Fatal Shooting," *Sulphur Valley News*, November 16, 1897.

12. "Burt Kills a Mexican," *Florence Tribune*, May 14, 1898; "Black Jack Says Burt Must Die," *Florence Tribune*, December 25, 1897.

13. "Train Robbers in Arizona," *Railway and Engineering Review* 39 (September 1899): 513; "The Hold-Up," *Tombstone Weekly Epitaph*, September 17, 1899; "Pursuit of Bandits," *Arizona Republic*, September 12, 1899; Smith, *Fun on the Run*, 4–10.

14. "Bold Train Robbery," *Arizona Republic*, September 11, 1899.

15. "Sensational Case," *Tombstone Weekly Epitaph*, March 4, 1900.

16. Ibid.

17. "More Testimony in the Cochise Hold-Up," *Tombstone Weekly Epitaph*, March 4, 1900.

18. "Sensational Case," *Tombstone Weekly Epitaph*, March 4, 1900.

19. Captured after the February 1900 Fairbank robbery attempt, the Owens (Owings, Owints) brothers provided the information that Alvord's plan for that robbery was to alibi them as playing cards in the backroom of a saloon. It seems likely he would have used a similar alibi for the Cochise robbery. "A Confession of the Fairbank Train Robbery," *Tombstone Weekly Epitaph*, October 14, 1900.

20. I believe that Kathy Klump of the Sulphur Springs Valley Historical Society and Chiricahua Mountain Museum in Willcox told me this some years ago. I can't locate my notes.

21. "Bold Train Robbery," *Arizona Republic*, September 11, 1899; "Train Robbers in Arizona," 513; "The Hold-Up," *Tombstone Weekly Epitaph*, September 17, 1899; "Pursuit of Bandits," *Arizona Republic*, September 12, 1899; Smith, *Fun on the Run*, 4–10.

22. "More Testimony in the Cochise Hold-Up," *Tombstone Weekly Epitaph*, March 4, 1900.

23. "Some Theories Regarding the Supposed Cochise Robbers," *Tombstone Weekly Epitaph*, September 17, 1899.

24. "No Trace, Lost at Willcox," *Tombstone Weekly Epitaph*, September 17, 1899.

25. "Pursuit of Bandits," *Arizona Republic*, September 12, 1899.

26. "The Trail Lost," *Arizona Daily Star*, September 19, 1899.

27. "Detective J.N. Thacker Surprised Burt Alvord of Willcox," *Florence Tribune*, March 3, 1900.

28. "An Outlaw Captured," *Arizona Republic*, October 25, 1899; "Three-Fingered Jack in Jail," *Arizona Range News*, July 31, 1894; "Three-Fingered Jack," *Arizona Republic*, November 6, 1899.

29. "A Fairbanks Hold-Up," *Arizona Republic*, February 16, 1900.

30. Kathy Klump, Sulphur Spring Valley Historical Society, has court documents that show the correct spelling of the name as Owings.

31. Bailey, *Mines, Camps, Ranches and Characters of the Dragoon Mountains*, 124.

32. This is a Spanish variant spelling of *Quixote*, as in Don Quixote, meaning a champion or defender. Presumably, Billy Stiles meant the Quijotoa Mountains in Pima County.

33. Smith, *Fun on the Run*.

34. Now known as Middle March Pass between Pearce and Tombstone.

35. "Details of the Fairbank Hold-Up," *Copper Era and Morenci Leader*, April 12, 1900.

36. "Owing's Story," *Tombstone Weekly Epitaph*, October 14, 1900.

37. There is some confusion about what direction the train was traveling, north or south. If Milton got the telegram at Imuris, he must have come from there to Benson and been returning to Nogales. Since he got the message at Imuris, many writers think he was headed north from Nogales to Benson. However, three contemporary sources all say that after Milton was wounded the train "backed to Benson," indicating it went backward to the north. The train was carrying mail, which is more likely to have come from Benson and the Southern Pacific Railroad than from Mexico. The *Weekly Journal-Miner* said that it was southbound from Benson to Nogales. "A Hold-Up at Benson," *Weekly Journal-Miner*, February 21, 1900. The *Arizona Republic*, apparently quoting from the same press release, says the same. "A Fairbanks Hold-Up," *Arizona Republic*, February 16, 1900. The train schedule for the New Mexico and Arizona Railroad published on February 10, 1900, gives the train's departure from Benson at 5:30 p.m. and its arrival at Fairbank as 6:13 p.m. Going north, arrivals are in the morning. "New Mex. & Ariz. & Son. Ry," *Oasis*, February 10, 1900.

38. "Some Examples Made of Arizona Outlaws," *Arizona Republican*, October 18, 1900.

39. The *Epitaph* reported that three buckshot were removed from Jack Dunlap. "Three-Fingered Jack," *Tombstone Weekly Epitaph*, February 25, 1900. The newspapers at the time reported that Jeff Milton used a pistol or a Winchester rifle to fight the outlaws. Since buckshot was removed from Jack and Jeff was the only one shooting at him, I conclude that he must have started out with a shotgun. Milton later reported that he was annoyed that Bravo Juan had stolen his pistol, apparently taking it from his hand. *Arizona Daily Star*, February 21, 1900.

40. "A Fairbanks Hold-Up," *Arizona Republic*, February 16, 1900; "A Hold Up," *Tombstone Weekly Epitaph*, February 18, 1900.

41. "The Alvord Case in Hands of Jury," *Bisbee Daily Review*, July 15, 1903.

42. Names change over time. I can no longer identify Sycamore Spring. I assume it was one of the springs near Middle March Pass. "Tom Broderick," *Arizona Daily Star*, February 21, 1900; "A Fairbanks Hold-Up," *Graham Guardian*, February 23, 1900.

43. Tom Broderick," *Arizona Daily Star*, February 21, 1900; J. Evetts Haley, *Jeff Milton, a Good Man with a Gun* (Norman: University of Oklahoma Press, 1948); "Some Examples Made of Arizona Outlaws," *Arizona Republican*, October 18, 1900; Smith, *Fun on the Run*; "A Fairbanks Hold-Up," *Arizona Republic*, February 16, 1900; "A Hold Up," *Tombstone Weekly Epitaph*, February 18, 1900.

44. "Former Plot Revealed," *Tombstone Weekly Epitaph*, March 4, 1900; "Posse Bring Two Charged with the Hold-Up," *Tombstone Weekly Epitaph*, February 25, 1900.

45. "Cachise" is the old spelling of Cochise.

46. "Reign of Terror,." *Arizona Daily Star*, April 8, 1900.

47. "Burts Captured in Utah," *Oasis*, April 14, 1900.

48. "Paid the Penalty," *Tombstone Weekly Epitaph*, November 18, 1900; "Plea for Two Lives," *Arizona Republic*, July 25, 1900; "The Tightened Noose," *Arizona Republic*, July 27, 1900.

49. "Returned the Keys—Letter," *Oasis*, April 28, 1900.

50. "The Train Robbers," *Arizona Daily Star*, June 8, 1900.

51. Ibid.

52. "Stiles on the Interview," *Florence Tribune*, September 1, 1900; "Burt Alvord's Skull," *Arizona Republic*, November 15, 1900.

53. "Stiles Surrenders," *Oasis*, July 7, 1900; "Stiles in Town," *Arizona Daily Star*, July 3, 1900; "Stiles to Yuma," *Arizona Daily Star*, July 10, 1900.

54. "A Confession of the Fairbank Train Robbery," *Tombstone Weekly Epitaph*, October 14, 1900; "Some Examples Made of Arizona Outlaws," *Arizona Republican*, October 18, 1900; "Three of the Fairbank Hold Up, Off to Penitentiary," *Arizona Weekly Journal-Miner*, October 24, 1900.

55. "United States vs. William Downing," *Tucson Citizen*, April 6, 1901.

56. "Proceedings of the Court," *Cochise Review*, December 8, 1900; "The First of the Cochise Train Cases on Trial," *Tombstone Weekly Epitaph*, December 9, 1900; "Matt Burts in Court, Creates a Sensation," *Tombstone Weekly Epitaph*, December 9, 1900; "Matt Burts Sentenced," *Cochise Review*, December 22, 1900; "Stiles Testimony," *Cochise Review*, December 15, 1900; "Cut Out Stiles," *Cochise Review*, December 22, 1900; "Downing Verdict," *Arizona Daily Star*, December 14, 1900.

57. "Change the Law," *Tombstone Weekly Epitaph*, December 30, 1900.

58. "Cut Out Stiles," *Cochise Review*, December 22, 1900; "Downing Verdict," *Arizona Daily Star*, December 14, 1900.

59. "Billy Stiles Again," *Cochise Review*, January 26, 1901.

60. "Matt Burts Pardoned," *Arizona Republic*, April 18, 1901.

61. "Burt Alvord," *Tucson Citizen*, March 8, 1901, pp. 1 and 4; "Alvord Again," *Tombstone Weekly Epitaph*, March 10, 1901; "Alvord at It Again," *Arizona Republic*, March 13, 1901; "Alvord Again," *Cochise Review*, March 9, 1901; "Henry Shwink," *Arizona Silver Belt*, April 25, 1901.

62. Bill O'Neal, *The Arizona Rangers* (Austin: Eakin Press, 1987), 26–29.

63. Grassé, *True Story of Notorious Arizona Outlaw Augustine Chacón*.

64. "Burt Alvord," *Tucson Citizen*, March 8, 1901, pp. 1 and 4; "Alvord Again," *Tombstone Weekly Epitaph*, March 10, 1901; "Alvord at It Again," *Arizona Republic*, March 13, 1901; "Alvord Again," *Cochise Review*, March 9, 1901; "Henry Shwink," *Arizona Silver Belt*, April 25, 1901.

65. "Burt Alvord May Come In," *Tucson Citizen*, May 1, 1901; "Alvord May Come In," *Arizona Republic*, May 13, 1901.

66. "Alvord Seen," *Tombstone Weekly Epitaph*, July 14, 1901.

67. "The Alvord Story," *Arizona Republic*, December 2, 1901.

68. "Alvord, Bravo John & the Rurales," *Weekly Journal-Miner*, February 26, 1902; "Probably a Myth," *Bisbee Daily Review*, February 25, 1902; "Smooth Escape," *Graham Guardian*, March 7, 1902.

69. "Particulars of Train Robbery," *Tombstone Weekly Epitaph*, September 7, 1902.

70. "Burt Alvord Is in Custody: Surrenders to Sheriff Lewis at Naco," *Bisbee Daily Review*, September 12, 1902.

71. Ibid.; "Burt Alvord," *Tucson Citizen*, September 11, 1902; Grassé, *True Story of Notorious Arizona Outlaw Augustine Chacón*, 132–47.

72. "Alvord Is Innocent: At Least He Says So, and He Ought to Know," *Arizona Republic*, September 18, 1902.

73. "Burt Alvord's Case," *Arizona Republic*, December 4, 1902.

74. "Burt Alvord Indicted," *Arizona Sentinel*, July 15, 1903; "Alvord Indicted," *Arizona Republic*, July 12, 1902; "Burt Alvord," *Arizona Daily Star*, December 5, 1902.

75. "The Alvord Case in Hands of Jury," *Bisbee Daily Review*, July 15, 1903.

76. "Stiles Loses First Inning," *Bisbee Daily Review*, December 12, 1903.

77. "Burt Alvord Has Pled Guilty," *Bisbee Daily Review*, December 9, 1903; "Alvord Pleads Guilty Gets Two Years at Yuma," *Tucson Citizen*, December 10, 1903; "The Passing of Alvord," *Bisbee Daily Review*, December 10, 1903; "Returned to Tombstone Alvord and Stiles Trials," *Tucson Citizen*, December 7, 1903.

78. "Stiles and Alvord Again Break Jail," *Arizona Daily Star*, December 16, 1903; "The Way It Was Done," *Arizona Republic*, December 18, 1903; "Not a Word from the Escapes," *Bisbee Daily Review*, December 17, 1903.

79. "Tener Was Not in Tucson: That Robbery of $8000," *Tucson Citizen*, March 7, 1904.

80. "Capt Rynning Has Returned," *Bisbee Daily Review*, February 18, 1904.

81. "Bullion Found and Returned," *Arizona Sentinel*, March 9, 1904.

82. "Was Not Game," *Border Vidette*, February 27, 1904.

83. "Alvord's Sentence When It Expired," *Arizona Republic*, October 25, 1905.

84. "Ranger Brooks Close to Billy Stiles," *Bisbee Daily Review*, April 17, 1904.

85. "Billy Stiles Enter Once More," *Border Vidette*, November 12, 1904.

86. "Billy Stiles Makes Escape and Takes Passage for China,," *Bisbee Daily Review*, December 18, 1904.

87. "Billy Stiles Reported to Have Cashed In," *Arizona Daily Star*, December 23, 1908.

88. "Billy Stiles Has Perished by Violence," *Arizona Daily Star*, December 22, 1908.

89. "Pardoned Convicts," *Arizona Sentinel*, November 19, 1903.

90. "The Facts about the Owens Brothers," *Bisbee Daily Review*, November 29, 1903.

91. "Downing to Be Released," *Tombstone Weekly Epitaph*, September 15, 1907; "Receives His Sentence: Dowing Gets 10 Years—Breaks Down in Court," *Tombstone Weekly Epitaph*, April 14, 1901.

92. "Mrs. Downing's Death, Wife of the Convicted Train Robber Dies in Tucson," *Bisbee Daily Review*, February 21, 1902.

93. "Dead Outlaw Wm. Downing," *Arizona Republic*, August 6, 1908.

94. "The Trainor Killing," *Tombstone Weekly Epitaph*, May 28, 1899; "Dead Outlaw Wm. Downing," *Arizona Republic*, August 6, 1908.

95 "Dead Outlaw Wm. Downing," *Arizona Republic*, August 6, 1908.

96. Personal communication, Kathy Klump, Sulphur Springs Valley Historical Society, June 2022.

97. Courtesy of Kathy Klump at the Sulphur Springs Valley Historical Society, which retains copies of the *Arizona Range News* not otherwise available.

CHAPTER NINE

1. "Says Arizona Is the Place to Acquire Wealth,." *Arizona Daily Star*, June 2, 1910.

2. "Beardless Boy Bandits," *Arizona Republic*, May 12, 1910.

3. Ibid.

4. Ibid.

5. "The More Conspicuous Incidents," *Arizona Republic*, May 12, 1910.

6. "Description of Bandits," *Arizona Republic*, May 12, 1910.

7. "Beardless Boy Bandits," *Arizona Republic*, May 12, 1910. I keep adding the same note so that you won't think I'm making any of this up.

8. "Carl Trumbull Hayden," Wikipedia, https://en.wikipedia.org/wiki/Carl_Hayden.

9. "The Arrival of the Broke," *Arizona Republic*, May 12, 1910.

10. "The Women Were Cool," *Arizona Republic*, May 12, 1910.

11. "Beardless Boy Bandits," *Arizona Republic*, May 12, 1910.

12. "Woodson Brothers Lions of the Hour," *Arizona Republic*, May 14, 1910.

13. Ibid.

14. Ibid.

15. Ibid.

16. "Busy Day around the Court House," *Arizona Republic*, November 15, 1910.

17. "Woodson Brothers Given Ten Years," *Arizona Republic*, November 18, 1910.

18. "Parole Given Train Robbers," *Arizona Republic*, March 31, 1914.

CHAPTER TEN

1. "Apache Elementary School," http://www.apacheelementary.org/.

2. Myrick, *Railroads of Arizona*, 1:179–80, 183–84, 192, 196, 199.

3. "Skeleton Canyon Treasure," Wikipedia, https://en.wikipedia.org/wiki /Skeleton_Canyon_treasure.

4. "Skeleton Canyon Massacres," Wikipedia, https://en.wikipedia.org/wiki /Skeleton_Canyon_massacres.

5. "That Train Robbery, All for an Empty Safe Which They Couldn't Open. Many Bisbeeites Have Thrills," *Bisbee Daily Review*, September 8, 1916.

6. Bill O'Neal, *Captain Harry Wheeler: Arizona Lawman* (Austin: Eakin Press, 2003), 26.

7. Ibid., 25–44.

8. "A Detachment of Cavalry," *Tombstone Weekly Epitaph*, November 5, 1916.

9. "Bandit Charged with Holding Up Train at Apache Now in State," *Bisbee Daily Review*, December 12, 1916.

10. "Doc Pardee," *New York Times*, July 21, 1975.

11. "'Doc' Pardee Is Indicted for Aiding Davis," *Tombstone Weekly Epitaph*, February 25, 1917, 25 March 1917; "Lulu Cobb Is Freed: Bond Is Not Required," *Arizona Daily Star*, March 1 and 13, 1917; "Pardee Is Facing Conspiracy Charge," *Weekly Journal-Miner*, March 21, 1917.

12. John "Rusty" Tulk, *Ride 'em as They Come: The Life of John "Rusty" Tulk* (Deming, NM: NWJ, 2005).

13. "Davis' Private Letters Will Not Be Returned, Court Rules," *Arizona Daily Star*, February 23, 1917.

14. "Soldier Identifies Davis as Man Who Held Up Train," *Arizona Daily Star*, February 22, 1917.

15. "Davis' Private Letters Will Not Be Returned, Court Rules," *Arizona Daily Star*, February 23, 1917.

16. "Davis-Spurlock Case Closes Suddenly When Defense Fails to Offer Evidence," *Arizona Daily Star*, February, 24, 1917.

17. "Davis' Private Letters Will Not Be Returned, Court Rules," *Arizona Daily Star*, February 23, 1917.

18. "That Train Robbery, All for an Empty Safe Which They Couldn't Open. May Bisbeeites Have Thrills," *Bisbee Daily Review*, September 8, 1916.

19. Ibid.

20. "Soldier Identifies Davis as Man Who Held Up Train," *Arizona Daily Star*, February 22, 1917.

21. Ibid.

22. "Sheriff Wheeler Returns," *Tombstone Weekly Epitaph*, September 24, 1916.

23. "Will Defend Felk," *Bisbee Daily Review*, September 27, 1916.

24. "Soldier Identifies Davis as Man Who Held Up Train.," *Arizona Daily Star*, February 22, 1917.

25. "Davis' Private Letters Will Not Be Returned, Court Rules," *Arizona Daily Star*, February 23, 1917.

26. "Bandit Charged with Holding Up Train at Apache Now in State," *Bisbee Daily Review*, December 12, 1916.

27. "Jury Chose to Try Alleged Train Robbers," *Arizona Daily Star*, February 20, 1917.

28. Ibid.

29. "Davis and Spurlock Guilty on All Five Counts, Verdict of Jury in Robbery Case," *Arizona Daily Star*, February 25, 1917.

30. "Golden State Robbers Get Sentences in Federal Pen," *Tombstone Weekly Epitaph*, March 4, 1917.

CHAPTER ELEVEN

1 *Bisbee Daily Review*, March 30, 1922.

2. "El Paso and Southwestern Railroad," Wikipedia, https://en.wikipedia.org/wiki/El_Paso_and_Southwestern_Railroad.

3. "Two Masked Bandits Stage Train Hold-Up," *Copper Era and Morenci Leader*, May 12, 1922.

4. Ibid.

5. "Deputy Sheriff Resigns," *Copper Era and Morenci Leader*, May 19, 1922.

6. "Fulcher Bros. and Bradberry Bros. Fight to a Finish," *Copper Era and Morenci Leader*, July 14, 1922.

7. Ibid.

8. Ibid.

9. "Alleges Killers Ambush Victims," *Deming Headlight*, July 28, 1922.

10. "Tom Fulcher and His Son Charged with E.P.& S.W. Train Robbery Last May," *Copper Era and Morenci Leader*, July 28, 1922.

11. "Fulcher Sister Gives Alibi in Robbery Trail," *Arizona Daily Star*, April 6, 1926.

12. "Fulcher Held to Grand Jury on Murder Charge," *Deming Headlight*, August 25, 1922.

13. "Witnesses in Fulcher Trial Coming Friday," *Arizona Daily Star*, March 24, 1926.

14. "Peculiar Tracks of Fulcher's Horse and Memory of Voice of Hold-Up Man Factors at Trial," *Tucson Citizen*, March 31, 1926.

15. Ibid.

16. "Government Rests Today in Prosecution of 2 Fulchers," *Tucson Citizen*, April 5, 1926.

17. "Wife Tells of Her Husband's Break in Luck," *Arizona Daily Star*, May 16, 1922.

18. "Jaynes Holdup, Train Robber and Pursuit," *Tucson Citizen*, May 15, 1922.

19. "Steward Exonerated for Killing Bandit by Coroner's Jury," *Arizona Daily Star*, May 18, 1922.

20. "Wife Tells of Her Husband's Break in Luck," *Arizona Daily Star*, May 16, 1922.

21. "Body of Train Robber Viewed by Officials," *Tucson Citizen*, May 15, 1922.

22. This refers to what today we call a hobo and not to an enthusiast of the band Grateful Dead, which would not appear for many decades.

23. "Steward Exonerated for Killing Bandit by Coroner's Jury," *Arizona Daily Star*, May 18, 1922.

24. "Golden State Limited," Wikipedia, https://en.wikipedia.org/wiki/Golden _State_(train).

25. "Steward Exonerated for Killing Bandit by Coroner's Jury," *Arizona Daily Star*, May 18, 1922; "Winkler Trial Now Under Way in Pima Court," *Tucson Citizen*, November 21, 1922.

26. "Jirou Bound Over on Charge of Holding Up Limited Train," *Arizona Daily Star*, May 28, 1922.

27. "Dugat Turned Train Robber to Provide for His Family," *Arizona Daily Star*, May 16, 1922; "Steward Exonerated for Killing Bandit by Coroner's Jury," *Arizona Daily Star*, May 19, 1922.

28. "Steward Exonerated for Killing Bandit by Coroner's Jury," *Arizona Daily Star*, May 18, 1922; "Express Messenger Has 'Bad Eye' Say Friends," *Tucson Citizen*, May 15, 1922; "Dugat Turned Train Robber to Provide for His Family," *Arizona Daily Star*, May 16, 1922; "Edward Winkler Is in Custody at Albuquerque for Attempted Robbery of S.P. Train in May," *Tucson Citizen*, September 18, 1922; "Jaynes Holdup," *Tucson Citizen*, May 15, 1922.

29. "Steward Exonerated for Killing Bandit by Coroner's Jury," *Arizona Daily Star*, May 18, 1922; "Winkler Trial Now Under Way in Pima Court," *Tucson Citizen*, November 21, 1922.

30. "Steward Exonerated for Killing Bandit by Coroner's Jury," *Arizona Daily Star*, May 18, 1922; "Winkler Trial Now Under Way in Pima Court," *Tucson Citizen*, November 21, 1922.

31. "Steward Exonerated for Killing Bandit by Coroner's Jury," *Arizona Daily Star*, May 18, 1922.

32. "Dugat Turned Train Robber to Provide for His Family," *Arizona Daily Star*, May 16, 1922.

33. "Wife Tells of Her Husband's Break in Luck," *Arizona Daily Star*, May 16, 1922.

34. "Dugat Turned Train Robber to Provide for His Family," *Arizona Daily Star*, May 16, 1922.

35. "Tucson Man Arrested in Connection with Attempted Hold-Up of Golden State Limited: Fix Bond at $10,000," *Bisbee Daily Review*, May 19, 1922.

36. "Suit Grew out of Arrest of Plaintiff by Daniels," *Arizona Daily Star*, February 18, 1923.

37. Ibid.; "Tucson Man Arrested in Connection with Attempted Hold-Up of Golden State Limited: Fix Bond at $10,000," *Bisbee Daily Review*, May 19, 1922; "Richard Starr Sues Sheriff Daniels for $10,250 on Libel," *Arizona Daily Star*, June 2, 1922.

38. "Jirou Bound Over on Charge of Holding Up Limited Train," *Arizona Daily Star*, May 28, 1922; "Tucson Man Arrested Charged with Jaynes Train Hold Up," *Tombstone Weekly Epitaph*, May 22, 1922; "Alleged Train Bandits Named in Information," *Tucson Citizen*, July 2, 1922; "Guilt Admitted by Frank Jirou in Local Court," *Tucson Citizen*, July 27, 1922.

39. "Missing Robbers Reported to Be on West Coast," *Tucson Citizen*, July 30, 1922; "Geo. Winkler, St., Pleads Not Guilty to Charge of Having Participated in Train Holdup," *Arizona Daily Star*, September 8, 1922; "Edward Winkler Is in Custody at Albuquerque for Attempted Robbery of S.P. Train in May," *Tucson Citizen*, September 18, 1922.

40. "Attorney Loses Battle to Keep out Confession," *Tombstone Weekly Epitaph*, November 26, 1922; "Confession Is Admitted into Court Records," *Tucson Citizen*, November 23, 1922.

41. Ex-Pvt. Harold L. Henry, "Mother Asks for Clemency for Son, Facing Sentence; Valiant War Record Cited," *Tucson Citizen*, November 28, 1922.

42. "Silver Star," Wikipedia, https://en.wikipedia.org/wiki/Silver_Star.

43. "Winkler Gets 10 Years in Prison for S.P. Holdup," *Arizona Republic*, December 9, 1922; "Ten-Year Suspended Given to Son, Edward Winkler," *Arizona Daily Star*, December 9, 1922; "Frank Jirou, Member of Hold-Up Gang, Exiled From State," *Arizona Daily Star*, December 12, 1922.

EPILOGUE

1. Lathrop, *Rio Grande Glory Days*, 21.

Index

Agua Zarca massacre, 80–87, *82, 86*

airplanes, 203

Akimel O'odham, 166

alcaldes, 76–77

Alvord, Albert Wright "Burt" (sometimes deputy sheriff), 83–84, 99, 122, *155*; alibis role of, 140–41; alleged robberies of Stiles and, 134, 141; arrest of, 133; background, 136; "crimes" of Chacón and, 156–57; in Fairbank attempted robbery of 1900, 146, 150; gold bullion stolen by Stiles and, 160; growing legend of Yoas (Bravo Juan) and, 158; jail keys letter from Stiles and, 151–52; King, B., shot by, 138; as outlaw and sheriff, 136; prison time and release of, 160–61; shootings by, 116, 138; Stiles and, 140, 150, 156, 158–60

Apache, Arizona, 1916: EPSW and, 176–77; Golden State Limited hold-up, 178–79; history associated with, 178; posse and pursuit of outlaws, 186–87; town of, 176; train robbery at, 179–86; train station today, *177*; trial and sentence of outlaws, 188

Apache Indians, 46, 190; Bull Run and, 43; cavalry tactic, 23

The Apache problem, 21

Arizona: Confederate, 20; depot at Dragoon, *102*; drought of 1892, 7, 94; first Congress representative from, 170; first paved road in, 172, 204; hanging law passed in, 68; heat bets, 167; state status issues, 66; Union admission of, 114. *See also specific towns*

Arizona-New Mexico line, 3; incorporation, 44

Arizona Rangers, 16, 156, 160; captains of, 207; founding and disbanding of, 179. *See also 26 Men*

Arizona Supreme Court, 89, 94

Huachuca Siding and, 48, *49*;
Mexico route of, 45; Pumpelly
account of shooting on, 46;
schedule, *145*; winnings
hidden by gamblers aboard,
49
New Mexico Territory, US
Marshals of, 208
newspapers: "accuracy" of old
time, 17–18, 114; alleged
Stiles interview in, 152;
editor imagination and,
135; hangings viewed by
Phoenix *vs.* Tucson, 194;
on Maricopa plundered
passengers, 170; memory
and fantasy, 156–57; name
mistakes in, 107, 220n27;
names of outlaws assigned by,
115; past events confused by,
70; on posse arrest in Mexico,
74; questionable story of
riot over Chinese labor, 45;
research method using, 17–18;
on Silver City arrival of
Cleveland, 32; on train scenes,
11–12; way to spot errors in,
18
nitroglycerin, 187
Nogales, Arizona, 49; 1888, 79–87;
1896, 122; Tullier and, 79–81,
82, 82–83, 85, *86*
Nogales Gang, 111–12; High Fives
and, 123

old timers, 67
open ranges, 8, 33; of 1880s, 21;
violence and, 22
OSHA, 162
outlaws: caboose as home for,
63; Cleveland confession to
sheriff, 31; county jurisdiction
issue for capture of, 29,
70, 73, 83; "cowboys" as, 9;
crimes miles apart attributed
to famous, 115; engine
wrecking and, 48; express
mail car targeted by, 12–14,
101; famous, 115; fate of
Gage robbery, 31; Gadsden
Purchase hideout for, 9; labor
disdained by, 23; names of,
107, 115, 121, 186, 220n27;
payrolls sought by, 135–36,
140; rancher sympathy with,
9, 33; safe blowing by, 12,
135; sheriffs as, 136; solidarity
between proletariat and, 185;
stupidest or cleverest, 134,
137; sympathy with, 110, 163;
train robbing techniques of,
13–14; train wrecking by, 3–4,
88; turning in comrades, 34.
See also specific outlaws
Owens boys, 133–34
Owings, George, 145–51, 162;
newspaper version of ranch
shooting, 163
Owings, Lewis, 145–51, 162, 163

railroad workers: red lanterns
carried by, 13. *See also* train
crew, late nineteenth-century
ranchers: capital offense law
disliked by, 7; cooperation
and firepower of, 33; land
purchase from railroads,
8; outlaws sympathy of, 9,
33; sympathy toward Texas
drovers, 8
ranches: cattle ownership on, 21;
cowboy tasks on, 96–97;
homestead claims of, 99; land
claims and, 33
Ranch Rodeo, in Wilcox, 96–97
red light district, 13
Red River Railway, 5
regulation cowboy, 36
Rennick, "Cowboy Bob," 55
research method: memoirs
as resource in, 18–19;
newspapers and, 17–18
resources, best documents as, 18
rewards, 15, 28, 42, 54. *See also*
bounty hunters
riding the "blind," 196, 197
Rio Grande Glory Days, 2
Rio Puerco Station, Mexican
meaning of name, 122
river, named Bull Run, 43
rodeo: cowboy Tulk, *180*; oldest,
96; origins, 96; Wheeler as
hero of, 97–98, 105–6; in
Wilcox, 96–97

Rodger, R. M., 128, 129
Rogers, Oscar, 93, 94, 95
Rohling, Conrad, 80, 81, 83, 85, 86
Rough Riders, 164
roundup, 21–22, 99, 100
the Rurales, 157, 160

safes, blowing, 12, 135
sailors, 68
Salome, 130, 131
Sam Bass Gang, 117
San Simon Gang, 67
Santa Cruz County, sheriffs of, 207
Santa Fe penitentiary, 129
Santa Fe Railroad (the Short
Line), 80
Santa Fe short line, 44
Santa Fe system, 6, 124; tracks
shared by, 23
sentences: commuted, 10, 41, 95; of
Fulcher trio, 202; salt mines,
85; of Winkler brothers, 201.
See also hangings; pardons
Separ, New Mexico, 123; 1896
robbery of, 121–22; Gage and,
23
Shanghai Noon, 116
Shaw, Sheriff William, Sr., 72–74
Sheehan, "Red Larry," 68; capture
and shooting of, 77; self-
inflicted shooting injury, 69,
71; Steins Pass robbery and,
70–71

About the Author

DOUG HOCKING IS THE AUTHOR OF SEVERAL AWARD-WINNING HISTO-ries of the American Southwest. He serves on the governing boards of many historical societies. Living in southeast Arizona, he visits the sites he writes about seeing them through the eyes of historian, ethnographer and historical archaeologist.